T0076505

Get the eBook FREE!

(PDF, ePub, Kindle, and liveBook all included)

We believe that once you buy a book from us, you should be able to read it in any format we have available. To get electronic versions of this book at no additional cost to you, purchase and then register this book at the Manning website.

Go to https://www.manning.com/freebook and follow the instructions to complete your pBook registration.

That's it!
Thanks from Manning!

Learn Concurrent Programming with Go

Learn Concurrent Programming with Go

JAMES CUTAJAR

MANNING
SHELTER ISLAND

For online information and ordering of this and other Manning books, please visit
www.manning.com. The publisher offers discounts on this book when ordered in quantity.
For more information, please contact

    Special Sales Department
    Manning Publications Co.
    20 Baldwin Road
    PO Box 761
    Shelter Island, NY 11964
    Email: orders@manning.com

 Manning Publications Co.
    20 Baldwin Road
    PO Box 761
    Shelter Island, NY 11964

Development editor:	Becky Whitney
Technical editor:	Steven Jenkins
Review editor:	Mihaela Batinić
Production editor:	Kathy Rossland
Copy editor:	Andy Carroll
Proofreader:	Melody Dolab
Technical proofreader:	Nicolas Modrzyk
Typesetter:	Gordan Salinovic
Cover designer:	Marija Tudor

ISBN 9781633438385
Printed in the United States of America

brief contents

PART 1 FOUNDATIONS..1

1 ▪ Stepping into concurrent programming 3
2 ▪ Dealing with threads 16
3 ▪ Thread communication using memory sharing 42
4 ▪ Synchronization with mutexes 66
5 ▪ Condition variables and semaphores 89
6 ▪ Synchronizing with waitgroups and barriers 114

PART 2 MESSAGE PASSING 139

7 ▪ Communication using message passing 141
8 ▪ Selecting channels 163
9 ▪ Programming with channels 187

PART 3 MORE CONCURRENCY 215

10 ▪ Concurrency patterns 217
11 ▪ Avoiding deadlocks 245
12 ▪ Atomics, spin locks, and futexes 273

contents

preface xi
acknowledgments xiii
about this book xv
about the author xix
about the cover illustration xx

PART 1 FOUNDATIONS 1

1 **Stepping into concurrent programming 3**

   1.1 About concurrency 5

   1.2 Interacting with a concurrent world 5

   1.3 Increasing throughput 6

   1.4 Improving responsiveness 8

   1.5 Programming concurrency in Go 9

       Goroutines at a glance 9 ▪ *Modeling concurrency with CSP
       and primitives 9* ▪ *Building our own concurrency tools 10*

   1.6 Scaling performance 11

       Amdahl's law 11 ▪ *Gustafson's law 13*

2 Dealing with threads   16

2.1   Multiprocessing in operating systems   17

2.2   Abstracting concurrency with processes and threads   20

Concurrency with processes   20 • Creating processes   22 • Using multiprocessing for common tasks   23 • Concurrency with threads   24 A multithreaded application in practice   28 • Using multiple processes and threads together   29

2.3   What's so special about goroutines?   29

Creating goroutines   29 • Implementing goroutines in the user space   33 • Scheduling goroutines   37

2.4   Concurrency versus parallelism   38

2.5   Exercises   39

3 Thread communication using memory sharing   42

3.1   Sharing memory   43

3.2   Memory sharing in practice   46

Sharing a variable between goroutines   46 • Escape analysis   47 Updating shared variables from multiple goroutines   49

3.3   Race conditions   55

Stingy and Spendy: Creating a race condition   56 • Yielding execution does not help with race conditions   60 • Proper synchronization and communication eliminate race conditions   61 The Go race detector   62

3.4   Exercises   63

4 Synchronization with mutexes   66

4.1   Protecting critical sections with mutexes   67

How do we use mutexes?   67 • Mutexes and sequential processing   70 • Non-blocking mutex locks   74

4.2   Improving performance with readers–writer mutexes   77

Go's readers–writer mutex   77 • Building our own read-preferred readers–writer mutex   83

4.3   Exercises   87

5 *Condition variables and semaphores 89*

5.1   Condition variables 90

Combining mutexes with condition variables 90 ▪ Missing the signal 96 ▪ Synchronizing multiple goroutines with waits and broadcasts 99 ▪ Revisiting readers–writer locks using condition variables 102

5.2   Counting semaphores 108

What's a semaphore? 108 ▪ Building a semaphore 109 ▪ Never miss a signal with semaphores 110

5.3   Exercises 112

6 *Synchronizing with waitgroups and barriers 114*

6.1   Waitgroups in Go 115

Waiting for tasks to complete with waitgroups 115 ▪ Creating a waitgroup type using semaphores 118 ▪ Changing the size of our waitgroup while waiting 120 ▪ Building a more flexible waitgroup 122

6.2   Barriers 126

What is a barrier? 126 ▪ Implementing a barrier in Go 127 Concurrent matrix multiplication using barriers 130

6.3   Exercises 136

PART 2   MESSAGE PASSING 139

7 *Communication using message passing 141*

7.1   Passing messages 142

Passing messages with channels 142 ▪ Buffering messages with channels 146 ▪ Assigning a direction to channels 149 Closing channels 150 ▪ Receiving function results with channels 153

7.2   Implementing channels 154

Creating a channel with semaphores 155 ▪ Implementing the Send() function in our channel 157 ▪ Implementing the Receive() function in our channel 158

7.3   Exercises 161

8 Selecting channels   163

8.1 Combining multiple channels   163

Reading from multiple channels   164 ▪ Using select for non-blocking channel operations   166 ▪ Performing concurrent computations on the default case   167 ▪ Timing out on channels   170 ▪ Writing to channels with select   172 ▪ Disabling select cases with nil channels   174

8.2 Choosing between message passing and memory sharing   178

Balancing code simplicity   179 ▪ Designing tightly versus loosely coupled systems   179 ▪ Optimizing memory consumption   180 Communicating efficiently   182

8.3 Exercises   183

9 Programming with channels   187

9.1 Communicating sequential processes   188

Avoiding interference with immutability   189 ▪ Concurrent programming with CSP   189

9.2 Reusing common patterns with channels   190

Quitting channels   191 ▪ Pipelining with channels and goroutines   193 ▪ Fanning in and out   198 ▪ Flushing results on close   202 ▪ Broadcasting to multiple goroutines   204 Closing channels after a condition   208 ▪ Adopting channels as first-class objects   210

9.3 Exercises   213

PART 3 MORE CONCURRENCY 215

10 Concurrency patterns   217

10.1 Decomposing programs   217

Task decomposition   219 ▪ Data decomposition   220 ▪ Thinking about granularity   221

10.2 Concurrency implementation patterns   222

Loop-level parallelism   222 ▪ The fork/join pattern   227 ▪ Using worker pools   230 ▪ Pipelining   235 ▪ Pipelining properties   240

10.3 Exercises   242

11   *Avoiding deadlocks   245*

   11.1   Identifying deadlocks   245

          Picturing deadlocks with resource allocation graphs   247
          Deadlocking in a ledger   251

   11.2   Dealing with deadlocks   255

          Detecting deadlocks   255 ▪ Avoiding deadlocks   258
          Preventing deadlocks   264

   11.3   Deadlocking with channels   267

   11.4   Exercises   271

12   *Atomics, spin locks, and futexes   273*

   12.1   Lock-free synchronization with atomic variables   274

          Sharing variables with atomic numbers   274 ▪ Performance
          penalty when using atomics   276 ▪ Counting using atomic
          numbers   278

   12.2   Implementing a mutex with spin locks   280

          Comparing and swapping   282 ▪ Building a mutex   284

   12.3   Improving on spin locking   286

          Locking with futexes   286 ▪ Reducing system calls   289 ▪ Go's
          mutex implementation   291

   12.4   Exercises   294

          index   297

"Can you describe a situation in which two threads of execution would cause a dead-lock?" asked my interviewer. After I gave the correct answer, he probed further: "And what would you do in that situation to make sure the code avoids the deadlock?" Luck-ily, I also knew the solution. The interviewer proceeded to show me some code and inquire whether I could spot anything wrong with it. The code had a bad race condi-tion, which I highlighted, and I suggested ways to resolve the problem.

This exchange came up during my third and final interview for a core backend developer position at an international tech company in London. In this role, I was exposed to some of the most challenging problems in programming—problems requiring that I sharpen my skills in developing concurrent, low-latency, and high-throughput services. That was more than 15 years ago.

Throughout my career in technology, over 20+ years, many circumstances have changed: developers can now work from anywhere, computer languages have evolved to model more-complex businesses, and geeks have become cool since they now run the giant tech companies. However, a few aspects have remained constant: program-mers will always struggle to name variables, a great many problems can be solved by turning systems off and then on again, and concurrent programming skills are still in short supply.

The tech industry lacks programmers skilled in concurrency because concurrent programming is perceived as extremely challenging. Many developers even dread using concurrent programming to solve problems. The perception in the tech indus-try is that this is an advanced topic, reserved only for hard-core computer nerds.

There are many reasons for this. Developers are not familiar with the concepts and tools available for managing concurrency, and sometimes they fail to recognize how concurrency can be modeled programmatically. This book is my attempt to address this problem and explain concurrent programming in a pain-free manner.

acknowledgments

I am grateful for the significant contributions of those who helped during the writing of this book.

First, I want to thank Joe Cordina, who introduced me to concurrent programming early in my studies and sparked my interest in this subject.

I also want to thank Miguel David for planting the idea to publish material using Go.

I am indebted to Russ Cox for providing me with valuable pointers on Go's history.

Special thanks go to development editor Becky Whitney, technical proofreader Nicolas Modrzyk, and technical editor Steven Jenkins, who is a senior engineer at a global financial services company and has designed, built, and supported systems from startups to global enterprises. He finds Go useful for efficiently building and delivering scalable solutions. Their professionalism, expertise, and dedication ensured that this book meets the highest standards of quality.

To all the reviewers: Aditya Sharma, Alessandro Campeis, Andreas Schroepfer, Arun Saha, Ashish Kumar Pani, Borko Djurkovic, Cameron Singe, Christopher Bailey, Clifford Thurber, David Ong Da Wei, Diego Stamigni, Emmanouil Chardalas, Germano Rizzo, Giuseppe Denora, Gowtham Sadasivam, Gregor Zurowski, Jasmeet Singh, Joel Holmes, Jonathan Reeves, Keith Kim, Kent Spillner, Kévin Etienne, Manuel Rubio, Manzur Mukhitdinov, Martin Czygan, Mattia Di Gangi, Miki Tebeka, Mouhamed Klank, Nathan B. Crocker, Nathan Davies, Nick Rakochy, Nicolas Modrzyk, Nigel V. Thomas, Phani Kumar Yadavilli, Rahul Modpur, Sam Zaydel, Samson Desta, Sanket Naik, Satadru Roy, Serge Simon, Serge Smertin, Sergio Britos Arévalo, Slavomir Furman, Steve Prior, and Vinicios Henrique Wentz, your suggestions helped make this a better book.

Finally, I would like to thank Vanessa, Luis, and Oliver for their unwavering support throughout this project. Their encouragement and enthusiasm kept me motivated and inspired me to give my best.

about this book

Learn Concurrent Programming with Go was written to help developers increase their programming skills with more advanced programming in concurrency. Go was chosen as the language in which to present examples because it provides a wide range of tools for fully exploring this concurrent programming world. In Go, these tools are quite intuitive and easy to grasp, letting us focus on the principles and best practices of concurrency.

After reading this book, you will be able to

- Use concurrent programming to write software that is responsive, high-performance, and scalable
- Grasp the advantages, limits, and properties of parallel computing
- Distinguish between memory sharing and message passing
- Utilize goroutines, mutexes, readers-writer locks, waitgroups, channels, and condition variables—and, additionally, understand how to build some of these tools
- Identify typical errors to watch for when dealing with concurrent executions
- Improve your programming skills in Go with more advanced, multithreading topics

Who should read this book

This book is for readers who already have some programming experience and would like to learn about concurrency. The book assumes no prior knowledge of concurrent programming. Though the ideal reader would already have some experience with Go or another C-syntax-like language, this book is also well suited for developers coming from any language—if some effort is spent learning Go's syntax.

Concurrent programming adds another dimension to your programming: programs stop being a set of instructions executing one after the other. This makes it a challenging topic, and it requires you to think about programs in a different way. Thus, being already proficient in Go is not as important as possessing curiosity and drive.

This book does not focus on explaining Go's syntax and features but instead uses Go to demonstrate concurrency principles and techniques. Most of these techniques can be applied to other languages. For Go tutorials and documentation, see https://go.dev/learn.

How this book is organized: A road map

This book has three parts with 12 chapters. Part 1 introduces the fundamentals of concurrent programming and communication using memory sharing:

- Chapter 1 introduces concurrent programming and talks about some of the laws governing parallel execution.
- Chapter 2 discusses the various ways we can model concurrency and the abstractions provided by operating systems and the Go runtime. The chapter also compares concurrency and parallelism.
- Chapter 3 talks about inter-thread communication using memory sharing, and it introduces race conditions.
- Chapter 4 explores different types of mutexes as solutions to some race conditions. It also shows how to implement a basic readers-writer lock.
- Chapter 5 shows how to use condition variables and semaphores to synchronize concurrent executions. This chapter also describes how to build a semaphore from scratch and improve the readers-writer lock developed in the previous chapter.
- Chapter 6 demonstrates how to build and use more complex synchronization mechanisms, such as waitgroups and barriers.

Part 2 discusses how multiple executions can communicate using message passing instead of memory sharing:

- Chapter 7 describes message passing using Go's channels. This chapter shows the various ways channels can be used, and it illustrates how channels can be built on top of memory sharing and synchronization primitives.
- Chapter 8 explains how we can combine multiple channels by using Go's select statement. In addition, this chapter gives some guidelines on choosing memory sharing versus message passing when developing concurrent programs.
- Chapter 9 provides examples and best practices for reusing common message-passing patterns. This chapter also demonstrates the flexibility of having a language (such as Go) where channels are first-class objects.

Part 3 explores common concurrency patterns and some more advanced topics:

- Chapter 10 lists techniques for breaking down problems so that programs can run more efficiently by employing concurrent programming.
- Chapter 11 illustrates how deadlock situations can develop when we have concurrency and describes various techniques for avoiding them.
- Chapter 12 deals with the internals of mutexes. It explains how mutexes are implemented in both the kernel and user space.

How to read the book

Developers with no experience in concurrency should view the book as a journey, starting with the first chapter and following through to the end. Each chapter teaches new skills and techniques that build on the knowledge acquired in previous ones.

Developers who already have some experience with concurrency can read chapters 1 and 2 as a refresher on how operating systems model concurrency and then decide whether to skip to some of the more advanced topics. For example, a reader who is already familiar with race conditions and mutexes may choose to continue learning about condition variables in chapter 5.

About the code

The source code in the book's listings is in a `fixed-width font` to distinguish it from the rest of the document, with keywords in Go set in **bold**. Code annotations accompany many of the listings, highlighting important concepts.

To download all the source code in the book, including the exercise solutions, go to https://github.com/cutajarj/ConcurrentProgrammingWithGo. The complete code for the examples in the book is also available for download from the Manning website at https://www.manning.com/books/learn-concurrent-programming-with-go. You can get executable snippets of code from the liveBook (online) version of this book at https://livebook.manning.com/book/learn-concurrent-programming-with-go.

The source code in this book requires the Go compiler, which can be downloaded from https://go.dev/doc/install. Note that some of the source code in this book will not work correctly on Go's online playground—the playground is blocked from certain operations, such as opening web connections.

liveBook discussion forum

Purchase of *Learn Concurrent Programming with Go* includes free access to liveBook, Manning's online reading platform. Using liveBook's exclusive discussion features, you can attach comments to the book globally or to specific sections or paragraphs. It's a snap to make notes for yourself, ask and answer technical questions, and receive help from the author and other users. To access the forum, go to https://livebook .manning.com/book/learn-concurrent-programming-with-go/discussion. You can also learn more about Manning's forums and the rules of conduct at https://livebook .manning.com/discussion.

Manning's commitment to our readers is to provide a venue where a meaningful dialogue between individual readers and between readers and the author can take place. It is not a commitment to any specific amount of participation on the part of the author, whose contribution to the forum remains voluntary (and unpaid). We suggest you try asking the author some challenging questions lest his interest stray! The forum and the archives of previous discussions will be accessible from the publisher's website as long as the book is in print.

about the author

 **JAMES CUTAJAR** is a software developer with an interest in scalable, high-performance computing and distributed algorithms. He has worked in the field of technology in various industries for more than 20 years. During his career, James has been an open source contributor, blogger (http://www.cutajarjames.com), tech evangelist, Udemy instructor, and author. When he isn't writing software, he enjoys riding his motorbike, surfing, scuba diving, and flying light aircraft. Born in Malta, James lived in London for almost a decade and now lives and works in Portugal.

about the cover illustration

The figure on the cover of *Learn Concurrent Programming with Go* is "Homme Tschou-kotske," or "Man from Chukotka," taken from a collection by Jacques Grasset de Saint-Sauveur, published in 1788. Each illustration is finely drawn and colored by hand.

In those days, it was easy to identify where people lived and what their trade or station in life was just by their dress. Manning celebrates the inventiveness and initiative of the computer business with book covers based on the rich diversity of regional culture centuries ago, brought back to life by pictures from collections such as this one.

Part 1

Foundations

How can we write instructions so that some actions are performed at the same time as others? In part 1 of this book, we'll explore the basics of how we can model concurrency in our programming. We'll see how modeling and executing concurrent programs require help from the hardware, the operating system, and the programming language.

When we develop concurrent programs, we encounter a new set of programming errors that are not present in sequential code. Known as race conditions, these errors can be some of the most difficult to identify and fix. A huge part of concurrent programming involves learning how to prevent these types of bugs in our code. In this part of the book, we'll learn about race conditions and then discuss various techniques for avoiding them.

Stepping into concurrent
programming

This chapter covers

- Introducing concurrent programming
- Improving performance with concurrent execution
- Scaling our programs

Meet Jane Sutton. Jane has been working at HSS International Accountancy as a software developer for three months. In her latest project, she has been looking at a problem in the payroll system. The payroll software module runs at the end of the month after the close of business, and it computes all the salary payments for the HSS clients' employees. Jane's manager has arranged a meeting with the product owner, the infrastructure team, and a sales representative to try to get to the bottom of the problem. Unexpectedly, Sarika Kumar, CTO, has joined the meeting room via video call.

Thomas Bock, the product owner, starts: "I don't understand. The payroll module has been working fine for as long as I can remember. Suddenly, last month, the payment calculations weren't completed on time, and we got loads of complaints from our clients. It made us look really unprofessional to Block Entertainment, our new and biggest client yet, with them threatening to go to our competitor."

Jane's manager, Francesco Varese, chimes in: "The problem is that the calculations are too slow and take too long. They are slow because of their complex nature, considering many factors such as employee absences, joining dates, overtime, and a thousand other factors. Parts of the software were written more than a decade ago in C++. There are no developers left in the firm who understand how this code works."

"We're about to sign up our biggest client ever, a company with over 30,000 employees. They've heard about our payroll problem, and they want to see it resolved before they proceed with the contract. It's really important that we fix this as soon as possible," replies Rob Gornall from the Sales and Acquisitions department.

"We've tried adding more processor cores and memory to the server that runs the module, but this made absolutely no difference. When we execute the payroll calculation using test data, it's taking the same amount of time, no matter how many resources we allocate. It's taking more than 20 hours to calculate all the clients' payrolls, which is too long for our clients," continues Frida Norberg from Infrastructure.

It's Jane's turn to finally speak. As the firm's newest employee, she hesitates a little but manages to say, "If the code is not written in a manner that takes advantage of the additional cores, it won't matter if you allocate multiple processors. The code needs to use concurrent programming for it to run faster when you add more processing resources."

Everyone seems to have acknowledged that Jane is the most knowledgeable about the subject. There is a short pause. Jane feels as if everyone wants her to come up with some sort of answer, so she continues. "Right. Okay. I've been experimenting with a simple program written in Go. It divides the payroll into smaller employee groups and then calls the payroll module with each group as input. I've programmed it so that it calls the module concurrently using multiple goroutines. I'm also using a Go channel to load-balance the workload. At the end, I have another goroutine that collects the results via another channel."

Jane looks around quickly and sees blank looks on everyone's faces, so she adds, "In simulations, it's at least five times faster on the same multicore hardware. There are still a few tests to run to make sure there are no race conditions, but I'm pretty sure that I can make it run even faster, especially if I get some help from accounting to migrate some of the old C++ logic into clean Go concurrent code."

Jane's manager has a big smile on his face now. Everyone else in the meeting seems surprised and speechless. The CTO finally speaks up and says, "Jane, what do you need to get this done by the end of the month?"

Concurrent programming is a skill that is increasingly sought after by tech companies. It is a technique used in virtually every field of development, from web development to game programming, backend business logic, mobile applications, crypto, and many others. Businesses want to utilize hardware resources to their full capacity, as this saves them time and money. To accomplish this, they understand that they have to hire the right talent—developers who can write scalable concurrent applications.

1.1 About concurrency

In this book, we will focus on principles and patterns of concurrent programming. How can we program instructions that happen at the same time? How can we manage concurrent executions so they don't step over each other? What techniques should we use to have executions collaborate toward solving a common problem? When and why should we use one form of communication over another? We will answer all these questions and more by making use of the Go programming language. Go gives us a full set of tools to illustrate these concepts.

If you have little or no experience in concurrency but have some experience in Go or a similar C-style language, this book is ideal. This book starts with a gentle introduction to concurrency concepts in the operating system and describes how Go uses them to model concurrency. We'll then move on to explain race conditions and why they occur in some concurrent programs. Later, we'll discuss the two main ways we can implement communication between our executions: memory sharing and message passing. In the final chapters of this book, we'll discuss concurrency patterns, deadlocks, and some advanced topics such as spinning locks.

Apart from helping us to get hired or promoted as developers, knowing concurrent programming gives us a wider set of skills that we can employ in new scenarios. For example, we can model complex business interactions that happen at the same time. We can also use concurrent programming to improve our software's responsiveness by picking up tasks swiftly. Unlike sequential programming, concurrent programming can make use of multiple CPU cores, which allows us to increase the work done by our programs by speeding up their execution. Even with a single CPU core, concurrency offers benefits because it enables time-sharing and lets us perform tasks while we're waiting for I/O operations to complete. Let's now look at some of these scenarios in more detail.

1.2 Interacting with a concurrent world

We live and work in a concurrent world. The software that we write models complex business processes that interact concurrently. Even the simplest of businesses typically have many of these concurrent interactions. For example, consider multiple people ordering online at the same time or a consolidation process grouping packages together while coordinating with ongoing shipments, as shown in figure 1.1.

In our everyday life, we deal with concurrency all the time. Every time we drive a car, we interact with multiple concurrent actors, such as other cars, cyclists, and pedestrians. At work, we may put a task on hold while we're waiting for an email reply and pick up the next task. When cooking, we plan our steps so we maximize our productivity and shorten the cooking time. Our brain is perfectly comfortable managing concurrent behavior. In fact, it does this all the time without us even noticing.

Concurrent programming is about writing code so that multiple tasks and processes can execute and interact at the same time. If two customers place an order simultaneously and only one stock item remains, what happens? If the price of a flight ticket goes up every time a client buys a ticket, what happens when multiple tickets are

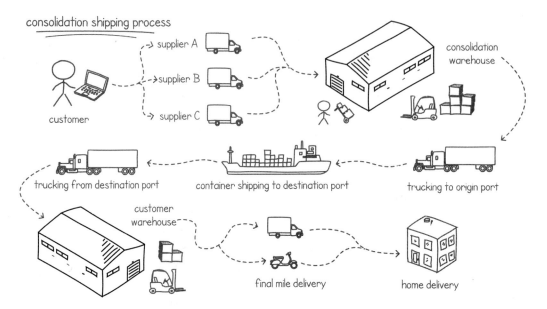

Figure 1.1   A consolidation shipping process showing complex concurrent interactions

booked at the same exact instant? If we have a sudden increase in load due to extra demand, how will our software scale when we increase the processing and memory resources? These are all scenarios that developers deal with when they are designing and programming concurrent software.

1.3   *Increasing throughput*

For the modern developer, it is increasingly important to understand how to program concurrently. This is because the hardware landscape has changed over the years to benefit this type of programming.

Prior to multicore technology, processor performance increased proportionally to clock frequency and transistor count, roughly doubling every two years. Processor engineers started hitting physical limits due to overheating and power consumption, which coincided with the explosion of more mobile hardware, such as notebooks and smartphones. To reduce excessive battery consumption and CPU overheating while increasing processing power, engineers introduced multicore processors.

In addition, the rise of cloud computing services has given developers easy access to large, cheap processing resources where they can run their code. This extra computational power can only be harnessed effectively if our code is written in a manner that takes full advantage of the extra processing units.

DEFINITION   *Horizontal scaling* is when we improve system performance by distributing the load over multiple processing resources, such as processors and server machines (see figure 1.2). *Vertical scaling* is when we improve the existing resources, such as by getting a faster processor.

Figure 1.2 Improving performance by adding more processors

Having multiple processing resources means we can scale horizontally. We can use the extra processors to execute tasks in parallel and finish them more quickly. This is only possible if we write code in a way that takes full advantage of the extra processing resources.

What about a system that has only one processor? Is there any advantage to writing concurrent code if our system does not have multiple processors? It turns out that writing concurrent programs has a benefit even in this scenario.

Most programs spend only a small proportion of their time executing computations on the processor. Think, for example, about a word processor that waits for input from the keyboard, or a text-file search utility that spends most of its running time waiting for portions of the text files to load from disk. We can have our program perform different tasks while it's waiting for I/O. For example, the word processor could perform a spell check on the document while the user is thinking about what to type next. We can have the file search utility look for a match with the file that we already loaded in memory while we are reading the next file into another portion of memory.

As another example, think of cooking or baking a favorite dish. We can make more effective use of our time if, while the dish is in the oven or on the stove, we perform some other actions instead of just waiting around (see figure 1.3). In this way, we are making more effective use of our time, and we are more productive. This is analogous to our program executing other instructions on the CPU while it waits for a network message, user input, or a file to be written. This means our program can get more work done in the same amount of time.

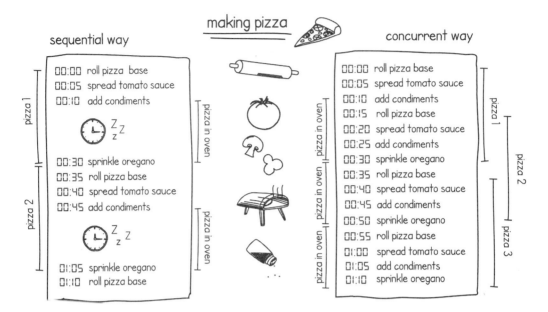

Figure 1.3   Even with one processor, we can improve performance if we utilize idle times.

1.4   *Improving responsiveness*

Concurrent programming makes our software more responsive because we don't need to wait for one task to finish before responding to a user's input. Even if we have one processor, we can always pause the execution of a set of instructions, respond to the user's input, and then continue with the execution while we're waiting for the next user's input.

If we again think of a word processor, multiple tasks might be running in the background while we are typing. There is a task that listens to keyboard events and displays each character on the screen. We might also have a task that checks our spelling and grammar in the background. Another task might be running to give us stats on our document (word count, page count, etc.). Periodically, we may have another task that autosaves our document. All these tasks running together give the impression that they are somehow running simultaneously, but what's happening is that these tasks are being fast-switched by the operating system on CPUs. Figure 1.4 illustrates a simplified timeline showing these three tasks executing on a single processor. This interleaving system is implemented by using a combination of hardware interrupts and operating system traps.

We'll go into more detail on operating systems and concurrency in the next chapter. For now, it's important to realize that if we didn't have this interleaving system, we would have to perform each task one after the other. We would have to type a sentence, then click the spell check button, wait for it to complete, and then click another button and wait for the document stats to appear.

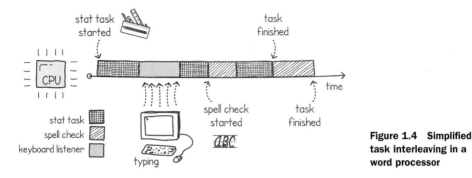

Figure 1.4 Simplified task interleaving in a word processor

1.5 Programming concurrency in Go

Go is a very good language to use when learning about concurrent programming because its creators designed it with high-performance concurrency in mind. Their aim was to produce a language that was efficient at runtime, readable, and easy to use.

1.5.1 Goroutines at a glance

Go uses a lightweight construct, called a *goroutine*, to model the basic unit of concurrent execution. As we shall see in the next chapter, goroutines give us a system of user-level threads running on a set of kernel-level threads and managed by Go's runtime.

Given the lightweight nature of goroutines, the premise of the language is that we should focus mainly on writing correct concurrent programs, letting Go's runtime and hardware mechanics deal with parallelism. The principle is that if you need something to be done concurrently, create a goroutine to do it. If you need many things done concurrently, create as many goroutines as you need, without worrying about resource allocation. Then, depending on the hardware and environment that your program is running on, your solution will scale.

In addition to goroutines, Go provides us with many abstractions that allow us to coordinate the concurrent executions on a common task. One of these abstractions is known as a *channel*. Channels allow two or more goroutines to pass messages to each other. This enables the exchange of information and synchronization of the multiple executions in an easy and intuitive manner.

1.5.2 Modeling concurrency with CSP and primitives

In 1978, C.A.R. Hoare first described *communicating sequential processes* (CSP) as a formal language for expressing concurrent interactions. Many languages, such as Occam and Erlang, have been influenced by CSP. Go tries to implement many of CSP's ideas, such as the use of synchronized channels.

This concurrency model of having isolated goroutines communicating and synchronizing using channels (see figure 1.5) reduces the risk of race conditions—types of programming errors that occur in bad concurrent programming and that are typically very hard to debug and lead to data corruption and unexpected behavior. This type of modeling concurrency is more akin to how concurrency happens in our everyday lives, such as when we have isolated executions (people, processes, or machines) working concurrently, communicating with each other by sending messages back and forth.

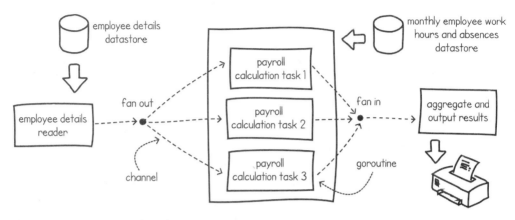

Figure 1.5   A concurrent Go application using CSP

Depending on the problem, the classic concurrency primitives used with memory sharing (such as mutexes and condition variables, found in many other languages) will sometimes do a better job and result in better performance than using CSP-style programming. Luckily for us, Go provides us with these tools in addition to the CSP-style tools. When CSP is not the appropriate model to use, we can fall back on the other classic primitives.

In this book, we will purposely start with memory sharing and synchronization using classic primitives. The idea is that by the time we get to discussing CSP-style concurrent programming, you will have a solid foundation in the traditional locking and synchronization primitives.

1.5.3   *Building our own concurrency tools*

In this book, you will learn how to use various tools to build concurrent applications. This includes concurrency constructs such as mutex, condition variables, channels, semaphores, and so on.

Knowing how to use these concurrency tools is good, but what about understanding their inner workings? Here, we'll go one step further and take the approach of building them together from scratch, even if they are available in Go's libraries. We will pick common concurrency tools and see how they can be implemented using other concurrency primitives as building blocks. For example, Go doesn't come with a bundled semaphore implementation, so apart from understanding how and when to use semaphores, we'll go about implementing one ourselves. We'll also do this for some of the tools that are available in Go, such as waitgroups and channels.

This idea is analogous to having the knowledge to implement well-known algorithms. We might not need to know how to implement a sorting algorithm to use a sorting function; however, learning how the algorithm works exposes us to different scenarios and new ways of thinking, making us better programmers. We can then apply those scenarios to different problems. In addition, knowing how a concurrency tool is built allows us to make better-informed decisions about when and how to use it.

1.6 Scaling performance

Performance scalability is the measure of how well a program speeds up in proportion to the increase in the number of resources available to the program. To understand this, let's try to make use of a simple analogy.

Imagine a world where we are property developers. Our current project is to build a small multi-story residential house. We give the architectural plan to a builder, and they set off to finish the small house. The work is all completed in a period of eight months.

As soon as that project is finished, we get another request for the same build but in another location. To speed things up, we hire two builders instead of one. This time around, the builders complete the house in just four months.

The next time we are asked to build the same house, we hire even more help, so that the house is finished quicker. This time we pay four builders, and it takes them two and a half months to complete. The house has cost us a bit more to build than the previous one. Paying four builders for two and a half months costs more than paying two builders for four months (assuming they all charge the same rate).

We repeat the experiment twice more, once with 8 builders and then with 16. With both 8 and 16 builders, the house takes two months to complete. It seems that no matter how many hands we put on the job, the build cannot be completed in less than two months. In geek speak, we say that we have hit our *scalability limit*. Why does this happen? Why can't we continue to double our resources (people, money, or processors) and always reduce the time spent by half?

1.6.1 Amdahl's law

In 1967, Gene Amdahl, a computer scientist, presented a formula at a conference that measured speedup with regard to a problem's parallel-to-sequential ratio. This became known as Amdahl's law.

> **DEFINITION** *Amdahl's law* states that the overall performance improvement gained by optimizing a single part of a system is limited by the fraction of time that the improved part is actually used.

In our house build scenario, the scalability is limited by various factors. For starters, our approach to solving the problem might be limiting us. For example, one cannot construct the second floor before constructing the first. In addition, several parts of the build can only be done sequentially. For example, if a single road leads to the building site, only one transport can use the road at any point in time. In other words, some parts of the building process are sequential (one after the other), and other parts can be done in parallel (at the same time). These factors influence and limit the scalability of our task.

Amdahl's law tells us that the non-parallel parts of an execution act as a bottleneck and limit the advantage of parallelizing the execution. Figure 1.6 shows this relationship between the theoretical speedup obtained as we increase the number of processors.

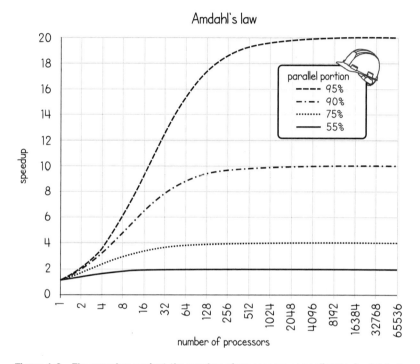

Figure 1.6   The speedup against the number of processors according to Amdahl's law

If we apply this chart to our construction problem, when we use a single builder and they spend 5% of their time on the parts that can only be done sequentially, the scalability follows the topmost line in our chart (95% parallel). This sequential portion is the part that can only be done by one person, such as trucking in the building materials through a narrow road.

As you can see from the chart, even with 512 people working on the construction, we would only finish the job about 19 times faster than if we had just 1 person. After this point, the situation does not improve much. We'll need more than 4,096 builders to finish the project just 20 times faster. We hit a hard limit around this number. Contracting more workers does not help at all, and we would be wasting our money.

The situation is even worse if a lower percentage of work is parallelizable. With 90%, we would hit this scalability limit around the 512-workers mark. With 75%, we get there at 128 workers, and with 50% at just 16 workers. Notice that it's not just this limit that goes down—the speedup is also greatly reduced. When the work is 90%, 75%, and 50% parallelizable, we get maximum speedups of 10, 4, and 2, respectively.

Amdahl's law paints a pretty bleak picture of concurrent programming and parallel computing. Even with concurrent code that has a tiny fraction of serial processing, the scalability is greatly reduced. Thankfully, this is not the full picture.

1.6.2　Gustafson's law

In 1988, two computer scientists, John L. Gustafson and Edwin H. Barsis, reevaluated Amdahl's law and published an article addressing some of its shortcomings ("Reevaluating Amdah's Law," https://dl.acm.org/doi/pdf/10.1145/42411.42415). The article gives an alternative perspective on the limits of parallelism. Their main argument is that, in practice, the size of the problem changes when we have access to more resources.

To continue with our house-building analogy, if we did have thousands of builders available at our disposal, it would be wasteful to put them all into building a small house when we have future projects in the pipeline. Instead, we would try to put the optimal number of builders on our house construction and allocate the rest of the workers to other projects.

Suppose we were developing software and we had a large number of computing resources. If we noticed that utilizing half the resources resulted in the same software performance, we could allocate the extra resources to do other things, such as increasing the accuracy or quality of that software in other areas.

The second argument against Amdahl's law is that when you increase the problem's size, the non-parallel part of the problem typically does not grow in proportion with the problem size. In fact, Gustafson argues that for many problems, this remains constant. Thus, when you take these two points into account, the speedup can scale linearly with the available parallel resources. This relationship is shown in figure 1.7.

Gustafson's law tells us that as long as we find ways to keep our extra resources busy, the speedup should continue to increase and not be limited by the serial part of the problem. However, this is only true if the serial part stays constant as we increase the problem size, which, according to Gustafson, is the case in many types of programs.

To fully understand both Amdahl's and Gustafson's laws, let's take a computer game as an example. Let's say a particular computer game with rich graphics was written to make use of multiple computing processors. As time goes by and computers become more powerful, with more parallel processing cores, we can run that same game with a higher frame rate, giving us a smoother experience. Eventually, we get to a point where we're adding more processors, but the frame rate is not increasing further. This happens when we hit the speedup limit. No matter how many processors we add, the game won't run with higher frame rates. This is what Amdahl's law is telling us—that there is a speedup limit for a particular problem of fixed size if it has a non-parallel portion.

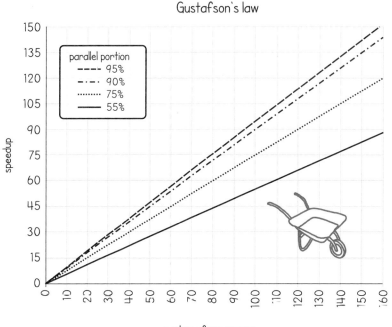

Figure 1.7   The speedup against the number of processors according to Gustafson's law

However, as technology improves and processors get more cores, the game designers will put those extra processing units to good use. Although the frame rate might not increase, the game can now contain more graphic detail and higher resolution due to the extra processing power. This is Gustafson's law in action. When we increase the resources, there is an expectation of an increase in the system's capabilities, and the developers will make good use of the extra processing power.

Summary

- Concurrent programming allows us to build more responsive software.
- Concurrent programs can also provide increased speedup when running on multiple processors.
- We can increase throughput even when we have only one processor if our concurrent programming makes effective use of the I/O wait times.
- Go provides us with goroutines, which are lightweight constructs for modeling concurrent executions.
- Go provides us with abstractions, such as channels, that enable concurrent executions to communicate and synchronize.
- Go allows us the choice of building our concurrent application either using the communicating sequential processes (CSP)-style model or using the classical primitives.

- Using a CSP-style model, we reduce the chance of certain types of concurrent errors; however, for certain problems, using the classical primitives will give us better results.
- Amdahl's law tells us that the performance scalability of a fixed-size problem is limited by the non-parallel parts of an execution.
- Gustafson's law tells us that if we keep on finding ways to keep our extra resources busy, the speedup should continue to increase and not be limited by the serial part of the problem.

Dealing with threads

This chapter covers

- Modeling concurrency in operating systems
- Differentiating between processes and threads
- Creating goroutines
- Differentiating between concurrency and parallelism

The operating system is the gatekeeper of our system resources. It decides when and which processes are given access to the various system resources, including processing time, memory, and network. As developers, we don't necessarily need to be experts on the inner workings of the operating system. However, we need to have a good understanding of how it operates and the tools it provides to make our lives as programmers easier.

We'll start this chapter by looking at how the operating system manages and allocates resources to run multiple jobs concurrently. In the context of concurrent programming, the operating system gives us various tools to help manage this concurrency. Two of these tools, processes and threads, represent the concurrent actors in our code. They may execute in parallel or interleave and interact with each other. We will look, in some detail, at the differences between the two. Later,

16

we will also discuss goroutines and where they sit in this context, and then we'll create our first concurrent Go program using goroutines.

2.1   Multiprocessing in operating systems

How does an operating system provide abstractions to build and support concurrent programs? *Multiprocessing* (sometimes referred to as multiprogramming) is the term used when an operating system can handle more than one task at a time. This is important because it enables us to make effective use of the CPU. Whenever the CPU is idling, such as when the current job is waiting for user input, we can have the operating system choose another job to run on the CPU.

> **NOTE**   When it comes to multiprocessing, modern operating systems have various procedures and components to manage their multiple jobs. Understanding this system and how it interacts with our programming can help us program in a more effective manner.

Whenever we execute a job on our system, whether it's our home laptop or a cloud server, that execution transitions through various states. To fully understand the life cycle that a job goes through, let's pick an example and walk through these states. Let's say we run a command on our system to search for a particular string in a large text file. Suppose our system is a UNIX platform, and we use this command:

```
grep 'hello' largeReadme.md
```

Figure 2.1 shows an example of the path taken by this job.

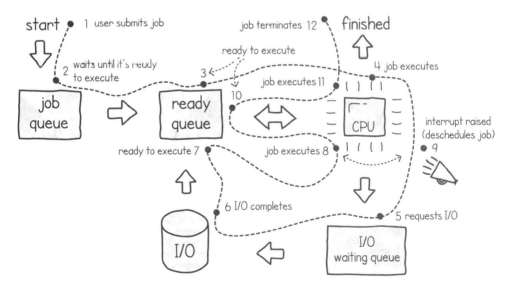

Figure 2.1   The operating system's job states in a single-CPU system

NOTE   On some operating systems (such as Linux), the ready queue is known as the *run queue.*

Let's have a look at each of these states, one step at a time:

1   A user submits the string-search job for execution.

2   The operating system places this job in the job queue. The job goes into this queue in cases when it is not yet ready to run.

3   Once our text search is in a ready-to-run state, it moves to the ready queue.

4   At some point, when the CPU is free, the operating system picks up the job from the ready queue and starts executing it on the CPU. At this stage, the processor is running the instructions contained in the job.

5   As soon as our text-search job requests an instruction to read from a file, the operating system removes the job from the CPU and places it in an I/O waiting queue. Here it waits until the requested I/O operation returns data. If another job is available in the ready queue, the OS will pick it up and execute it on the CPU, thus keeping the processor busy.

6   The device will perform and complete the I/O operation (reading some bytes from the text file).

7   Once the I/O operation is complete, the job moves back to the ready queue. It's now waiting for the operating system to pick it up so that it can continue its execution. The reason for this wait period is that the CPU might be busy executing other jobs.

8   At some point, the CPU is free again, and the OS picks up the text-search job and continues executing its instructions on the CPU. The typical instructions in this case would be to try to find a match in the loaded text from the file.

9   At this point, the system might raise an interrupt while the job is in execution. An *interrupt* is a mechanism used to stop the current execution and notify the system of a particular event. A piece of hardware called the *interrupt controller* handles all interrupts coming from multiple devices. This controller then notifies the CPU to stop the current job and start on another task. Typically, this task involves a call to a device driver or the operating system scheduler. This interrupt can be raised for many reasons, such as

   – An I/O device completes an operation such as reading a file or network or even a keystroke on a keyboard.

   – Another program requests a software interrupt.

   – A hardware clock (or timer) tick occurs, interrupting the current execution. This ensures that other jobs in the ready queue also get their own chance to execute.

10 The operating system pauses the execution of the current job and puts the job back on the ready queue. The OS will also pick up another item from the ready queue and execute it on the CPU. The job of the OS scheduling algorithm is to determine which job from the ready queue to pick up for execution.

11 At some point, our job is picked up again by the OS scheduler, and its execution resumes on the CPU. Steps 4 through 10 will typically repeat multiple times during the execution, depending on the size of the text file and how many other jobs are running on the system.

12 Our text search finishes its programming (completing the search) and terminates.

DEFINITION Steps 9 and 10 are an example of a *context switch*, which occurs whenever the system interrupts a job and the operating system steps in to schedule another one.

A bit of overhead occurs on every context switch—the OS needs to save the current job state so that it can later resume where it left off. The OS also needs to load the state of the next job to be executed. This state is referred to as the *process context block* (PCB). It is a data structure used to store all the details about a job, such as the program counter, CPU registers, and memory information.

This context switching creates the impression that many tasks are happening at the same time, even when we have only one CPU. When we write concurrent code and execute it on a system with only one processor, our code creates a set of *jobs* that run in this fashion to give a quicker response. When we have a system with multiple CPUs, we can also have true parallelism, in that our jobs are running at the same time on different execution units.

In the 1990s, many systems came with dual-processor motherboards, although these were generally expensive. The first dual-core processor was available commercially (from Intel) in 2005. In the drive to increase processing power and lengthen battery life, most devices now come with multiple cores. This includes cloud server setups, home laptops, and mobile phones. Typically, the architecture of these processors is such that they share the main memory and a bus interface; however, each core has its own CPU and at least one memory cache. The role of the operating system remains the same as in a single-core machine, with the difference being that now the scheduler has to schedule jobs on more than one CPU. Interrupts are quite a bit more complex to implement, and these systems have an advanced interrupt controller, which can interrupt one processor or a group of processors together, depending on the scenario.

Multiprocessing and time sharing

Although many systems adopted multiprocessing in the 1950s, these were usually special purpose-built systems. One example is the Semi-Automatic Ground Environment (SAGE) system, which the US military developed in the 1950s to monitor airspace. SAGE consisted of many remote computers connected using telephone lines. The SAGE system was ahead of its time, and its development gave birth to many ideas in use today, such as real-time processing, distributed computing, and multiprocessing.

Later, in the 1960s, IBM introduced System/360. In various literature, this is referred to as the first real operating system, although similar systems available earlier were named and referred to differently (such as batch-processing systems).

(continued)

System/360, however, was one of the first commercially available systems that had the ability to perform multiprocessing. Prior to this, on some systems, when a job required loading data from or saving data to tape, all processing would stop until the system accessed the slow tape. This created inefficiencies in programs that performed a high proportion of I/O. During this time, the CPU was sitting idle and unable to do any useful work. The solution to this was to load more than one job at a time and allocate a chunk of fixed memory to each job. When one job was waiting for its I/O, the CPU was switched to execute another job.

Another solution that emerged about this time is the idea of time sharing. Prior to this, when computers were still large, shared mainframes, programming involved submitting the instructions and having to wait for hours for the job to compile and execute. If a submitted program had an error in the code, programmers would not know until late in the process. The solution to this was to have a *time-sharing* system, which is when many programmers are connected via terminals. Since programming is mostly a thinking process, only a small proportion of the connected users would be compiling and executing jobs. The CPU resources would be allocated alternately to this small proportion of users when they needed it, reducing the long feedback time.

So far, we have vaguely referred to these execution units managed by the operating system as system jobs. In the next section, we will go into a bit more detail to see how the OS provides us with two main abstractions to model these execution units.

2.2 Abstracting concurrency with processes and threads

When we need to execute our code and manage concurrency (with jobs running, or appearing to run, at the same time), or enable true parallelism in the case of a multi-core system, the operating system provides two abstractions: processes and threads.

A *process* represents a program that is currently running on the system. It is an essential concept in an operating system. The main purpose of an operating system is to efficiently allocate the system's resources (such as memory and CPUs) amongst the many processes that are executing. We can use multiple processes and have them run concurrently as outlined in the previous section.

A *thread* is an extra construct that executes within the process context to give us a more lightweight and more efficient approach to concurrency. As we shall see, each process is started with a single thread of execution, sometimes referred to as the primary or main thread. In this section, we'll look at the differences between modeling concurrency with multiple processes and having many threads running in a single process.

2.2.1 Concurrency with processes

How can we complete a large piece of work when multiple people are working on the task? To pick a concrete example, let's say we are a group of famous artists, and someone commissions us to paint a large piece of art. The deadline is tight, so it's essential we work together as a team to work efficiently and finish on time.

One way of having our artists work on the same picture is to give everyone a separate piece of paper and instruct them to draw a different feature of the finished painting. Each member of the team would draw their feature on their respective piece of paper. When everyone was finished, we would merge our work. We could stick our respective pieces of paper onto a blank canvas, paint over the paper edges, and consider the job done.

In this analogy, the various team members represent our CPUs. The instructions we are following are our programmed code. The execution of a task by the team members (such as painting on the paper) represents a process. We each have our own resources (paper, desk space, etc.), we work independently, and at the end, we come together to merge our work. In this example, we finish the work in two steps. The first step is creating the different parts of the painting in parallel. The second step is sticking the different parts together (see figure 2.2).

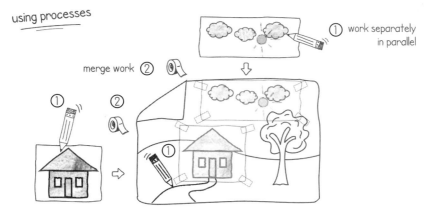

Figure 2.2 Having your own space while performing a task is analogous to using processes.

This is similar to what happens in the operating system with processes. The painter's resources (paper, pencil, etc.) represent the system resources, such as memory. Each operating system process has its own memory space, isolated from other processes. Typically, a process would work independently, having minimal interaction with other processes. Processes provide isolation at the cost of consuming more resources. If, for example, one process crashes due to an error, it will not affect other processes, since it has its own memory space. The downside of this isolation is that we end up consuming more memory. In addition, starting up processes takes a bit longer (compared to threads) since we need to allocate the memory space and other system resources.

Since processes do not share memory with each other, they tend to minimize communication with other processes. Just like our painter analogy, using processes to synchronize and merge work is, in the end, a bit more of a challenge. When processes do need to communicate and synchronize with each other, we program them to use operating system tools and other applications, such as files, databases, pipes, sockets, etc.

2.2.2   Creating processes

A process is an abstraction of how the system will execute our code. Telling the operating system when to create a process and which code it should execute is crucial if we want to execute our code in an isolated manner. Luckily, the operating system gives us system calls for creating, starting, and managing our processes.

For example, Windows has a `CreateProcess()` system call. This call creates the process, allocates the required resources, loads the program code, and starts executing the program as a process.

Alternatively, on UNIX systems, there is a `fork()` system call. Using this call, we can create a copy of an execution. When we make this system call from an executing process, the operating system makes a complete copy of the memory space and the process's resource handlers, including the registers, stack, file handlers, and even the program counter. The new process then takes over this new memory space and continues execution from that point onward.

> **DEFINITION**   We refer to the new process as the *child* and the process that created it as the *parent*. This child and parent terminology also applies to threads, which we shall explore in section 2.2.4.

The `fork()` system call returns the process ID on the parent process and a value of 0 on the child. After forking into two processes, each process can determine what instructions to run based on the return value of the `fork()` system call. A child process can decide to use the copied resources (such as data contained in memory) or to clear it and start anew. Because each process has its own memory space, if one process changes its memory contents (for example, changing a variable's value), the other process will not see this change. Figure 2.3 shows the result of the `fork()` system call on UNIX.

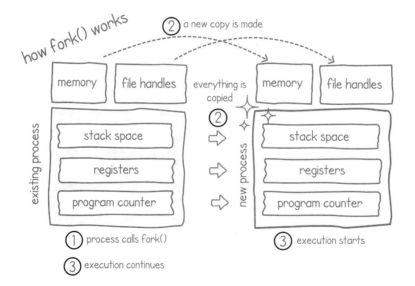

Figure 2.3   Using the `fork()` system call to create a new process

As you can imagine, since each process has its own memory space, the total memory consumed increases every time you spawn a new process. In addition to consuming more memory, copying and allocating system resources takes time and consumes precious CPU cycles. This means that creating too many processes takes a heavy toll on the system. For this reason, it's quite unusual for one program to use a large number of processes concurrently, all working on the same problem.

> **Copy on write for UNIX processes**
>
> Copy on write (COW) is an optimization introduced to the fork() system call. It reduces the time taken by not copying the entire memory space. For systems using this optimization, whenever fork() is called, both child and parent processes share the same memory pages. Then, if one of the processes tries to modify the contents of a memory page, that page is copied to a new location so that each process has its own copy. The OS only makes copies of the memory pages that are modified. This is a great way to save both memory and time, but if a process modifies large parts of its memory, the OS will end up copying most pages anyway.

Support for creating and forking processes in Go is limited to the syscall package and is OS-specific. If we look at the package, we'll find the CreateProcess() function on Windows and ForkExec() and StartProcess() on UNIX systems. Go also gives us the ability to run commands in a new process by calling the exec() function, abstracting some of the OS-specific functions in the syscall package. However, concurrent programming in Go does not typically rely on heavyweight processes. As we shall see, Go adopts a more lightweight threading and goroutine concurrency model instead.

A process will terminate when it has finished executing its code or has encountered an error it cannot handle. Once a process terminates, the OS reclaims all its resources so they are free to be used by other processes. This includes memory space, open file handles, network connections, etc. On UNIX and Windows, when a parent process finishes, it does not automatically terminate the child processes.

2.2.3 Using multiprocessing for common tasks

Have you ever considered what happens behind the scenes when you run a UNIX command like this?

```
$ curl -s https://www.rfc-editor.org/rfc/rfc1122.txt | wc
```

When we run this command on a UNIX system, the command line is forking two concurrent processes. We can check this by opening another terminal and running ps -a:

```
PID     TTY      TIME      CMD
. . .
26013  pts/49    00:00:00  curl
26014  pts/49    00:00:00  wc
. . .
```

The first process (PID 26013, in this example) will run the curl program, which will download the text file from the given URL. The second process (PID 26014) will run the word count program. In this example, we are feeding the output of the first process (curl) into the input of the second one (wc) through a buffer (see figure 2.4). Using the pipe operator, we are telling the operating system to allocate a buffer and to redirect the output of the curl process and the input of the word count to that buffer. The curl process blocks when this buffer is full and resumes when the word count process consumes it. The word count process blocks when the buffer is empty until curl piles up more data.

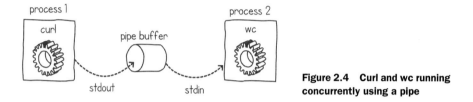

Figure 2.4   Curl and wc running concurrently using a pipe

Once curl reads all the text from the web page, it terminates and puts a marker on the pipe indicating that no more data is available. This marker acts as a signal to the word count process indicating that it can terminate since no more data will be coming.

2.2.4 *Concurrency with threads*

Processes are the heavyweight answer to concurrency. They provide us with good isolation, but they consume lots of resources and take a while to create.

Threads are the answer to some of the problems that come with using processes for concurrency. We can think of threads as the lightweight alternative to multiple processes. Creating a thread is much faster (sometimes 100 times faster), and a thread consumes fewer system resources than a process. Conceptually, threads are another execution context (kind of a microprocess) within a process.

Let's continue our simple analogy, where we're painting a picture with a team of people. Instead of each member of our team having their own piece of paper and drawing independently, we could have one large, empty canvas and hand everyone paintbrushes and pencils. Everyone would share space and draw directly on the large canvas (see figure 2.5).

This is similar to what happens when you use threads. Like when we are sharing the canvas, multiple threads will execute concurrently sharing the same memory space. This is more efficient because we're not consuming large amounts of memory for each execution. In addition, sharing memory space usually means that we don't have to merge our work at the end. Depending on the problem we're solving, we might reach the solution more efficiently by sharing memory with other threads.

When we discussed processes, we saw how a process contained both resources (program and data in memory) together with the execution that is running the program. Conceptually, we can separate the resources from the execution because this lets us

using threads

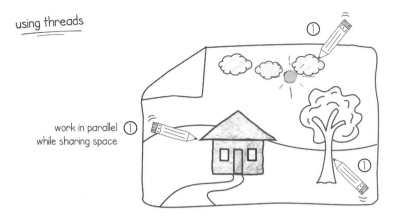

Figure 2.5 **Painting concurrently and sharing space is analogous to using threads.**

create more than one execution and share the resources between them. We call each single execution a *thread* (or *thread of execution*). When you start a process, it contains one main thread by default. When we have more than one thread in a single process, we say that the process is *multithreaded*. Multithreaded programming is when we code in a manner that has different threads working together in the same application. Figure 2.6 shows how two threads can share the same memory, contained in one process.

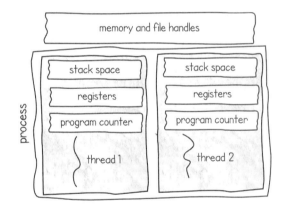

Figure 2.6 **Threads sharing the same process memory space**

When we create a new thread, the operating system needs to create only enough resources to manage the stack space, registers, and a program counter. The new thread runs inside the context of the same process. In contrast, when we create a new process, the OS needs to allocate a completely new memory space for it. For this reason, threads are a lot more lightweight than processes, and we can typically create many more threads than processes before the system starts running out of resources. In addition, because there are so few new resources to allocate, starting a thread is a lot faster than starting a process.

> ### What goes on the stack space?
> The *stack space* stores the local variables that live within a function. These are typically short-lived variables—when the function finishes, they are not used anymore. This space does not include variables that are shared between functions (using pointers), which are allocated on the main memory space, called the *heap*.

This extra performance comes at a price. Working in the same memory space means we don't get the isolation that processes offer. This can lead to one thread stepping over another thread's work. Communication between and synchronization of the multiple threads are important in avoiding this. It's much the same in our team-of-painters analogy. When we are working together on the same project and sharing the same resources, we need to have good communication and synchronization between the painters. We need to constantly talk to each other about what we are doing and when. Without this cooperation, we would risk painting over each other's art, giving us a poor result.

This is similar to how we manage concurrency with multiple threads. Since multiple threads are sharing the same memory space, we need to take care so that the threads are not stepping over each other and causing problems. We do this by using thread communication and synchronization. We'll examine the types of errors that can arise from sharing memory and provide solutions throughout this book.

Since threads share memory space, any change made in main memory by one thread (such as changing a global variable's value) is visible to every other thread in the same process. This is the main advantage of using threads—multiple threads can use this shared memory to work on the same problem together. This enables us to write concurrent code that is very efficient and responsive.

> **NOTE** Threads do not share stack space. Although threads share the same memory space, it's important to realize that each thread has its own private stack space (as was shown in figure 2.6).

Whenever we create a local non-shared variable in a function, we are placing this variable on the stack space. These local variables are thus visible only to the thread that creates them. It's important that each thread has its own private stack space because it might call completely different functions than other threads and will need its own private space to store the variables and return values used in these functions.

We also need each thread to have its own program counter. A *program counter* (also known as an *instruction pointer*) is simply a pointer to the instruction that the CPU will execute next. Since threads will likely execute different parts of our program, each thread needs to have a separate instruction pointer as well.

When we have multiple threads and only one core processor, each thread in a process gets a time slice of the processor. This improves responsiveness, and it's useful in applications where you need to respond to multiple requests concurrently (such as in a web server). If multiple processors (or processor cores) are present in a system, threads will get to execute in parallel with each other. This gives our application a speedup.

Earlier in this chapter, we discussed how the operating system manages multiprocessing, and we talked about jobs being in different states (such as ready to run, running, waiting for I/O, etc.). In a system that handles multithreaded programs, these states describe each thread of execution on the system. Only threads that are ready to run can be picked up and moved to the CPU for execution. If a thread requests I/O, the system will move it to the waiting for I/O state, and so on.

When we create a new thread, we give it an instruction pointer in our program from where the new execution should start. Many programming languages hide this pointer complexity and allow programs to specify target functions (or a method or procedure) where the threads should start executing. The operating system allocates space only for the new thread state, a stack, registers, and the program counter (pointing to the function). The child thread will then run concurrently with the parent, sharing the main memory and other resources, such as open files and network connections.

Once a thread finishes its execution, it terminates, and the operating system reclaims the stack memory space. Depending on the thread implementation, however, a thread terminating does not necessarily terminate the entire process. In Go, when the main thread of execution terminates, the entire process also terminates, even if other threads are still running. This is different than in some other languages. In Java, for instance, a process will terminate only when all the threads in the process have finished.

Operating systems and programming languages implement threads in different manners. For example, on Windows, we can create a thread using the `CreateThread()` system call. On Linux, we can use the `clone()` system call with the `CLONE_THREAD` option. There are also differences in how languages represent threads. For example, Java models threads as objects, Python blocks multiple threads from executing in parallel (using a global interpreter lock), and in Go, as we shall see, there is a finer-grained concept of the goroutine.

POSIX Threads

IEEE attempted to standardize thread implementations using a standard called POSIX Threads (pthreads for short). These threads are created, managed, and synchronized through the use of a standard POSIX Threads API. Various operating systems, including Windows and UNIX systems, offer implementations of this standard. Unfortunately, not all languages support the POSIX Thread standard.

Although differences exist in how threads are created, modeled, and destroyed, the concurrency concepts and techniques involved in coding concurrent programs will be very similar regardless of what technology you use. Thus, learning about the models, techniques, and tools of multithreaded programming in one language will be useful in whatever language you decide to use. The differences lie only in the language's multithreading implementation details.

2.2.5   *A multithreaded application in practice*

Let's now look at an example that makes use of multithreading in a web server application. Suppose we have developed an application that feeds users, via a service, information and scores from their favorite sports teams. This application lives on a server and handles users' requests through their mobile or desktop browsers. For example, Paul might want to know the latest score of a football game in which his favorite team, the New York Giants, are playing. One architecture for this application is shown in figure 2.7. It's composed of two main parts: the client handler's threads and a stream reader thread.

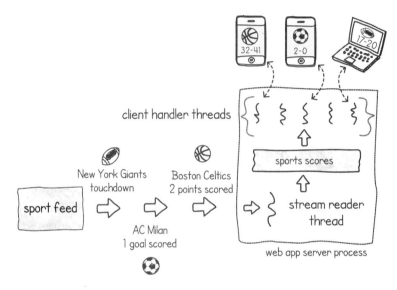

Figure 2.7   A web server application serving sports scores

The stream reader thread reads match events from a sports feed through a network connection. Each message received will tell the application what is happening in a particular game. Some examples are points scored, fouls committed, players on the field, etc. The stream reader thread uses this information to build a picture of the game, storing the score of each game in a shared sports scores data structure.

Each client handler thread takes care of user requests. Depending on the request coming from the user, the thread will look up and read the required match information from the sports scores data structure. It will then return the information to the user's device. We have a pool of these threads so that we're able to handle multiple requests at the same time without making users wait too long for a reply.

Using threads to implement this type of server application has two benefits:

- We consume fewer resources. We can spin up a number of client handler threads without taking up too much memory. In addition, we can size up this pool dynamically, increasing the thread count when we expect more traffic and reducing it during less busy periods. We can do this because spawning and terminating threads is cheap and fast (relative to using processes).
- We have the option to use memory to store and share the sports scores data structure. This is easy to do when using threads because they share the same memory space.

2.2.6 Using multiple processes and threads together

Let's now think of a hybrid example, such as a modern browser, that could use both processes and threads. When a browser is rendering a web page, it needs to download various resources for the downloaded page: text, images, videos, and so on. To do this efficiently, the browser can use multiple threads working concurrently to download and then render the various elements of the page. Threads are ideal for this kind of work since the result page can be kept in the threads' shared memory, and the threads can fill it with the various pieces as they complete their tasks.

If the page includes some scripting that requires heavy computation (such as graphics), we can allocate more threads to perform this computation, possibly in parallel on a multicore CPU. But what happens when one of those scripts misbehaves and crashes? Will it also kill all the other open windows and tabs of the browser?

This is where processes might come in handy. We can design the browser to take advantage of the isolation of processes, perhaps by using a separate process for each window or tab. This ensures that when one web page crashes due to an erroneous script, it doesn't bring down everything, ensuring that the tab containing your long draft email is not lost.

Modern browsers adopt a hybrid thread and process system for this reason. Typically, they have a limit on how many processes they can create, after which tabs start sharing the same process. This is done to reduce memory consumption.

2.3 What's so special about goroutines?

Go's answer to concurrency is the goroutine. As we shall see, it doesn't tie in directly with an operating system thread. Instead, goroutines are managed by Go's runtime at a higher level to give us an even more lightweight construct, consuming far fewer resources than an operating system thread. In this section, we'll start by looking at how we create goroutines before moving on to describe where goroutines sit in terms of operating system threads and processes.

2.3.1 Creating goroutines

Let's now look at how we can create goroutines in Go as we transform a sequential program into a concurrent one. We'll start with the following sequential program.

Listing 2.1   Function simulating some work being done

```go
package main

import (
    "fmt"
    "time"
)

func doWork(id int) {
    fmt.Printf("Work %d started at %s\n", id, time.Now().Format("15:04:05"))
    time.Sleep(1 * time.Second)
    fmt.Printf("Work %d finished at %s\n", id, time.Now().Format("15:04:05"))
}
```

> Simulates doing computation work by sleeping for 1 second

NOTE Visit http://github.com/cutajarj/ConcurrentProgrammingWithGo to see all the listings in this book.

As you can see, we have a function that simulates doing some work. This work could be anything, such as a long-running CPU computation or downloading something from a web page. In the function, we pass an integer as an identifier for the work. Then we simulate doing some work by putting the execution to sleep for 1 second. At the end of this sleep period, we print a message containing the work identifier to the console to signify that we have completed the work. We also print timestamps at the beginning and end to show how long the function takes to execute.

Let's run this function several times sequentially. In listing 2.2, we use a loop to call the function five times, each time passing a different value for i, starting at 0 and finishing at 4. This main() function will run in our main thread of execution, and the doWork() function will be called sequentially in the same execution, with one call after the other.

Listing 2.2   The main() thread calling the doWork() function sequentially

```go
func main() {
    for i := 0; i < 5; i++ {
        doWork(i)
    }
}
```

As you might expect, the output lists the work identifiers one after the other, each taking 1 second:

```
$ go run main.go
Work 0 started at 19:41:03
Work 0 finished at 19:41:04
Work 1 started at 19:41:04
Work 1 finished at 19:41:05
Work 2 started at 19:41:05
Work 2 finished at 19:41:06
Work 3 started at 19:41:06
```

```
Work 3 finished at 19:41:07
Work 4 started at 19:41:07
Work 4 finished at 19:41:08
```

The entire program takes around 5 seconds to complete. When the main thread has no more instructions to execute, it terminates the entire process.

How can we change our instructions so that we perform this work concurrently instead of sequentially? We can put the call to the doWork() function in a goroutine, as shown in listing 2.3. There are two main changes from our previous sequential program. The first is that we are calling the doWork() function with the keyword go. The result is that the function runs in a separate execution concurrently. The main() function does not wait for it to complete to continue. Instead, it goes on to the next instruction, which in this case is to create more goroutines.

Listing 2.3 Main thread calling the doWork() function in parallel

```
func main() {
    for i := 0; i < 5; i++ {
        go doWork(i)        ◁——     Starts a new goroutine that
    }                                calls the doWork() function
    time.Sleep(2 * time.Second)  ◁——┘  Waits for all of the work to
}                                        finish using a longer sleep
```

We can also refer to this manner of calling functions as an *asynchronous* call, meaning that we don't have to wait for the function to complete to continue executing. We can refer to a normal function call as synchronous because we need to wait for the function to return before proceeding with other instructions.

The second change to our main function is that after we call the doWork() function asynchronously, the main() function sleeps for 2 seconds. The sleep instruction needs to be there because in Go, when the main execution runs out of instructions to run, the process terminates. Without this sleep, the process would terminate without giving the goroutines a chance to run. If we try omitting this statement, the program outputs nothing on the console. The output of the program shown in listing 2.3 will look something like this:

```
$ go run main.go
Work 2 started at 20:53:10
Work 1 started at 20:53:10
Work 3 started at 20:53:10
Work 4 started at 20:53:10
Work 0 started at 20:53:10
Work 0 finished at 20:53:11
Work 2 finished at 20:53:11
Work 3 finished at 20:53:11
Work 4 finished at 20:53:11
Work 1 finished at 20:53:11
```

The first thing to notice is that the program completes in about 2 seconds instead of the 5 seconds it took to execute the sequential version. This is simply because we're now executing the work in parallel. Instead of working on one thing, finishing, and then starting another one, we're doing all of the work at once. You can see a representation of this in figure 2.8. In part a of the figure, we have the sequential version of this program, showing the doWork() function being called multiple times, one after the other. In part b, we have the goroutine executing the main() function and spawning five child goroutines, each calling the doWork() function concurrently.

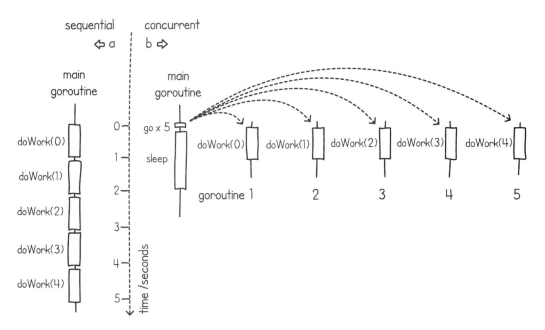

Figure 2.8   (a) The doWork() function called sequentially (b) and the function called concurrently

The second thing to notice when we run the Go program is that the order in which the function messages are output has changed. The program is no longer outputting the work identifiers in order. Instead, they seem to appear at random. Running the program again gives us a different ordering:

```
$ go run main.go
Work 0 started at 20:58:13
Work 3 started at 20:58:13
Work 4 started at 20:58:13
Work 1 started at 20:58:13
Work 2 started at 20:58:13
Work 2 finished at 20:58:14
Work 1 finished at 20:58:14
Work 0 finished at 20:58:14
Work 4 finished at 20:58:14
Work 3 finished at 20:58:14
```

This is because when we run jobs concurrently, we can never guarantee the execution order of those jobs. When our `main()` function creates the five goroutines and submits them, the operating system might pick up the executions in a different order than we created them in.

2.3.2 Implementing goroutines in the user space

Earlier in this chapter, we talked about operating system processes and threads, and we discussed their differences and roles. Where does a goroutine belong within this context? Is a goroutine a separate process or a lightweight thread?

It turns out that goroutines are neither OS threads nor processes. The specification for the Go language does not strictly specify how goroutines should be implemented, but the current Go implementations group sets of goroutine executions onto another set of OS thread executions. To better understand this, let's first talk about another way to model threads of execution, called *user-level* threads.

In the previous section, we talked about threads living inside processes and being managed by the operating system. The operating system knows all about the threads and decides when or whether each thread should execute. The OS also stores the context of each thread (registers, stack, and state) and uses it whenever the threads need executing. We refer to these types of threads as *kernel-level* threads because the operating system manages them. Whenever there is a need for a context switch, the operating system intervenes and chooses the next thread to execute.

Instead of implementing threads at the kernel level, we can have threads running completely in the *user space*, which means the memory space that is part of our application, as opposed to the operating system's space. Using user-level threads is like having different threads of execution running inside the main kernel-level thread, as shown in figure 2.9.

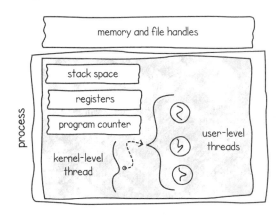

Figure 2.9   User-level threads executing within a single kernel-level thread

From an operating system point of view, a process containing user-level threads will appear to have just one thread of execution. The OS doesn't know anything about user-level threads. The process itself is responsible for managing, scheduling, and context switching its own user-level threads. To execute this internal context switch, there needs to be a separate runtime that maintains a table containing all the data (such as the state) of each user-level thread. We are replicating on a small scale what the OS does, in terms of thread scheduling and management, inside the main thread of the process.

The main advantage of user-level threads is performance. Context-switching a user-level thread is faster than context-switching a kernel-level one. This is because for kernel-level context switches, the OS needs to intervene and choose the next thread to execute. When we can switch execution without invoking any kernel, the executing process can keep hold of the CPU without needing to flush its cache and slow us down.

The downside of using user-level threads comes when they execute code that invokes blocking I/O calls. Consider the situation where we need to read from a file. Since the operating system sees the process as having a single thread of execution, if a user-level thread performs this blocking read call, the entire process is descheduled. If any other user-level threads are present in the same process, they will not get to execute until the read operation is complete. This is not ideal, since one of the advantages of having multiple threads is to perform computations when other threads are waiting for I/O. To work around this limitation, applications using user-level threads tend to use non-blocking calls to perform their I/O operations. However, using non-blocking I/O is not ideal, since not every device supports non-blocking calls.

Another disadvantage of user-level threads is that if we have a multiprocessor or a multicore system, we will be able to utilize only one of the processors at any point in time. The OS sees the single kernel-level thread, containing all the user-level threads, as a single execution. Thus, the OS executes the kernel-level thread on a single processor, so the user-level threads contained in that kernel-level thread will not execute in a truly parallel fashion.

What about green threads?

The term *green thread* was coined in version 1.1 of the Java programming language. The original green threads in Java were an implementation of user-level threads. They ran only on a single core and were managed completely by the JVM. In Java version 1.3, green threads were abandoned in favor of kernel-level threads. Since then, many developers have used the term to refer to other implementations of user-level threads. It is perhaps inaccurate to refer to Go's goroutines as green threads since, as we shall see, Go's runtime allows its goroutines to take full advantage of multiple CPUs.

To further complicate naming matters, a threading model similar to Go was introduced in later versions of Java. However, this time, instead of green threads, the name *virtual threads* was used.

Go provides a hybrid system that gives us the great performance of user-level threads without most of the downsides. It achieves this by using a set of kernel-level threads, each managing a queue of goroutines. Since we have more than one kernel-level thread, we can utilize more than one processor if multiple ones are available.

To illustrate this hybrid technique, suppose our hardware has just two processor cores. We can have a runtime system that creates and uses two kernel-level threads—one for each processor core—and each of these kernel-level threads can manage a set of user-level threads. At some point, the operating system will schedule the two kernel-level threads in parallel, each on a separate processor. We will then have a set of user-level threads running on each processor.

M:N hybrid threading

The system that Go uses for its goroutines is sometimes called the *M:N* threading model. This is when you have *M* user-level threads (goroutines) mapped to *N* kernel-level threads. This contrasts with normal user-level threads, which are referred to as an *N:1* threading model, meaning *N* user-level threads to 1 kernel-level thread. Implementing a runtime for *M:N* models is substantially more complex than other models since it requires many techniques to move around and balance the user-level threads on the set of kernel-level threads.

Go's runtime determines how many kernel-level threads to use based on the number of logical processors. This is set in the environment variable called GOMAXPROCS. If this variable is not set, Go populates this variable by querying the operating system to determine how many CPUs your system has. You can check how many processors Go sees and the value of GOMAXPROCS by executing the following code.

Listing 2.4 Checking how many CPUs are available

```
package main

import (
    "fmt"
    "runtime"
)

func main() {
    fmt.Println("Number of CPUs:", runtime.NumCPU())

    fmt.Println("GOMAXPROCS:", runtime.GOMAXPROCS(0))
}
```

Go defaults the value of **GOMAXPROCS** to the value of NumCPU().

Calling **GOMAXPROCS(n)** with n < 1 returns the current value without altering it.

The output of listing 2.4 will depend on the hardware it runs on. Here's an example of the output on a system with eight cores:

```
$ go run cpucheck.go
Number of CPUs: 8
GOMAXPROCS: 8
```

Go's runtime will assign a local run queue (LRQ) to each of these kernel-level threads. Each LRQ will contain a subset of the goroutines in the program. In addition, there is a global run queue (GRQ) for goroutines that Go hasn't yet assigned to a kernel-level thread (refer to the left side of figure 2.10). Each of the kernel-level threads running on a processor will take care of executing the goroutines present in its LRQ.

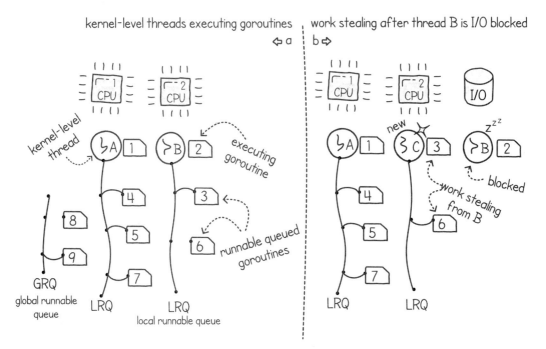

Figure 2.10 (a) Kernel-level threads A and B are executing goroutines from their respective LRQs; (b) a goroutine is waiting on I/O blocking thread B, resulting in the creation or reuse of a new thread C, stealing work from the previous thread.

To work around the problem of blocking calls, Go wraps any blocking operations so that it knows when a kernel-level thread is about to be descheduled. When this happens, Go creates a new kernel-level thread (or reuses an idle one from a pool) and moves the queue of goroutines to this new thread, which picks a goroutine from the queue and starts executing it. The old thread with its goroutine waiting for I/O is then descheduled by the OS. This system ensures that a goroutine making a blocking call will not block the entire local run queue of goroutines (refer to the right side of figure 2.10).

This system of moving goroutines from one queue to another is known in Go as *work stealing*. Work stealing does not just happen when a goroutine makes a blocking call. Go can also use this mechanism when there is an imbalance in the number of goroutines in the queues. For example, if a particular LRQ is empty and the kernel-level thread has no more goroutines to execute, it will steal work from the queue of another thread. This ensures that our processors are balanced with work and that none are idle when there is more work to execute.

Locking to a kernel-level thread

In Go, we can force a goroutine to lock itself to an OS thread by calling the `runtime.LockOSThread()` function. This call binds the goroutine exclusively to its kernel-level thread. No other goroutines will run on the same OS thread until the goroutine calls `runtime.UnlockOSThread()`.

These functions can be used when we need specialized control over the kernel-level threads—for example, when we are interfacing with an external C library and need to make sure that the goroutine does not move to another kernel-level thread, causing problems accessing the library.

2.3.3 *Scheduling goroutines*

After a kernel-level thread has had its fair share of time on the CPU, the OS scheduler context switches the next thread from the run queue. This is known as *preemptive scheduling*. It's implemented using a system of clock interrupts that stops the executing kernel-level thread and calls the OS scheduler. Since the interrupt calls only the OS scheduler, the Go scheduler, which runs in the user space, needs a different system.

The Go scheduler needs to execute to perform its context switching. Thus, the Go scheduler needs user-level events to trigger its execution (see figure 2.11). These events include starting a new goroutine (using the keyword `go`), making a system call (for example, reading from a file), or synchronizing goroutines.

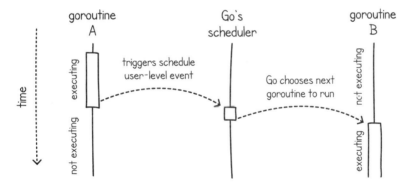

Figure 2.11 Context switching in Go requires user-level events.

We can also call the Go scheduler in our code to try to get the scheduler to context-switch to another goroutine. In concurrency lingo, this is usually called a *yield* command. It's when a thread decides to yield control so that another thread gets its turn on the CPU. In the following listing, we are using the command `runtime.Gosched()` to call the scheduler directly in our `main()` goroutine.

Listing 2.5   Calling the Go scheduler

```go
package main

import (
    "fmt"
    "runtime"
)

func sayHello() {
    fmt.Println("Hello")
}

func main() {
    go sayHello()
    runtime.Gosched()      ◁——┐  Calling the Go scheduler
    fmt.Println("Finished")      gives the other goroutine
}                                a chance to run.
```

Without calling the scheduler directly, we have very little chance of getting the
sayHello() function executed. The main() goroutine will terminate before the goroutine calling the sayHello() function gets any time to run on the CPU. Since in Go we
exit the process when the main() goroutine terminates, we wouldn't get to see the text
"Hello" printed.

> **WARNING** We have no control over which goroutine the scheduler will select
> to execute. When we call the Go scheduler, it might pick up the other goroutine
> and start executing it, or it might continue the execution of the goroutine that
> called the scheduler.

In listing 2.5, the scheduler may very well select the main() goroutine again, and we
may never see the "Hello" message. In fact, by calling runtime.Gosched() in the listing,
we are only increasing the chances that sayHello() will be executed. There is no guarantee that it will.

As with the OS scheduler, we cannot predictably determine what the Go scheduler
will execute next. As programmers writing concurrent programs, we must never write
code that relies on an apparent scheduling order, because the next time we run the
program, the ordering might be different. If you try executing listing 2.5 several
times, you will eventually get an execution that will output Finished without executing
the sayHello() function. If we need to control the order of execution of our threads,
we'll need to add synchronization mechanisms to our code instead of relying on the
scheduler. We'll discuss these techniques starting in chapter 4.

2.4   *Concurrency versus parallelism*

Many developers use the terms *concurrency* and *parallelism* interchangeably, sometimes
referring to them as the same concept. However, many textbooks make a clear distinc-
tion between the two.

We can think of *concurrency* as an attribute of the program code and *parallelism* as a property of the executing program. Concurrent programming occurs whenever we write our programs in a way that groups instructions into separate tasks, outlining the boundaries and synchronization points. These are some examples of such tasks:

- Handle one user's request.
- Search one file for some text.
- Calculate the result of one row in a matrix multiplication.
- Render one frame of a video game.

These tasks then may or may not execute in parallel. Whether they execute in parallel will depend on the hardware and environment where we execute the program. For example, if our concurrent matrix multiplication program runs on a multicore system, we might be able to perform more than a single row calculation at the same time. For parallel execution to happen, we require multiple processing units. Otherwise, the system can interleave between the tasks, giving the impression that it is doing more than one task at the same time. For example, two threads can take turns and share a single processor, each taking a time share. Because the OS switches the threads often and quickly, they both seem to be running at the same time.

NOTE Concurrency is about *planning* how to do many tasks at the same time. Parallelism is about *performing* many tasks at the same time.

Obviously, definitions overlap. In fact, we can say that parallelism is a subset of concurrency. Only concurrent programs can execute in parallel, but not all concurrent programs will execute in parallel.

Can we have parallelism when we have only one processor? You have seen that parallelism requires multiple processing units, but if we widen our definition of a processing unit, a thread that is waiting for an I/O operation to complete is not really idling. Isn't writing to disk still part of the program's work? If we have two threads, where one is writing to disk and another is executing instructions on the CPU, should we consider this to be parallel execution? Other components, such as disk and network, can also be working at the same time with the CPU for the program. Even in this scenario, we typically reserve the term *parallel execution* to refer to computations and not to I/O. However, many textbooks mention the term *pseudo-parallel execution* in this context. This refers to a system with one processor giving the impression that multiple jobs are being executed at the same time. The system does this by frequently context-switching jobs either on a timer or whenever an executing job requests a blocking I/O operation.

2.5 Exercises

NOTE Visit http://github.com/cutajarj/ConcurrentProgrammingWithGo to see all the code solutions.

1 Write a program similar to the one in listing 2.3 that accepts a list of text filenames as arguments. For each filename, the program should spawn a new
   goroutine that will output the contents of that file to the console. You can use
   the `time.Sleep()` function to wait for the child goroutines to complete (until
   you know how to do this better). Call the program `catfiles.go`. Here's how you
   can execute this Go program:

```
go run catfiles.go txtfile1 txtfile2 txtfile3
```

2 Expand the program you wrote in the first exercise so that instead of printing
   the contents of the text files, it searches for a string match. The string to search
   for is the first argument on the command line. When you spawn a new goroutine, instead of printing the file's contents, it should read the file and search for
   a match. If the goroutine finds a match, it should output a message saying that
   the filename contains a match. Call the program `grepfiles.go`. Here's how you
   can execute this Go program ("bubbles" is the search string in this example):

```
go run grepfiles.go bubbles txtfile1 txtfile2 txtfile3
```

3 Change the program you wrote in the second exercise so that instead of passing
   a list of text filenames, you pass a directory path. The program will look inside
   this directory and list the files. For each file, you can spawn a goroutine that will
   search for a string match (the same as before). Call the program `grepdir.go`.
   Here's how you can execute this Go program:

```
go run grepdir.go bubbles ../../commonfiles
```

4 Adapt the program in the third exercise to continue searching recursively in
   any subdirectories. If you give your search goroutine a file, it should search for a
   string match in that file, just like in the previous exercises. Otherwise, if you
   give it a directory, it should recursively spawn a new goroutine for each file or
   directory found inside. Call the program `grepdirrec.go`, and execute it by running this command:

```
go run grepdirrec.go bubbles ../../commonfiles
```

Summary

- Multiprocessing operating systems and modern hardware provide concurrency
  through their scheduling and abstractions.
- Processes are the heavyweight way of modeling concurrency; however, they provide isolation.
- Threads are lightweight and share the same process memory space.

- User-level threads are even more lightweight and performant, but they require complex handling to prevent the process managing all the user-level threads from being descheduled.
- User-level threads contained in a single kernel-level thread will use only one processor at a time, even if the system has multiple processors.
- Goroutines adopt a hybrid threading system with a set of kernel-level threads containing a set of goroutines apiece. With this system, multiple processors can execute the goroutines in parallel.
- Go's runtime uses a system of work stealing to move goroutines to other kernel-level threads whenever there is a load imbalance or a descheduling takes place.
- Concurrency is about planning how to do many tasks at the same time.
- Parallelism is about performing many tasks at the same time.

Thread communication using memory sharing

3

This chapter covers

- Using inter-thread communication with our hardware architecture
- Communicating with memory sharing
- Recognizing race conditions

Threads of execution working together to solve a common problem require some form of communication. This is what is known as *inter-thread communication* (ITC), or *inter-process communication* (IPC) when referring to processes. This type of communication falls under two main classes: memory sharing and message passing. In this chapter, we will focus on the former.

Memory sharing is similar to having all our executions share a large, empty canvas (the process's memory) on which each execution gets to write the results of its own computation. We can coordinate the executions in such a way that they collaborate using this empty canvas. In contrast, message passing is exactly what it sounds like. Just like people, threads can communicate by sending messages to each other. In chapter 8, we'll investigate message passing in Go using channels.

The type of thread communication we use in our applications will depend on the type of problem we're trying to solve. Memory sharing is a common approach to ITC, but as we shall see in this chapter, it comes with a certain set of challenges.

3.1 Sharing memory

Communication via memory sharing is like trying to talk to a friend, but instead of exchanging messages, we're using a whiteboard (or a large piece of paper), and we're exchanging ideas, symbols, and abstractions (see figure 3.1).

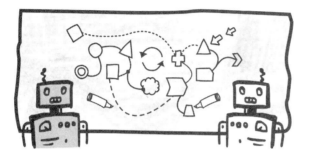

Figure 3.1   Communication via memory sharing

In concurrent programming using memory sharing, we allocate a part of the process's memory—for example, a shared data structure or a variable—and we have different goroutines work concurrently on this memory. In our analogy, the whiteboard is the shared memory used by the various goroutines.

In Go, our goroutines may live under several kernel-level threads. Thus, the hardware and operating system architecture on which we run our multithreaded application needs to enable this type of memory sharing between threads belonging to the same process. If our system has only a single processor, the architecture can be simple. We can give the same memory access to all kernel-level threads on the same process, and we can context-switch between threads, letting each thread read and write to memory as it pleases. However, the situation grows more complex when we have a system with more than one processor (or a multicore system) because computer architecture usually involves various layers of caches between the CPUs and main memory.

Figure 3.2 shows a simplified example of a typical bus architecture. Here, the processor uses a system bus when it needs to read or write from main memory. Before a processor uses the bus, it listens to make sure the bus is idle and not in use by another processor. Once the bus is free, the processor places a request for a memory location and goes back to listening and waiting for a reply on the bus.

As we scale the number of processors in the system, this bus becomes busier and acts as a bottleneck on our ability to add more processors. To reduce the load on the bus, we can use caches to bring memory contents closer to where they're needed and thus improve performance. The caches also reduce the load on the system bus since the CPU can now read most of the required data from cache instead of querying the memory. This prevents the bus from acting as a bottleneck. The example shown in figure 3.2

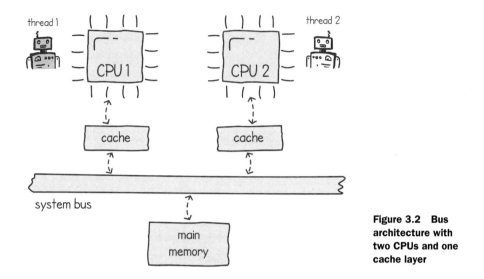

Figure 3.2   Bus architecture with two CPUs and one cache layer

is a simplified architecture with two CPUs and one layer of caching. Typically, modern architectures contain many more processors and multiple layers of caching.

In figure 3.2, we have two threads running in parallel that want to communicate via memory sharing. Let's assume that thread 1 tries to read a variable from main memory. The system will bring the contents of a block of memory, containing the variable, into a cache closer to the CPU (via the bus). Then, when thread 1 needs to read again or update that variable, it will be able to perform that operation faster using the cache. It will not need to overload the system bus by trying to read the variable from the main memory again. This is shown in figure 3.3.

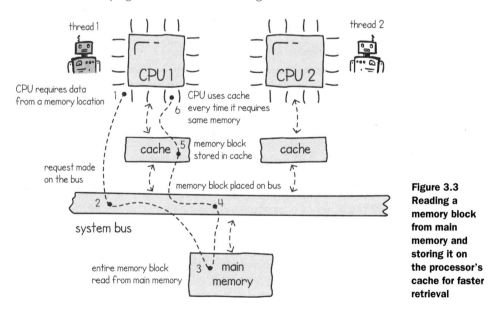

Figure 3.3 Reading a memory block from main memory and storing it on the processor's cache for faster retrieval

Let's now suppose thread 1 decides to update the value of this variable. This results in the contents of the cache being updated with this change. If we don't do anything else, thread 2 might want to read this very same variable, and when it fetches it from main memory, it will have an outdated value, without the changes made by thread 1.

One solution to this problem is to perform what is known as a *cache write-through*: when thread 1 updates the cache contents, we mirror the update back to the main memory. However, this doesn't solve the problem if thread 2 has an outdated copy of the same memory block in another local CPU cache. To address this case, we can make caches listen to bus memory update messages. When a cache notices an update to the memory that it has replicated in its cache space, it either applies the update or invalidates the cache line containing the updated memory. If we invalidate the cache line, the next time the thread requires the variable, it will have to fetch it from memory, obtaining an updated copy. This system is shown in figure 3.4.

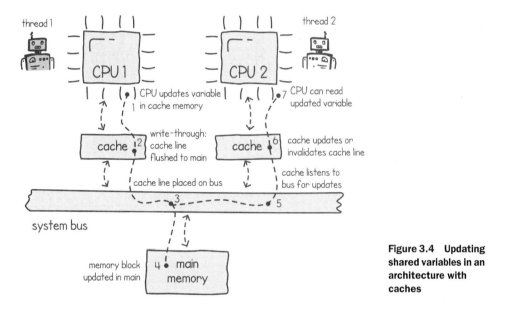

Figure 3.4 Updating shared variables in an architecture with caches

The mechanism for dealing with reads and writes on memory and caches in a multiprocessor system is known as the *cache-coherency protocols*. The write-back with invalidation, mentioned previously, is an outline of one such protocol. Modern architectures typically use a mixture of these protocols.

Coherency wall

Microchip engineers worry that cache coherence will be the limiting factor as they scale the number of processor cores. With many more processors, implementing cache coherence will become a lot more complex and costly and might eventually limit performance. This limit is known as the *coherency wall*.

3.2   *Memory sharing in practice*

Let's examine a couple of examples showing how we can use shared memory amongst goroutines in our concurrent Go programs. First, we'll look at simple variable sharing between two goroutines, illustrating the concept of memory escape analysis. Then we'll look at a more complex application where multiple goroutines work together to download and process several web pages in parallel.

3.2.1   *Sharing a variable between goroutines*

How do we get two goroutines to share memory? In this first example, we'll create one goroutine that will share a variable in memory with the `main()` goroutine (executing the `main()` function). The variable will act like a countdown timer. One goroutine will decrease the value of this variable every second, and another goroutine will read the variable more frequently and output it on the console. Figure 3.5 shows the two goroutines doing this.

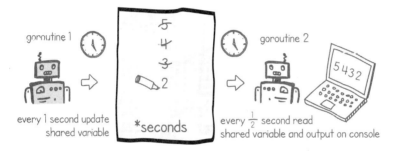

Figure 3.5   Two goroutines sharing a countdown timer variable

In listing 3.1, the main thread allocates space for an integer variable, called `count`, and then shares a memory pointer reference, called `*seconds`, with a newly created goroutine, calling the `countdown()` function. This function updates the shared variable every 1 second, decreasing its value by `1` until it's `0`. The `main()` goroutine reads this shared variable every half second and outputs it. In this way, the two goroutines share the memory at the pointer location.

Listing 3.1   Goroutines sharing a variable in memory

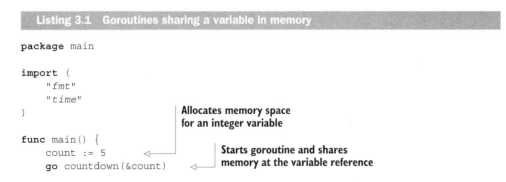

```
package main

import (
    "fmt"
    "time"
)

func main() {
    count := 5
    go countdown(&count)
```

Allocates memory space
for an integer variable

Starts goroutine and shares
memory at the variable reference

```
    for count > 0 {
        time.Sleep(500 * time.Millisecond)          The main() goroutine reads the value of
        fmt.Println(count)                           the shared variable every half second.
    }
}

func countdown(seconds *int) {
    for *seconds > 0 {
        time.Sleep(1 * time.Second)       The goroutine updates the
        *seconds -= 1            ◁──────   value of the shared variable.
    }
}
```

> **NOTE** You can visit http://github.com/cutajarj/ConcurrentProgramming-WithGo to see any of the listings in this book.

Since we read the value for the shared variable more frequently than we update it, the same value is recorded more than once in our console output:

```
$ go run countdown.go
5
4
4
3
3
2
2
1
1
0
```

What happens here is that we have a very simple memory-sharing concurrent program. One goroutine updates the contents of a particular memory location, and another thread reads its contents.

If you removed the go keyword from listing 3.1, the program would become sequential. It would create the variable count on the main stack, and it would pass a reference to it to the countdown() function. The countdown() function would take 5 seconds to return, during which it would update the value on the main() function's stack every second by subtracting 1. When the function returns, the count variable would have a value of 0 and the main() function would not enter the loop but instead would terminate since the count's value would be 0.

3.2.2 Escape analysis

Where should we allocate memory space for the variable count? This is a decision that the Go compiler must make for every new variable we create. It has two choices: allocate space on the function's stack or in the main process's memory, which we call the *heap space*.

In the previous chapter, we talked about threads sharing the same memory space, and we saw that each thread has its own stack space but shares the main memory of the process. When we execute the `countdown()` function in a separate goroutine, the `count` variable cannot exist on the `main()` function's stack. It doesn't make sense for Go's runtime to allow a goroutine to read or modify the memory contents of another goroutine's stack because the goroutines might have completely different lifecycles. One goroutine's stack might not be available anymore by the time another goroutine needs to modify it. Go's compiler is smart enough to realize when we are sharing memory between goroutines. When it notices this, it allocates memory on the heap instead of the stack, even though our variables might look like they are local ones belonging on the stack.

> **DEFINITION**   In technical speak, when we declare a variable that looks like it belongs to the local function's stack but instead is allocated in the heap memory, we say that the variable has *escaped* to the heap. *Escape analysis* consists of the compiler algorithms that decide whether a variable should be allocated on the heap instead of the stack.

There are many instances where a variable escapes to the heap. Anytime a variable is shared outside the scope of a function's stack frame, the variable is allocated on the heap. Sharing a variable's reference between goroutines is one such example, as illustrated in figure 3.6.

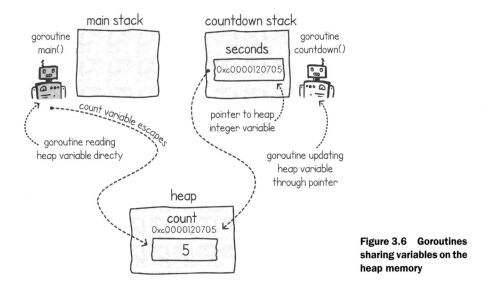

Figure 3.6   Goroutines sharing variables on the heap memory

In Go, there is an additional small cost to using memory on the heap as opposed to the stack. This is because when we are done using the memory, the heap needs to be cleaned up by Go's garbage collection. The garbage collector goes through the objects in the heap that are no longer referenced by any goroutine and marks the space as free so that it can be reused. When we use space on the stack, this memory is reclaimed when the function finishes.

We can tell that a variable has escaped to heap memory by asking the compiler to show its optimization decisions. We can do this by using the -m compile-time option:

```
$ go tool compile -m countdown.go
countdown.go:7:6: can inline countdown
countdown.go:7:16: seconds does not escape
countdown.go:15:5: moved to heap: count
```

Here the compiler is telling us which variables are escaping to heap memory and which ones are staying on the stack. At line 7, the seconds pointer variable is not escaping to the heap and is thus staying on the stack of our countdown() function. However, the compiler is placing the count variable on the heap since we are sharing the variable with another goroutine.

If we remove the go call from our code, turning it into a sequential program, the compiler will not move the count variable to the heap. Here is the output after we remove the go keyword:

```
$ go tool compile -m countdown.go
countdown.go:7:6: can inline countdown
countdown.go:16:14: inlining call to countdown
countdown.go:7:16: seconds does not escape
```

Notice that we no longer get the message moved to heap for the count variable. The other change is that we now get a message saying the compiler is inlining the function call to countdown(). *Inlining* is an optimization where, under certain conditions, the compiler replaces the function call with the contents of the function. The compiler does this to improve performance since calling a function has a slight overhead, which comes from preparing the new function stack, passing the input params onto the new stack, and making the program jump to the new instructions on the function. When we execute the function in parallel, it doesn't make sense to inline the function, since the function is executed using a separate stack, potentially on another kernel-level thread.

By using goroutines, we are forfeiting some compiler optimizations, such as inlining, and we are increasing overhead by putting our shared variable on the heap. The tradeoff is that by executing our code concurrently, we potentially achieve a speedup.

3.2.3 *Updating shared variables from multiple goroutines*

Let's now look at an example involving more than two goroutines, where the goroutines are updating the same variables at the same time. For this example, we'll write a program to find out how often the English alphabet letters appear in common text. The program will process web pages by downloading them and then counting how often each letter in the alphabet appears on the pages. When the program completes, it should give us a frequency table with a count of how often each character occurs.

Let's start by first developing this in a normal sequential manner and then changing our code so that it runs in a concurrent fashion. The steps and data structures needed to develop such a program are shown in figure 3.7. We'll use a slice integer data structure as our letter table, containing the results of each letter count. Our program will examine a list of web pages, one at a time, downloading and scanning the web page's contents, and reading and updating the count of each English letter encountered on the page.

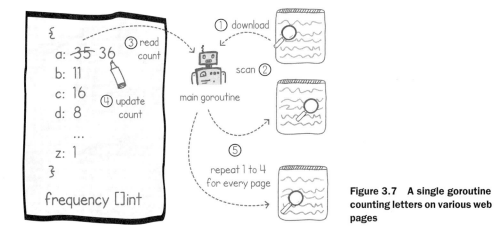

Figure 3.7   **A single goroutine counting letters on various web pages**

We can start by writing a simple function that downloads all the text from a URL and then iterates over every character in the downloaded text, as shown in the next listing. While we're doing this, we can update the letter frequency count table for any characters in the English alphabet (excluding punctuation marks, spaces, etc.).

Listing 3.2   Function producing a letter-frequency count for a web page

```
package main

import (
    "fmt"
    "io "
    "net/http"
    "strings"
)

const allLetters = "abcdefghijklmnopqrstuvwxyz"

func countLetters(url string, frequency []int) {
    resp, _ := http.Get(url)
    defer resp.Body.Close()
    if resp.StatusCode != 200 {
        panic("Server returning error status code: " + resp.Status)
    }
```

Downloads the web page from the given URL

Closes the response at the end of the function

```
    body, _ := io.ReadAll(resp.Body)
    for _, b := range body {              ⟵——— Iterates over every downloaded character
        c := strings.ToLower(string(b))
        cIndex := strings.Index(allLetters, c)  ⟵┐
        if cIndex >= 0 {                          │  Finds the index of the
            frequency[cIndex] += 1   ⟵┐          │  character in the alphabet
        }                             │
    }                                 │  If the character is part of the alphabet,
    fmt.Println("Completed:", url)    │  increments the count by 1
}
```

NOTE   For the sake of conciseness, we are ignoring some error handling in these listings.

The function starts by downloading the contents of the URL in its input argument. It then iterates over every single character, using the `for` loop, and converts each to lowercase. We do this so that we count uppercase and lowercase characters as equivalent. If we find the character in the string containing the English alphabet, then we increment the count of that character in the Go slice entry represented by that character. Here we are using the Go slice as our character frequency table. In this table, the element 0 represents the count of the letter *a*, element 1 is *b*, 2 is *c*, and so on. At the end of our function, after we have processed the entire downloaded document, we output a message showing which URL the function completed.

Let's run this function using some web pages. Ideally, we want static pages that never change. It would also be good if the contents of the web pages were just text with no document formatting, images, links, etc. For example, a news web page would not suffice, since the content changes frequently and is rich in formatting.

The www.rfc-editor.org website contains a database of technical documents (called *requests for comments*, or RFCs) about the internet, including specifications, standards, policies, and memos. It's a good source for this exercise because the documents do not change, and we can download text-only documents with no formatting. The other advantage is that the URLs have incremental document IDs, which make them predictable. We can use the URL format of `rfc-editor.org/rfc/rfc{ID}.txt`. For example, we can get document ID 1001 with the URL `rfc-editor.org/rfc/rfc1001.txt`.

Now we just need a `main()` function that runs our `countLetters()` function many times, each time with a different URL, passing in the same frequency table and letting it update the character counts. The following listing shows this `main()` function.

Listing 3.3   `main()` function calling `countLetters()` with different URLs

```
                                                Initializes slice space for the frequency table
func main() {
    var frequency = make([]int, 26)   ⟵┘    Iterates from document ID 1000
    for i := 1000; i <= 1030; i++ {   ⟵┘    to 1030 to download 31 docs
        url := fmt.Sprintf("https://rfc-editor.org/rfc/rfc%d.txt", i)
        countLetters(url, frequency)  ⟵┐
    }                                  │  Calls the countLetters()
                                       │  function sequentially
```

```
    for i, c := range allLetters {
        fmt.Printf("%c-%d ", c, frequency[i])  ⏴┐
    }                                               │  Outputs each letter with its frequency
}
```

In the `main()` function, we create a new slice that will store the results, containing the letter frequency table. Then we specify downloading 31 documents from `rfc1000.txt` to `rfc1030.txt`. The program calls our `countLetters()` function sequentially to download and process each web page (i.e., one after the other). Depending on the speed of our internet connection, the program can take anywhere from a few seconds to a couple of minutes. Once it's finished, the `main()` function will output the contents of the `frequency` slice variable:

```
$ time go run charcountersequential.go
Completed: https://rfc-editor.org/rfc/rfc1000.txt
Completed: https://rfc-editor.org/rfc/rfc1001.txt
. . .
Completed: https://rfc-editor.org/rfc/rfc1028.txt
Completed: https://rfc-editor.org/rfc/rfc1029.txt
Completed: https://rfc-editor.org/rfc/rfc1030.txt
a-103445 b-23074 c-61005 d-51733 e-181360 f-33381 g-24966 h-47722 i-103262 j-
    3279 k-8839 l-49958 m-40026 n-108275 o-106320 p-41404 q-3410 r-101118 s-
    101040 t-136812 u-35765 v-13666 w-18259 x-4743 y-18416 z-1404
real    0m17.035s
user    0m0.447s
sys     0m0.308s
```

The last line of the program output (before the times) contains the count of each letter in all 31 documents. The first entry in the list represents the count for the letter *a*, the second for *b*, and so on. A quick glance tells us that the letter *e* is the most frequent letter in our documents. The program took about 17 seconds to complete.

Let's now try to improve the speed of our program by using concurrent programming. Figure 3.8 shows how we can use multiple goroutines to download and process each web page concurrently instead of one after the other. The trick here is to run our `countLetters()` function concurrently by using the `go` keyword.

To implement this, we have to make two changes to our `main()` function, as shown in listing 3.4. The first is that we'll add `go` to our `countLetters()` function call. This just means that we will be creating 31 goroutines, one per web page. Each goroutine will then download and process its document concurrently (i.e., all at the same time, instead of one after the other). The second change is that we'll wait for a few seconds until all the goroutines are complete. We need this step; otherwise, when the `main()` goroutine finishes, the process would terminate before we had finished processing all the downloads. This is because in Go, when the `main()` goroutine completes, the entire process terminates. This happens even if other goroutines are still executing.

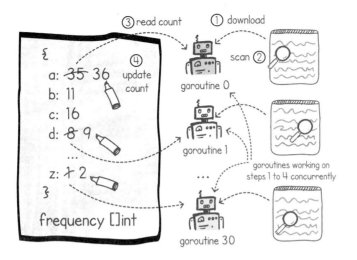

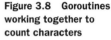

Figure 3.8   Goroutines working together to count characters

WARNING   Using the `countLetters()` function from multiple goroutines will produce erroneous results due to a race condition that will be discussed in the next section. We are doing this here for demonstration purposes only.

Listing 3.4   `main()` function creating goroutines and sharing the frequency slice

```
func main() {
    var frequency = make([]int, 26)
    for i := 1000; i <= 1030; i++ {
        url := fmt.Sprintf("https://rfc-editor.org/rfc/rfc%d.txt", i)
        go countLetters(fmt.Sprintf(url), frequency)
    }
    time.Sleep(10 * time.Second)
    for i, c := range allLetters {
        fmt.Printf("%c-%d ", c, frequency[i])
    }
}
```

Waits for the goroutines to finish → `time.Sleep(10 * time.Second)`

Starts a goroutine that calls the countLetters() function

Outputs each letter with its frequency

NOTE   Using `Sleep()` is not a great way to wait for another goroutine to complete. In fact, if you have a slow internet connection, you might need to increase the wait time in listing 3.4. In chapter 5, we'll discuss how to use condition variables and semaphores for this task. Additionally, in chapter 6, we will introduce the concept of waitgroups, which allow us to block the execution of a goroutine until certain tasks have completed.

Notice how, in this example, the goroutines all share the same data structure in memory. When we initialize the Go slice in the `main()` function, we allocate space for it on the heap. When we create the goroutines, we pass them all the same reference to the memory location containing the Go slice. The 31 goroutines then go about reading and writing to the same frequency slice concurrently. In this way, the threads are cooperating and working together to update the same memory space. That's all there is to thread memory sharing. You have a data structure or a variable that you're sharing with other threads. The difference compared to sequential programming is that a goroutine might write a value to a variable, but when it reads it back, the value might be different since another goroutine might have changed it.

If you ran this program, you might have noticed a problem with it. Here's what the output looks like after running it:

```
$ time go run charcounterconcurrent.go
Completed: https://rfc-editor.org/rfc/rfc1022.txt
Completed: https://rfc-editor.org/rfc/rfc1019.txt
. . .
Completed: https://rfc-editor.org/rfc/rfc1012.txt
Completed: https://rfc-editor.org/rfc/rfc1021.txt
Completed: https://rfc-editor.org/rfc/rfc1010.txt
a-103074 b-23054 c-60854 d-51609 e-179936 f-33356 g-24933 h-47637 i-102856 j-
    3279 k-8835 l-49873 m-39962 n-107840 o-105948 p-41334 q-3408 r-100730 s-
    100659 t-136100 u-35709 v-13659 w-18240 x-4743 y-18411 z-1404
real    0m11.485s
user    0m0.940s
sys     0m0.430s
```

First, you'll notice that the downloads finish much faster than in the sequential version. We were expecting this. Doing the downloads all in one go should be faster than doing them one after the other. Second, the output messages are no longer in order. Since we start downloading all the documents at the same time, some will finish earlier than others because they all have different sizes. The ones that finish earlier output their completed messages first. The order in which we process the pages doesn't really matter for this application.

The problem is in the result. When we compare the character counts of the sequential run against the concurrent one, we notice a difference: most characters have a lower count in the concurrent version. For example, the letter *e* has a count of 181,360 in the sequential run and a count of 179,936 in the concurrent one (your concurrent results may differ).

We can try running both the sequential and concurrent programs multiple times. The results will vary depending on the computer setup, such as the internet connection and processor speed. However, when we compare them, we'll see that the sequential version gives us the same results each time, but the parallel version gives us slightly different values on each run. What is going on?

This is the result of what's known as a *race condition*—when we have multiple threads (or processes) sharing a resource and they step over each other, giving us unexpected results. Let's go into more detail on why race conditions happen. (In the next chapter, we'll see how we can fix this problem with our concurrent letter frequency program.)

3.3   *Race conditions*

Race conditions are what happens when your program is trying to do many things at the same time, and its behavior is dependent on the exact timing of independent unpredictable events. As we saw in the previous section, our letter frequency program ends up giving unexpected results, but sometimes the outcome is even more dramatic. Our concurrent code might be happily running for a long period, and then one day it may crash, resulting in more serious data corruption. This can happen because the concurrent executions are lacking proper synchronization and are stepping over each other.

System-wide outage

The mood in the meeting on the 24th floor of Turner Belfort, a huge international investment bank, was as bleak as it gets. The firm's software developers met to discuss the best way forward after a critical core application failed and caused a system-wide outage. The system failure caused client accounts to report erroneous amounts in their holdings.

"Guys, we have a serious issue here. I found that the outage was caused by a race condition in our code, introduced a while ago and triggered last night," said Mark Adams, senior developer.

The room went silent. The tiny cars outside the floor-to-ceiling windows slowly and silently crept along in the heavy city traffic. The senior developers immediately understood the severity of the situation, realizing that they would now be working around the clock to fix the problem and sort out the mess in the datastore. The less experienced developers understood that a race condition was serious, but they didn't know exactly what caused it and, therefore, kept their mouths shut.

Eventually, David Holmes, delivery manager, broke the silence with this question: "The application has been running for months without any problems, and we haven't released any code recently, so how on earth is it possible that the software just broke down?"

Everyone shook their heads and returned to their desks, leaving David in the room alone, puzzled. He took out his phone and searched for the term "race condition."

This type of error doesn't just apply to computer programs. Sometimes we see examples of this in real life when we have concurrent actors interacting. For example, a couple might share a household shopping list, such as a list of groceries written on the fridge door. In the morning, before both head out to the office, they independently decide that they'll shop for groceries after work. The two take a picture of the list and later drop by the shops to purchase all the items. Unbeknownst to each, the other has decided to do the same thing. This is how they end up with two of everything they need (see figure 3.9).

Figure 3.9   Race conditions happen in real life too, sometimes.

Other race conditions

A *software race condition* is one that occurs in a concurrent program. Race conditions occur in other environments as well, such as in distributed systems, electronic circuits, and sometimes even in human interactions.

In the letter-frequency application, we had a race condition that resulted in the program underreporting the letter counts. Let's write a simpler concurrent program that highlights a race condition so that we can understand this problem better. In the upcoming chapters, we'll discuss different ways to avoid race conditions, such as fixing the letter counter program using mutexes (discussed in the next chapter).

3.3.1   *Stingy and Spendy: Creating a race condition*

Stingy and Spendy are two separate goroutines. Stingy works hard and earns the cash but never spends a single dollar. Spendy is the opposite, spending money without earning anything. Both goroutines share a common bank account. To demonstrate a race condition, we'll make Stingy and Spendy earn and spend 10 dollars each time for 1 million times. Since Spendy is spending the same exact amount that Stingy is earning, we should finish with the same amount we started with if our programming is correct (see figure 3.10).

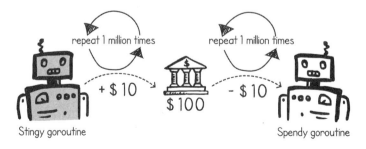

Figure 3.10   A race condition with two goroutines

In listing 3.5, we first create the Stingy and Spendy functions. Both `stingy()` and `spendy()` iterate 1 million times, adjusting a shared money variable each time—the `stingy()` function adding 10 dollars each time and the `spendy()` function subtracting it.

> **WARNING** Using the following `stingy()` and `spendy()` functions from multiple goroutines will produce race conditions. We are doing it here for demonstration purposes only.

Listing 3.5   Stingy and Spendy functions

stingy()
function
adds 10
dollars

```
func stingy(money *int) {
    for i := 0; i < 1000000; i++ {
        *money += 10
    }
    fmt.Println("Stingy Done")
}

func spendy(money *int) {
    for i := 0; i < 1000000; i++ {
        *money -= 10
    }
    fmt.Println("Spendy Done")
}
```

The function accepts a pointer to the variable holding the sum in the bank account.

spendy() function subtracts 10 dollars

We now need to call these two functions using a separate goroutine for each. We can write a `main()` function that initializes the shared `money` variable, creates the goroutines, and passes the variable reference to the newly created goroutines.

In listing 3.6, we initialize the common bank account to have 100 dollars. We also have the `main()` goroutine sleep for 2 seconds after creating the goroutines to wait for them to terminate. (In chapter 6, we will discuss waitgroups, which will allow us to block until a task has finished instead of having to sleep for several seconds.) After the main thread reawakens, it prints the amount of money in the `money` variable.

Listing 3.6   Stingy and Spendy `main()` function

```
package main

import (
    "fmt"
    "time"
)
. . .

func main() {
    money := 100
    go stingy(&money)
    go spendy(&money)
```

Initializes money value to have 100 dollars

Starts goroutines and passes a reference to the money variable

```
    time.Sleep(2 * time.Second)            ◁            Waits for 2 seconds for the
    println("Money in bank account: ", money)           goroutines to complete
}
```

In this listing, we expect that it will output 100 dollars as a result. After all, we are just adding and subtracting 10 to the variable 1 million times. This is simulating Stingy earning 10 million and Spendy spending the same amount, leaving us with the initial value of 100. However, here's the output of the program:

```
$ go run stingyspendy.go
Spendy Done
Stingy Done
Money in bank account: 4203750
```

More than $4 million remains in the account! Stingy would be very happy with this outcome. However, this result was pure chance. In fact, if we run it again, our account might end up below zero:

```
$ go run stingyspendy.go
Stingy Done
Spendy Done
Money in bank account: -1127120
```

Heisenbugs

We can try to debug what is going on in our Stingy and Spendy program by putting some breakpoints in key places. However, it would be very unlikely that we would spot the problem, since pausing on the breakpoints would slow down the execution, making it less likely for the race condition to occur.

A race condition is a good example of a *Heisenbug*. Named after the physicist Werner Heisenberg, with reference to his quantum mechanics uncertainty principle, a Heisenbug is a bug that disappears or changes behavior when we attempt to debug and isolate it. Since they're very hard to debug, the best way to deal with Heisenbugs is to not have them at all. Thus, it's vital to understand what causes race conditions and learn techniques for preventing them in our code.

Let's try to understand why we're getting these weird results by walking through a scenario. To keep things simple for now, let's assume we have only one processor, so no processing is happening in parallel. Figure 3.11 shows one such race condition that is happening in our Stingy and Spendy program.

At timestamps 1 through 3, Spendy is executing. The thread reads the value of 100 from shared memory and puts it on the processor's register. Then it subtracts 10 and writes back 90 dollars to the shared memory. At timestamps 4 through 6, it's Stingy's turn. It reads the value of 90, adds 10, and writes back 100 to the shared variable on the heap. Timestamps 7 through 11 are when things start to go bad. At timestamp 7, Spendy reads the value of 100 from main memory and writes this value to its processor registers.

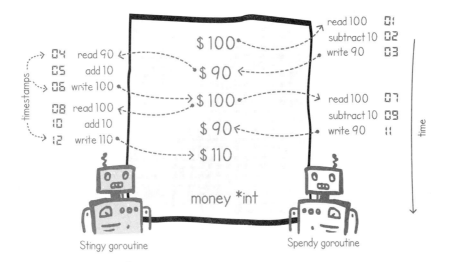

Figure 3.11 Race condition between Stingy and Spendy explained

At timestamp 8, a context switch happens, and Stingy's goroutine starts executing on the processor. It goes about reading the value of 100 from the shared variable since Stingy's thread didn't get the chance to update it yet. At timestamps 9 and 10, the goroutines subtract and add 10. Spendy then writes back the value of 90, and at time 11, Stingy's thread overwrites this by writing 110 to the shared variable. In total, we have spent $20 and earned back $20, but we ended up with an extra $10 in our account.

> **DEFINITION** The word *atomic* has its origins in the ancient Greek language, meaning "indivisible." In computer science, when we mention an *atomic operation*, we mean an operation that cannot be interrupted.

We are having this problem because the operations *money += 10 and *money -= 10 are not atomic; after compilation, they translate to more than one instruction. An interruption in the execution can occur in between the instructions. Different instructions from another goroutine can interfere and cause race conditions. When this overstepping happens, we get unpredictable results.

> **DEFINITION** A *critical section* in our code is a set of instructions that should be executed without interference from other executions affecting the state used in that section. When this interference is allowed to happen, race conditions may arise.

Even if the instructions were atomic, we might still run into issues. Remember how at the start of this chapter, we talked about processor caches and registers? Each processor core has a local cache and registers to store the variables that are used frequently. When we compile our code, the compiler sometimes applies optimizations to keep the variables on the CPU registers or caches before giving instructions to flush them back to memory. This means that there is a possibility that the two goroutines operating on separate CPUs are not seeing each other's changes until they complete the periodic flush to memory.

When we are executing a badly written concurrent program in a parallel environment, it is even more likely that these types of errors will arise. Goroutines running in parallel increase the chance of these types of race conditions happening since now we will be performing some steps at the same time. In our Stingy and Spendy program, the two goroutines are more likely to read the money variable at the same time before writing it back when running in parallel.

When we are using goroutines (or any user-level threads) and we are running only on a single processor, it is unlikely that the runtime will interrupt the execution in the middle of these instructions. This is because user-level scheduling is usually non-preemptive; it will only do a context switch in specific cases such as I/O or when the application calls a thread yield (`Gosched()` in Go). This is unlike the OS scheduling, which is usually preemptive and can interrupt the execution at any time. It's also unlikely that any goroutine will see an outdated version of a variable, since all the goroutines will be running on the same processor, using the same caches. In fact, if you try listing 3.6 with `runtime.GOMAXPROCS(1)`, you probably won't see the same issue.

Obviously, this is not a good solution, mainly because we would be giving up the advantage of having multiple processors, but also because there is no guarantee that it will solve the problem completely. A different or a future version of Go might do scheduling differently and then break our program. Regardless of the scheduling system we are using, we should guard against race conditions. This way, we are safe from problems regardless of the environment that the program will run on.

3.3.2 *Yielding execution does not help with race conditions*

What if we tell Go's runtime exactly when it should run the scheduler? In the previous chapter, we saw how we could use the `runtime.Gosched()` call to invoke the scheduler so that we might yield execution to another goroutine. The following listing shows how we could modify our two functions and make this call.

> **Listing 3.7 Stingy and Spendy functions invoking Go's scheduler**

```
func stingy(money *int) {
    for i := 0; i < 1000000; i++ {
        *money += 10
        runtime.Gosched()        ⟵──── Calls the Go scheduler after
    }                                   we perform the addition
    fmt.Println("Stingy Done")
}

func spendy(money *int) {
    for i := 0; i < 1000000; i++ {
        *money -= 10
        runtime.Gosched()        ⟵──── Calls the Go scheduler after
    }                                   we perform the subtraction
    fmt.Println("Spendy Done")
}
```

Unfortunately, this does not solve our problem. The output of this listing will vary depending on system differences (the number of processors, the Go version and implementation, the type of operating system, etc.). However, on a multicore system, this was the output:

```
$ go run stingyspendysched.go
Stingy Done
Spendy Done
Money in bank account: 170
```

Running this one more time produced this result:

```
$ go run stingyspendysched.go
Spendy Done
Stingy Done
Money in bank account: -190
```

It looks like the race condition is happening less frequently, but it's still occurring. In this snippet, the two goroutines were running in parallel on separate processors. There are various reasons why the race condition might occur less frequently, but it's unlikely to be because we are instructing the scheduler when to run. Let's first remind ourselves what this call does by looking at the Go documentation at https:// pkg.go.dev/runtime#Gosched:

> func Gosched()
>
> *Gosched yields the processor, allowing other goroutines to run. It does not suspend the current goroutine, so execution resumes automatically.*

Our program is now spending a smaller proportion of time on the critical sections (addition and subtraction). It's spending a considerable amount of time invoking the Go scheduler, so it's much less likely that the two goroutines read or write the shared variable at the same time.

Another reason why the race condition happens less often might be that the compiler has fewer options to optimize the code in the loop since we're now calling `runtime.Gosched()`.

> **WARNING** Never rely on telling the runtime when to yield the processor to solve race conditions. There is no guarantee that another parallel thread will not interfere. In addition, even if the system has one processor, if we were using more than one kernel-level thread—for example, by setting a different value using `runtime.GOMAXPROCS(n)`—the OS could interrupt the execution at any time.

3.3.3 *Proper synchronization and communication eliminate race conditions*

How can we write concurrent programs that avoid race conditions? There is no magic bullet here. There is no single technique best used to solve every case.

The first step is to make sure that we're using the right tool for the job. Is memory sharing really needed for the problem? Is there another way we can communicate between goroutines? In chapter 7 of this book, we will look at a different way of communicating—using channels and communicating sequential processes. This manner of modeling concurrency eliminates many of these types of errors.

The second step to good concurrent programming is recognizing when a race condition can occur. We must be mindful when we are sharing resources with other goroutines. Once we know where these critical code parts are, we can think about the best practices to employ so that the resources are shared safely.

Earlier we discussed a real-life race condition involving two people sharing a shopping list. This led to them buying the groceries twice since they didn't know that the other person had also decided to do the shopping. We can prevent this situation from occurring again by having a better way of synchronizing and communicating, as shown in figure 3.12.

Figure 3.12   Proper synchronization and communication eliminates race conditions.

For example, we could leave a note or a mark on the shopping list to show that someone is already doing the shopping. This would indicate to others that there is no need to shop again. To avoid race conditions in our programming, we need good synchronization and communication with the rest of the goroutines to make sure they don't step over each other. Good concurrent programming involves effectively synchronizing your concurrent executions to eliminate race conditions while improving performance and throughput. In later chapters of this book, we'll use different techniques and tools to synchronize and coordinate the threads in our programs. In this way, we can work around these race conditions and synchronization problems, sometimes avoiding them altogether.

3.3.4   *The Go race detector*

Go gives us a tool to detect race conditions in our code: we can run the Go compiler with the -race command-line flag. With this flag, the compiler adds special code to all memory accesses to track when different goroutines are reading from and writing to memory. When we use this flag and a race condition is detected, it outputs a warning message on the console. If we try running with this flag on our Stingy and Spendy program (listings 3.5 and 3.6), we'll get this result:

```
$ go run -race stingyspendy.go
===================
WARNING: DATA RACE
Read at 0x00c00001a0f8 by goroutine 7:
  main.spendy()
      /home/james/go/stingyspendy.go:21 +0x3b
  main.main.func2()
      /home/james/go/stingyspendy.go:29 +0x39

Previous write at 0x00c00001a0f8 by goroutine 6:
  main.stingy()
      /home/james/go/stingyspendy.go:14 +0x4d
  main.main.func1()
      /home/james/go/stingyspendy.go:28 +0x39

Goroutine 7 (running) created at:
  main.main()
      /home/james/go/stingyspendy.go:29 +0x116

Goroutine 6 (running) created at:
  main.main()
      /home/james/go/stingyspendy.go:28 +0xae
==================
Stingy Done
Spendy Done
Money in bank account:  -808630
Found 1 data race(s)
exit status 66
```

In this example, Go's race detector found our one race condition. It points to critical sections in our code on lines 21 and 14, the parts where we add to and subtract from the money variable in our stingy() and spendy() functions. It also gives us information about the reads from and writes to memory. In the preceding snippet, we can see that memory location 0x00c00001a0f8 was first written by goroutine 6 (running stingy()) and then later read by goroutine 7 (running spendy()).

> **WARNING** Go's race detector finds race conditions only when a particular race condition is triggered. For this reason, the detector is not infallible. When using the race detector, you should test your code with production-like scenarios, but enabling it in a production environment is usually not desirable, since it slows performance and uses a lot more memory.

Recognizing race conditions gets easier with experience as you write more concurrent code. It's important to remember that whenever you are sharing resources (such as memory) with other goroutines in a critical section of code, race conditions may arise unless you synchronize access to the shared resource.

3.4   *Exercises*

> **NOTE** Visit http://github.com/cutajarj/ConcurrentProgrammingWithGo to see all the code solutions.

1 Modify our sequential-letter frequency program to produce a list of word frequencies rather than letter frequencies. You can use the same URLs for the RFC web pages as were used in listing 3.3. Once it's finished, the program should output a list of words with the frequency with which each word appears in the web page. Here's some sample output:

```
$ go run wordfrequency.go
the -> 5
a -> 8
car -> 1
program -> 3
```

What happens when you try to convert the sequential program into a concurrent one, creating a goroutine for each page? We will fix these errors in the next chapter.

2 Run Go's race detector on listing 3.1. Does the result contain a race condition? If it does, can you explain why it happens?

3 Consider the following listing. Can you find the race condition in this program without running the race detector? Hint: Try running the program several times to see if it results in a race condition.

Listing 3.8 Find the race condition

```go
package main

import (
    "fmt"
    "time"
)

func addNextNumber(nextNum *[101]int) {
    i := 0
    for nextNum[i] != 0 { i++ }
    nextNum[i] = nextNum[i-1] + 1
}

func main() {
    nextNum := [101]int{1}
    for i := 0; i < 100; i++ {
        go addNextNumber(&nextNum)
    }
    for nextNum[100] == 0 {
        println("Waiting for goroutines to complete")
        time.Sleep(10 * time.Millisecond)
    }
    fmt.Println(nextNum)
}
```

Summary

- Memory sharing is one way in which multiple goroutines can communicate to accomplish a task.
- Multiprocessor and multicore systems give us hardware support and systems to share memory between threads.
- Race conditions are when unexpected results arise due to sharing resources, such as memory, between goroutines.
- A critical section is a set of instructions that should execute without interference from other concurrent executions. When interference is allowed to happen, race conditions might occur.
- Invoking the Go scheduler outside critical sections is not a solution to the problem of race conditions.
- Using proper synchronization and communication eliminates race conditions.
- Go gives us a race detector tool that helps us spot race conditions in our code.

Synchronization
with mutexes

This chapter covers

- Protecting critical sections with mutex locks
- Improving performance with readers–writer locks
- Implementing a read-preferred readers–writer lock

We can protect critical sections of our code with mutexes so that only one goroutine at a time accesses a shared resource. In this way, we eliminate race conditions.
Variations on mutexes, sometimes called locks, are used in every language that supports concurrent programming. In this chapter, we'll start by looking at the functionality that mutexes provide. Then we'll look at a variation on mutexes called
readers–writer mutexes.

Readers–writer mutexes give us performance optimizations in situations where
we need to block concurrency only when modifying the shared resource. They give
us the ability to perform multiple concurrent reads on shared resources while still
allowing us to exclusively lock write access. We will see a sample application of
readers–writer mutexes, and we'll learn about its internals and build one ourselves.

4.1 Protecting critical sections with mutexes

What if we had a way to ensure that only one thread of execution runs critical sections? This is the functionality that mutexes give us. Think of them as being physical locks that block certain parts of our code from more than one goroutine at any time. If only one goroutine is accessing a critical section at a time, we are safe from race conditions. After all, race conditions happen only when there is a conflict between two or more goroutines.

4.1.1 How do we use mutexes?

We can use mutexes to mark the beginnings and ends of our critical sections, as illustrated in figure 4.1. When a goroutine comes to a critical section of the code protected by a mutex, it first locks this mutex explicitly as an instruction in the program code. The goroutine then starts to execute the critical section's code, and when it's done, it unlocks the mutex so that another goroutine can access the critical section.

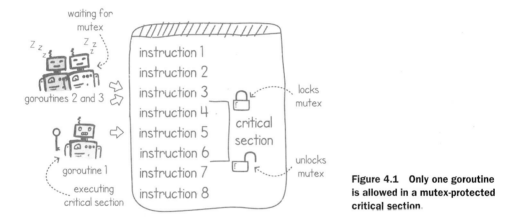

Figure 4.1 Only one goroutine is allowed in a mutex-protected critical section.

If another goroutine tries to lock a mutex that is already locked, the goroutine will be suspended until the mutex is released. If more than one goroutine is suspended, waiting for a lock to become available, only one goroutine is resumed, and it is the next to acquire the mutex lock.

> **DEFINITION** *Mutex*, short for *mutual exclusion*, is a form of concurrency control with the purpose of preventing race conditions. A mutex allows only one execution (such as a goroutine or a kernel-level thread) to enter a critical section. If two executions request access to the mutex at the same time, the semantics of the mutex guarantee that only one goroutine will acquire access to the mutex. The other execution will have to wait until the mutex becomes available again.

In Go, mutex functionality is provided in the `sync` package, under the type `Mutex`. This type gives us two main operations, `Lock()` and `Unlock()`, which we can use to mark the beginning and end of our critical code sections, respectively. As a simple example, we can modify our `stingy()` and `spendy()` functions from the previous chapter to protect our critical sections. In the following listing, we'll use the mutex to protect the shared `money` variable, preventing both goroutines from modifying it at the same time.

Listing 4.1   Stingy's and Spendy's functions using a mutex

```go
package main

import (
    "fmt"
    "sync"
    "time"
)

func stingy(money *int, mutex *sync.Mutex) {
    for i := 0; i < 1000000; i++ {
        mutex.Lock()
        *money += 10
        mutex.Unlock()
    }
    fmt.Println("Stingy Done")
}

func spendy(money *int, mutex *sync.Mutex) {
    for i := 0; i < 1000000; i++ {
        mutex.Lock()
        *money -= 10
        mutex.Unlock()
    }
    fmt.Println("Spendy Done")
}
```

Accepts a pointer to the shared mutex struct

Locks the mutex before entering the critical section

Unlocks after exiting the critical section

NOTE   All listings in this book are available on github.com/cutajarj/ ConcurrentProgrammingWithGo.

If both Stingy's and Spendy's goroutines attempt to lock the mutex at exactly the same time, we are guaranteed by the mutex that one and only one goroutine will be able to lock it. The other goroutine will have its execution suspended until the mutex becomes available again. So, for example, Stingy will have to wait until Spendy subtracts the money and releases the mutex. When the mutex becomes available again, Stingy's suspended goroutine will be resumed, acquiring the lock to the critical section.

The following listing shows the modified `main()` function creating a new mutex and passing a reference to `stingy()` and `spendy()`.

Listing 4.2   `main()` function creating the mutex

```go
func main() {
    money := 100
    mutex := sync.Mutex{}    
```

Creates a new mutex

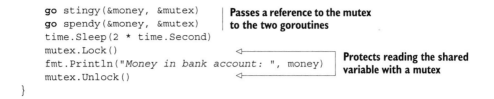

```
go stingy(&money, &mutex)          | Passes a reference to the mutex
go spendy(&money, &mutex)          | to the two goroutines
time.Sleep(2 * time.Second)
mutex.Lock()
fmt.Println("Money in bank account: ", money)    | Protects reading the shared
mutex.Unlock()                                    | variable with a mutex
}
```

NOTE When we create a new mutex, its initial state is always unlocked.

In our `main()` function, we're also using a mutex when we read the `money` variable after the goroutines finish. A race condition here is very unlikely since we sleep for a period to make sure that the goroutines are complete. However, it's always good practice to protect shared resources even if you're sure that there will be no conflict. Using mutexes (and other synchronization mechanisms covered in later chapters) ensures that the goroutine reads an updated copy of the variable.

NOTE We should protect all critical sections, including parts where the goroutine is only reading the shared resources. The compiler's optimizations might re-order instructions, causing them to execute in a different manner. Using proper synchronization mechanisms, such as mutexes, ensures that we're reading the latest copy of the shared resources.

If we now run listings 4.1 and 4.2 together, we can see that we have eliminated the race condition. The balance in the account is $100 after the Stingy and Spendy goroutines are complete. Here's the output:

```
$ go run stingyspendymutex.go
Stingy Done
Spendy Done
Money in bank account:  100
```

We can also try running this code with the `-race` flag to check that there are no race conditions.

How are mutexes implemented?

Mutexes are typically implemented with help from the operating system and hardware. If we had a system with just one processor, we could implement a mutex just by disabling interrupts while a thread is holding the lock. This way, another execution will not interrupt the current thread, and there is no interference. However, this is not ideal, because badly written code can end up blocking the entire system for all the other processes and threads. A malicious or poorly written program can have an infinite loop after acquiring a mutex lock and crash the system. Also, this approach will not work on a system with multiple processors, since other threads could be executing in parallel on another CPU.

(continued)
The implementation of mutexes involves support from the hardware to provide an atomic test and set operation. With this operation, an execution can check a memory location, and if the value is what it expects, it updates the memory to a locked flag value. The hardware guarantees that this test and set operation is atomic—that is, no other execution can access the memory location until the operation completes. Early hardware implementations guaranteed this atomicity by blocking the entire bus so that no other processor could use the memory at the same time. If another execution performed this operation and found it already set to a locked flag value, the operating system would block the execution of that thread until the memory location changed back to free.

We'll explore how mutexes can be implemented using atomics and operating system calls in chapter 12. In that chapter, we'll also examine how Go implements its own mutex.

4.1.2   Mutexes and sequential processing

We can, of course, also use mutexes when we have more than two goroutines. In the previous chapter, we implemented a letter-frequency program that used multiple goroutines to download and count the occurrence of characters in the English alphabet. The code lacked any synchronization and gave us erroneous counts when we ran the program. If we want to use mutexes to fix this race condition, at which point in our code should we lock and unlock the mutex (see figure 4.2.)?

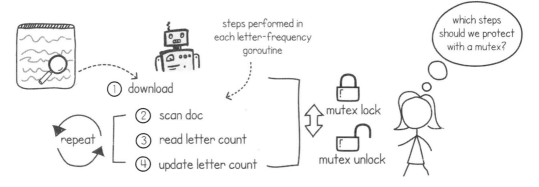

Figure 4.2   Deciding where to place the locking and unlocking of the mutex

NOTE Using mutexes has the effect of limiting concurrency. The code in between locking and unlocking a mutex is executed by one goroutine at any time, effectively turning that part of the code into sequential execution. As we saw in chapter 1, and according to Amdahl's law, the sequential-to-parallel ratio will limit the performance scalability of our code, so it's essential that we reduce the time spent holding the mutex lock.

Listing 4.3 shows how we can first modify the `main()` function to create the mutex and pass its reference to our `countLetters()` function. This is the same pattern we used for the Stingy and Spendy program, creating the mutex in the `main()` goroutine and sharing it with others. We are also protecting the read of the `frequency` variable at the end when we come to output the results.

Listing 4.3 `main()` function creating a mutex for letter frequency (imports omitted)

```
package main

import ( ... )

const AllLetters = "abcdefghijklmnopqrstuvwxyz"

func main() {
    mutex := sync.Mutex{}          // Creates new mutex
    var frequency = make([]int, 26)
    for i := 1000; i <= 1030; i++ {
        url := fmt.Sprintf("https://rfc-editor.org/rfc/rfc%d.txt", i)
        go CountLetters(url, frequency, &mutex)   // Passes a reference of the
    }                                             // mutex to the goroutines
    time.Sleep(60 * time.Second)
    mutex.Lock()
    for i, c := range AllLetters {                // Protects reading
        fmt.Printf("%c-%d ", c, frequency[i])     // the shared variable
    }                                             // with the mutex
    mutex.Unlock()
}
```

Waits for 60 seconds (annotation pointing to `time.Sleep(60 * time.Second)`)

What happens if we lock the mutex at the start of our `CountLetters()` function and release it at the very end? You can see this in the following listing, where we lock the mutex immediately after we call the function and release it after we output the completed message.

Listing 4.4 Incorrect (slow) way of locking and unlocking mutexes

```
func CountLetters(url string, frequency []int, mutex *sync.Mutex) {
    mutex.Lock()                              // Locks the mutex for the entire execution,
    resp, _ := http.Get(url)                  // making everything sequential
    defer resp.Body.Close()
    if resp.StatusCode != 200 {
        panic("Server returning error status code: " + resp.Status)
    }
    body, _ := io.ReadAll(resp.Body)
    for _, b := range body {
        c := strings.ToLower(string(b))
        cIndex := strings.Index(AllLetters, c)
        if cIndex >= 0 {
            frequency[cIndex] += 1
        }
    }
}
```

```
fmt.Println("Completed:", url, time.Now().Format("15:04:05"))
mutex.Unlock()                    ⟵──────┐
}                                         │   Unlocks the mutex
```

By using mutexes in this manner, we have changed our concurrent program into a sequential one. We will end up downloading and processing one web page at a time since we're needlessly blocking the entire execution. If we go ahead and run this, the time taken will be the same as the non-concurrent version of the program, although the order of execution will be random:

```
$ go run charcountermutexslow.go
Completed: https://rfc-editor.org/rfc/rfc1002.txt 08:44:21
Completed: https://rfc-editor.org/rfc/rfc1030.txt 08:44:23
. . .
Completed: https://rfc-editor.org/rfc/rfc1028.txt 08:44:33
Completed: https://rfc-editor.org/rfc/rfc1029.txt 08:44:34
Completed: https://rfc-editor.org/rfc/rfc1001.txt 08:44:34
Completed: https://rfc-editor.org/rfc/rfc1000.txt 08:44:35
a-103445 b-23074 c-61005 d-51733 e-181360 f-33381 g-24966 h-47722 i-103262 j-
    3279 k-8839 l-49958 m-40026 n-108275 o-106320 p-41404 q-3410 r-101118 s-
    101040 t-136812 u-35765 v-13666 w-18259 x-4743 y-18416 z-1404
```

Figure 4.3 shows a simplified scheduling chart of this manner of locking, using only three goroutines. The figure shows that our goroutines are spending most of their time downloading the document and a shorter time processing it. (In this figure, we are understating the proportion of time between the download and processing for illustration purposes. In reality, this difference is much bigger.) Our goroutines spend the vast majority of their time downloading the document and a tiny fraction of a second processing it. Performance-wise, it doesn't make sense to block the entire execution. The document download step doesn't share anything with other goroutines, so there is no risk of a race condition happening then.

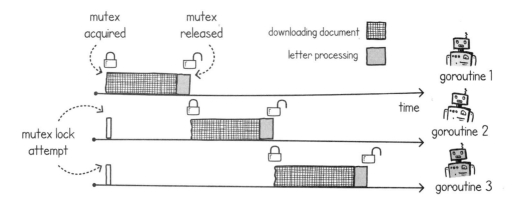

Figure 4.3   Locking too much code turns our letter-frequency concurrent program into a sequential one.

TIP When deciding how and when to use mutexes, it's best to focus on which resources we should protect and discover where critical sections start and end. Then we need to think about how to minimize the number of `Lock()` and `Unlock()` calls.

Depending on the mutex implementation, there is usually a performance cost if we call the `Lock()` and `Unlock()` operations too often. (In chapter 12, we'll see why.) In our letter-frequency program, we can try to use the mutex to protect just the one statement:

```
mutex.Lock()
frequency[cIndex] += 1
mutex.Unlock()
```

However, this means that we'll be calling these two operations for every letter in the downloaded document. Since processing the entire document is a very fast operation, it's probably more performant to call `Lock()` before the loop and `Unlock()` after we exit the loop. This is shown in the following listing.

Listing 4.5 Using mutexes on the processing part (imports omitted)

```
package listing4_5

import (...)

const AllLetters = "abcdefghijklmnopqrstuvwxyz"

func CountLetters(url string, frequency []int, mutex *sync.Mutex) {
    resp, _ := http.Get(url)                            // Performs the
    defer resp.Body.Close()                             // slow part of
    if resp.StatusCode != 200 {                         // the function
        panic("Server returning error code: " + resp.Status)  // (the download)
    }                                                   // concurrently
    body, _ := io.ReadAll(resp.Body)
    mutex.Lock()
    for _, b := range body {
        c := strings.ToLower(string(b))
        cIndex := strings.Index(AllLetters, c)          // Locks only the
        if cIndex >= 0 {                                // fast-processing
            frequency[cIndex] += 1                      // section of the
        }                                               // function
    }
    mutex.Unlock()
    fmt.Println("Completed:", url, time.Now().Format("15:04:05"))
}
```

In this version of the code, the download part, which is the lengthy part of our function, will execute concurrently. The fast letter-counting processing will then be done sequentially. We are basically maximizing the scalablity of our program by using the locks only on the code sections that run very quickly in proportion to the rest. We can run the preceding listing, and as expected, it runs much more quickly and gives us consistent correct results:

```
$ go run charcountermutex.go
Completed: https://rfc-editor.org/rfc/rfc1026.txt 08:49:52
Completed: https://rfc-editor.org/rfc/rfc1025.txt 08:49:52
. . .
Completed: https://rfc-editor.org/rfc/rfc1008.txt 08:49:53
Completed: https://rfc-editor.org/rfc/rfc1024.txt 08:49:53
a-103445 b-23074 c-61005 d-51733 e-181360 f-33381 g-24966 h-47722 i-103262 j-
    3279 k-8839 l-49958 m-40026 n-108275 o-106320 p-41404 q-3410 r-101118 s-
    101040 t-136812 u-35765 v-13666 w-18259 x-4743 y-18416 z-1404
```

The execution of the program is illustrated in figure 4.4. Again, the proportion between the downloading and processing parts is exaggerated for visual purposes. In reality, the time spent on processing is a tiny fraction of the time spent downloading the web page, so the speedup is more extreme. In fact, in our `main()` function, we can reduce the time spent sleeping to a few seconds (we had 60 seconds before).

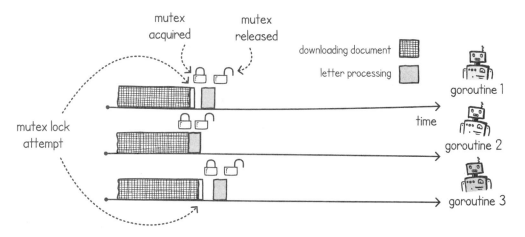

Figure 4.4   Locking only the processing part of our `countLetters()` function

This second solution is faster than our first attempt. If you compare figures 4.3 and 4.4, you'll see that we finish earlier when we're locking a smaller part of the code. The lesson here is to minimize the amount of time spent holding the mutex lock, while also trying to lower the number of mutex calls. This makes sense if you think back to Amdahl's law, which tells us that if our code spends more time on the parallel parts, we can finish faster and scale better.

4.1.3 *Non-blocking mutex locks*

A goroutine will block when it calls the `Lock()` operation if the mutex is already in use by another execution. This is what's known as a blocking function: the execution of the goroutine stops until `Unlock()` is called by another goroutine. In some applications, we might not want to block the goroutine, but instead perform some other work before attempting again to lock the mutex and access the critical section.

For this reason, Go's mutex provides another function called `TryLock()`. When we call this function, we can expect one of two outcomes:

- The lock is available, in which case we acquire it, and the function returns the Boolean value of `true`.
- The lock is unavailable because another goroutine is currently using the mutex, and the function will return immediately (instead of blocking) with a Boolean value of `false`.

Uses of non-blocking

Go added the `TryLock()` function for mutexes in version 1.18. Useful examples of this non-blocking call are hard to come by. This is because in Go, creating a goroutine is very cheap compared to creating a kernel-level thread in other languages. It doesn't make much sense to have a goroutine do something else if the mutex is not available, since in Go it's easier to just spawn another goroutine to do the work while we're waiting for the lock to be released. In fact, Go's mutex documentation mentions this (from `pkg.go.dev/sync#Mutex.TryLock`):

> *Note that while correct uses of TryLock do exist, they are rare, and use of TryLock is often a sign of a deeper problem in a particular use of mutexes.*

One example of using `TryLock()` is a monitor goroutine that checks the progress of a certain task without wanting to disrupt the task's progress. If we use the normal `Lock()` operation and the application is busy with many other goroutines wanting to acquire the lock, we are putting extra contention on the mutex just for monitoring purposes. When we use `TryLock()`, if another goroutine is busy holding a lock on the mutex, the monitor goroutine can decide to try again later when the system is not so busy. Think about going to the post office for a non-important errand and deciding to try again another day when you see the big queue at the entrance (see figure 4.5).

Figure 4.5 Try to acquire a mutex, and if it's busy, try again later.

We can modify our letter-frequency program to have the `main()` goroutine periodically monitor the frequency table while we are performing the downloads and document scanning with the other goroutines. Listing 4.6 shows the `main()` function printing the contents of the `frequency` slice every 100 ms. To do so, it must acquire a hold on the mutex lock; otherwise, we run the risk of reading erroneous data. However, we don't want to needlessly disrupt the `CountLetters()` goroutines if they are busy. For this reason, we're using the `TryLock()` operation, which attempts to acquire the lock, but if it's not available, it will try again in the next 100 ms cycle.

Listing 4.6 Using `TryLock()` to monitor the frequency table

```go
package main

import (
    "fmt"
    "github.com/cutajarj/ConcurrentProgrammingWithGo/chapter4/listing4.5"
    "sync"
    "time"
)

func main() {
    mutex := sync.Mutex{}
    var frequency = make([]int, 26)
    for i := 2000; i <= 2200; i++ {
        url := fmt.Sprintf("https://rfc-editor.org/rfc/rfc%d.txt", i)
        go listing4_5.CountLetters(url, frequency, &mutex)
    }
    for i := 0; i < 100; i++ {
        time.Sleep(100 * time.Millisecond)       ◁—— Sleeps for 100 ms
        if mutex.TryLock() {
            for i, c := range listing4_5.AllLetters {
                fmt.Printf("%c-%d ", c, frequency[i])
            }
            mutex.Unlock()
        } else {
            fmt.Println("Mutex already being used")
        }
    }
}
```

Tries to acquire the mutex

If the mutex lock is available, it outputs frequency counts and releases the mutex.

If the mutex is not available, it outputs a message and tries again later.

When we run listing 4.6, we can see in the output that the `main()` goroutine tries to acquire the lock to print out the frequency table. Sometimes it is successful; at other times, when it's not, it waits for the next 100 ms to try again:

```
$ go run nonblockingmutex.go
a-0 b-0 c-0 d-0 e-0 f-0 g-0 h-0 i-0 j-0 k-0 l-0 m-0 n-0 o-0 p-0 q-0 r-0 s-0
    t-0 u-0 v-0 w-0 x-0 y-0 z-0
. . .
Completed: https://rfc-editor.org/rfc/rfc2005.txt 11:18:39
a-2367 b-334 c-1270 d-1196 e-3685 f-1069 g-599 h-957 i-2537 j-22 k-112 l-1218
    m-927 n-2131 o-2321 p-722 q-64 r-1673 s-2188 t-2609 u-628 v-204 w-510 x-
    65 y-364 z-15
Completed: https://rfc-editor.org/rfc/rfc2122.txt 11:18:39
. . .
```

```
Completed: https://rfc-editor.org/rfc/rfc2027.txt 11:18:41
Mutex already being used
Completed: https://rfc-editor.org/rfc/rfc2006.txt 11:18:41
a-462539 b-90971 c-258306 d-235639 e-766999 f-142655 g-106497 h-212728 i-
      460748 j-10833 k-32495 l-213285 m-170227 n-433419 o-426131 p-174817 q-
      12578 r-419110 s-441282 t-597287 u-160276 v-60274 w-63028 x-28231 y-
      80664 z-6908
Completed: https://rfc-editor.org/rfc/rfc2178.txt 11:18:41
. . .
```

4.2 Improving performance with readers–writer mutexes

At times, mutexes might be too restrictive. We can think of mutexes as blunt tools that solve concurrency problems by blocking concurrency. Only one goroutine at a time can execute our mutex-protected critical section. This is great for guaranteeing that we don't suffer from race conditions, but this might needlessly restrict performance and scalability for some applications. Readers–writer mutexes give us a variation on standard mutexes that only block concurrency when we need to update a shared resource. Using readers–writer mutexes, we can improve the performance of read-heavy applications where we are doing a large number of read operations on shared data in comparison with updates.

4.2.1 Go's readers–writer mutex

What if we had an application serving mostly static data to many concurrent clients? We outlined one such application in chapter 2 when we had a web server application serving sports information. Let's take the example of a similar application serving users updates about a basketball game. One such application is illustrated in figure 4.6.

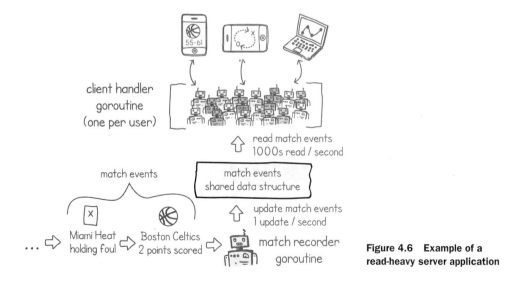

Figure 4.6 Example of a read-heavy server application

In this application, users are checking updates about a live basketball game from their devices. The Go application, running on our servers, serves these updates. In this application, we have a match-recorder goroutine that changes the content of the shared data every time an event happens in the game. An event can be a point scored, a foul committed, a ball passed, and so on.

Basketball is a fast-paced game, so on average, we get a few of these events every second. At the other end, we have a large set of goroutines serving the entire list of game events to a huge number of connected users. Users are using this data for various reasons: to display game stats, understand the match strategy, or just check the score and game time. The game is a popular one, so we should build something that can handle as many user requests per second as possible. We expect to have thousands of requests per second for our match event data.

Let's write the two different types of goroutines, starting with the match-recorder function, shown in listing 4.7. A goroutine running this function listens to events happening during the game, such as points scored, fouls committed, etc., and then appends them to a shared data structure. In this case, the shared data structure is a Go slice of `string` type. In our code, we are simulating an event happening every 200 milliseconds by adding a string containing `"Match Event i"`. In the real world, the goroutine would be listening to a sports feed or periodically polling an API, and the events would be of the type `"3 pointer from Team A"`.

Listing 4.7   Match recorder function simulating periodic game events

```go
package main

import (
    "fmt"
    "strconv"
    "sync"
    "time"
)

func matchRecorder(matchEvents *[]string, mutex *sync.Mutex) {
    for i := 0; ; i++ {
        mutex.Lock()                              // Protects access to matchEvents with a mutex
        *matchEvents = append(*matchEvents,
            "Match event " + strconv.Itoa(i))
        mutex.Unlock()                            // Unlocks the mutex
        time.Sleep(200 * time.Millisecond)
        fmt.Println("Appended match event")
    }
}
```

Adds a mock string containing a match event every 200 milliseconds

Listing 4.8 shows a client handler function together with a function that copies all the events in the shared slice. We can run the `clientHandler()` function as a goroutine, each handling a connected user. The function locks the shared slice containing the game events and makes a copy of every element in the slice. This function simulates building a response to send to the user. In the real world, we could send this response formatted in something like JSON. The `clientHandler()` function has a loop that repeats 100 times to simulate the same user making multiple requests.

Listing 4.8 Client handler using exclusive access to a shared list

```go
func clientHandler(mEvents *[]string, mutex *sync.Mutex, st time.Time) {
    for i := 0; i < 100; i ++ {
        mutex.Lock()                              ⟵ Protects access to the list of match events with the mutex
        allEvents := copyAllEvents(mEvents)       ⟵ Copies the entire contents of the match slice,
        mutex.Unlock()                                simulating building a response to the client
        timeTaken := time.Since(st)
        fmt.Println(len(allEvents), "events copied in", timeTaken)   ⟵
    }
}

func copyAllEvents(matchEvents *[]string) []string {
    allEvents := make([]string, 0, len(*matchEvents))
    for _, e := range *matchEvents {
        allEvents = append(allEvents, e)
    }
    return allEvents
}
```

Unlocks the mutex

Calculates the time taken since the start

Outputs to the console the time taken to serve the client

In listing 4.9, we connect everything together and start our goroutines in a `main()` function. In this `main()` function, after we create a normal mutex, we prepopulate the match event slice with many match events. This simulates a game that has been going on for a while. We do this so we can measure the performance of our code when the slice contains some events.

Listing 4.9 `main()` function prepopulating events and starting goroutines

```go
func main() {
    mutex := sync.Mutex{}                       ⟵ Initializes a new mutex
    var matchEvents = make([]string, 0, 10000)
    for j := 0; j < 10000; j++ {
        matchEvents = append(matchEvents, "Match event")
    }
    go matchRecorder(&matchEvents, &mutex)
    start := time.Now()                         ⟵ Records the start time before starting
    for j := 0; j < 5000; j++ {                     the client handler goroutines
        go clientHandler(&matchEvents, &mutex, start)   ⟵ Starts a large number of
    }                                                       client handler goroutines
    time.Sleep(100 * time.Second)
}
```

Starts the match-recorder Go routine

Prepopulates the events slice with many events, simulating an ongoing game

In the `main()` function, we then start a match-recorder goroutine and 5,000 client handler goroutines. Basically, we are simulating a game that is ongoing and that has a large number of users making simultaneous requests to get game updates. We also record the time before we start the client handler goroutines so that we can measure the time it takes to process all the requests. At the end, our `main()` function goes to sleep for a number of seconds to wait for the client hander goroutines to finish.

In comparison to the number of read queries, the data changes very slowly. When we use normal mutex locks, every time a goroutine reads the shared basketball data, it blocks all the other serving goroutines until it's finished. Even though the client handlers are just reading the shared slice without any modifications, we are still giving each one of them exclusive access to the slice. Note that if multiple goroutines are just reading shared data without updating it, there is no need for this exclusive access; concurrent reading of shared data does not cause any interference.

> **NOTE** Race conditions only happen if we change the shared state without proper synchronization. If we don't modify the shared data, there is no risk of race conditions.

It would be better if all client handler goroutines had non-exclusive access to the slice so that they could read the list at the same time if needed. This would improve performance, as it would allow multiple goroutines that are just reading the shared data to access it at the same time. We would only block access to the shared data if there was a need to update it. In this example, we are updating the data very infrequently (a few times per second) compared to the number of reads we're doing (thousands per second). Thus, we would benefit from a system that allows multiple concurrent reads but exclusive writes.

This is what the *readers–writer lock* gives us. When we just need to read a shared resource without updating it, the readers–writer lock allows multiple concurrent goroutines to execute the read-only critical section part. When we need to update the shared resource, the goroutine executing the write critical section requests the write lock to acquire exclusive access. This concept is depicted in figure 4.7. On the left side of the figure, a read lock allows for concurrent read access while blocking any write access. On the right side, obtaining a write lock blocks all other access, both read and write, just like a normal mutex.

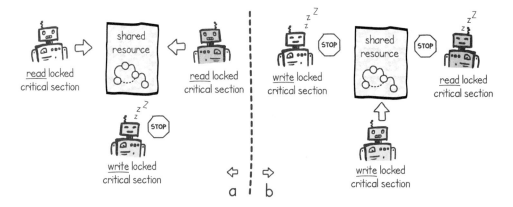

Figure 4.7   Goroutines using a readers–writer lock

Go comes with its own implementation of a readers–writer lock. In addition to offering the normal exclusive locking and unlocking functions, Go's `sync.RWMutex` gives us extra methods to use the reader's side of the mutex. Here's a list of the functions we can use:

```
type RWMutex
  //Locks mutex
  func (rw *RWMutex) Lock()
  //Locks read part of mutex
  func (rw *RWMutex) RLock()
  //Returns read part locker of mutex
  func (rw *RWMutex) RLocker() Locker
  //Unlocks read part of mutex
  func (rw *RWMutex) RUnlock()
  //Tries to lock mutex
  func (rw *RWMutex) TryLock() bool
  //Tries to lock read part of mutex
  func (rw *RWMutex) TryRLock() bool
  //Unlock mutex
  func (rw *RWMutex) Unlock()
```

The locking and unlocking functions that have an `R` in the function name, such as the `RLock()` functions, give us the reader's side of the `RWMutex`. Everything else, such as `Lock()`, lets us operate the writer part. We can now modify our application serving basketball updates to use these new functions. In the following listing, we'll initialize one of these readers–writer mutexes and pass it on to the other goroutines in our `main()` function.

Listing 4.10 `main()` function creating the `RWMutex`

```
func main() {
    mutex := sync.RWMutex{}          ⟵──┐  Initializes a new readers–writer mutex
    var matchEvents = make([]string, 0, 10000)
    for j := 0; j < 10000; j++ {
        matchEvents = append(matchEvents, "Match event")
    }
    go matchRecorder(&matchEvents, &mutex)     ⟵──┤  Passes readers–writer
    start := time.Now()                              mutex to match recorder
    for j := 0; j < 5000; j++ {
        go clientHandler(&matchEvents, &mutex, start)   ⟵──┐  Passes readers–writer
    }                                                        │  mutex to client handler
    time.Sleep(100 * time.Second)                            │  goroutine
}
```

Next, our two functions, the `matchRecorder()` and `clientHandler()`, need to be updated so that they call the write and read locks mutex functions, respectively. In listing 4.11, the `matchRecorder()` calls `Lock()` and `UnLock()` since it needs to update the shared data structure. The `clientHandler()` goroutines use `RLock()` and `RUnlock()` since they are only reading the shared data structure. The read locks used here are needed because we don't want the slice data structure to change while we are traversing it. For example, modifying the pointer and contents of the slice while another goroutine is traversing it might lead us to follow an invalid pointer reference.

Listing 4.11   Match-recorder and client handler functions calling the read-write mutex

```
func matchRecorder(matchEvents *[]string, mutex *sync.RWMutex) {
    for i := 0; ; i++ {
        mutex.Lock()
        *matchEvents = append(*matchEvents,          Protects critical section
            "Match event " + strconv.Itoa(i))        with a write mutex
        mutex.Unlock()
        time.Sleep(200 * time.Millisecond)
        fmt.Println("Appended match event")
    }
}

func clientHandler(mEvents *[]string, mutex *sync.RWMutex, st time.Time) {
    for i := 0; i < 100; i ++ {
        mutex.RLock()
        allEvents := copyAllEvents(mEvents)          Protects critical section
        mutex.RUnlock()                              with a read mutex
        timeTaken := time.Since(st)
        fmt.Println(len(allEvents), "events copied in", timeTaken)
    }
}
```

A goroutine executing the critical code section between `RLock()` and `RUnlock()`, in our `clientHandler()` function, blocks a goroutine from acquiring a write lock in our `matchRecorder()` function. However, it does not block another goroutine from also acquiring a readers' lock to a critical section. This means that we can have concurrent goroutines executing `clientHandler()` without any read goroutines blocking each other.

When there is a game update, the goroutine in the `matchRecorder()` acquires a write lock by calling the `Lock()` function on the mutex. The write lock will only be acquired when any active `matchRecorder()` goroutine releases its read lock. When the write lock is acquired, it will block any other goroutine from accessing the critical section in our `clientHandler()` function until we release the write lock by calling `UnLock()`.

If we have a system running multiple cores, this example should give us a speedup over a system with a single core. That's because we would be running a number of client handler goroutines in parallel since they can access the shared data at the same time. In a test run, I achieved a threefold increase in throughput performance using the readers–writer mutex:

```
$ go run matchmonitor.go
. . .
10064 events copied in 33.033974291s
Appended match event
Appended match event
. . .
```

```
$ go run matchmonitor.go
. . .
10033 events copied in 10.228970583s
Appended match event
Appended match event
. . .
```

Figure 4.8 converts the preceding result into requests per second and shows the advantage of using the readers–writer mutex for this simple application running on a 10-core machine. The chart assumes that the application handled a total of 500,000 requests (100 requests from 5,000 clients).

NOTE Running this application on different hardware will produce different results. Running on a slower machine might require changing the sleep period at the end or reducing the number of client handler goroutines.

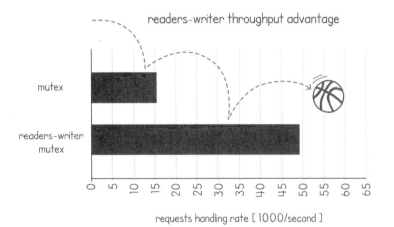

Figure 4.8 converts the preceding result into requests per second

Figure 4.8 Performance differences in our read-heavy server application running on a multicore processor

4.2.2 Building our own read-preferred readers–writer mutex

Now that we have seen how to use readers–writer mutexes, it would be good to see how they work internally. In this section, we'll try to build our own readers–writer mutex similar to the one bundled in Go's sync package. To keep things simple, we will build only the four important functions: ReadLock(), ReadUnlock(), WriteLock(), and WriteUnlock(). We named them slightly differently from the sync versions so that we can distinguish our implementations from the ones in Go's libraries.

To implement our readers–writer mutex, we need a system that, when a goroutine calls ReadLock(), blocks any access to the write part while allowing other goroutines to still call ReadLock() without blocking. We'll block the write part by making sure that a goroutine calling WriteLock() suspends execution. Only when all the read goroutines call ReadUnlock() will we allow another goroutine to unblock from WriteLock().

To help us visualize this system, we can think of goroutines as entities trying to access a room with two entrances. This room signifies access to a shared resource. The reader goroutines use a specific entrance, and the writers use another. Entrances only admit one goroutine at a time, although multiple goroutines can be in the room at the same time. We keep a counter that a reader goroutine increments by 1 when it enters via the reader's entrance and reduces by 1 when it leaves the room. The writer's entrance can be locked from the inside using what we call a global lock. This concept is shown on the left side of figure 4.9.

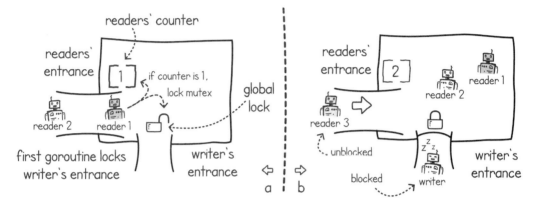

Figure 4.9   Locking the read part of a readers–writer mutex

The procedure is that when the first reader goroutine enters the room, it must lock the writers' entrance, as depicted on the right side of figure 4.9. This ensures that a writer goroutine will find access impassable, blocking the goroutine's execution. However, other reader goroutines will still have access through their own entrance. The reader goroutine knows that it's the first one in the room because the counter has a value of 1.

The writer's entrance here is just another mutex lock that we call the global lock. A writer needs to acquire this mutex in order to hold the writer's part of the readers-writer lock. When the first reader locks this mutex, it blocks any goroutine requesting the writer's part of the lock.

We need to make sure that only one goroutine is using the readers' entrance at any time because we don't want two simultaneous read goroutines to enter at the same time and believe they are both the first in the room. This would result in both trying to lock the global lock and only one succeeding. Thus, to synchronize access so only one goroutine can use the readers' entrance at any time, we can make use of another mutex. In the following listing, we'll call this mutex `readersLock`. The readers' counter is represented by the `readersCounter` variable, and we'll call the writer's lock `globalLock`.

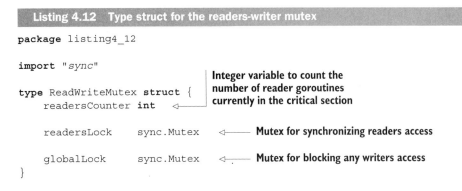

Listing 4.12   Type struct for the readers-writer mutex

```
package listing4_12

import "sync"

type ReadWriteMutex struct {
    readersCounter int          ◁──── Integer variable to count the
                                        number of reader goroutines
                                        currently in the critical section

    readersLock    sync.Mutex   ◁──── Mutex for synchronizing readers access

    globalLock     sync.Mutex   ◁──── Mutex for blocking any writers access
}
```

The following listing shows an implementation of the locking mechanism we've outlined. On the readers side, the ReadLock() function synchronizes access, using the readersLock mutex, to ensure that only one goroutine at a time is using the function.

Listing 4.13   Implementation of the `ReadLock()` function

```
func (rw *ReadWriteMutex) ReadLock() {          Synchronizes access so that only one
    rw.readersLock.Lock()          ◁──────────  goroutine is allowed at any time
    rw.readersCounter++
    if rw.readersCounter == 1 {                 If a reader goroutine is the first one
        rw.globalLock.Lock()        ◁─────────  in, it attempts to lock globalLock.
    }
    rw.readersLock.Unlock()         ◁─────────  Synchronizes access so that only one
}                                               goroutine is allowed at any time

func (rw *ReadWriteMutex) WriteLock() {
    rw.globalLock.Lock()            ◁─────────
}                                               Any writer access requires a lock on globalLock.
```

(annotation at left of ReadLock): **Reader goroutine increments readersCounter by 1**

Once the caller gets hold of the readersLock, it increments the readers' counter by 1, signifying that another goroutine is about to have read access to the shared resource. If the goroutine realizes that it's the first one to get read access, it tries to lock the globalLock so that it blocks access to any write goroutines. (The globalLock is used by the WriteLock() function when it needs to obtain the writer's side of this mutex.) If the globalLock is free, it means that no writer is currently executing its critical section. In this case, the first reader obtains the globalLock, releases the readersLock, and goes ahead to execute its reader's critical section.

When a reader goroutine finishes executing its critical section, we can think of it as exiting through the same passageway. On its way out, it decreases the counter by 1. Using the same passageway simply means that it needs to get hold of the readersLock when updating the counter. The last one out of the room (when the counter is 0), unlocks the global lock so that a writer goroutine can finally access the shared resource. This is shown on the left side of figure 4.10.

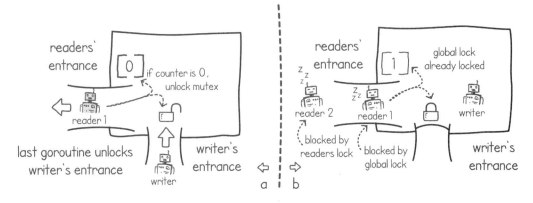

Figure 4.10 The read unlocking and locking of the write part in a readers–writer mutex

While a writer goroutine is executing its critical section, accessing the room in our analogy, it holds a lock on the globalLock. This has two effects. First, it blocks other writers' goroutines since writers need to acquire this lock before gaining access. Second, it also blocks the first reader goroutine when it tries to acquire the globalLock. The first reader goroutine will block and wait until the globalLock becomes available. Since the first reader goroutine also holds the readersLock, it will also block access to any other reader goroutine that follows while it waits. This is akin to the first reader goroutine not moving and thus blocking the readers' entrance, not letting any other goroutines in.

Once the writer goroutine has finished executing its critical section, it releases the globalLock. This has the effect of unblocking the first reader goroutine and later allowing in any other blocked readers.

We can implement this releasing logic in our two unlocking functions. Listing 4.14 shows both the ReadUnlock() and WriteUnlock() functions. ReadUnlock() again uses the readersLock to ensure that only one goroutine is executing this function at a time, protecting the shared readersCounter variable. Once the reader acquires the lock, it decrements the readersCounter count by 1, and if the count reaches 0, it also releases the globalLock. This allows the possibility of a writer gaining access. On the writer's side, WriteUnlock() simply releases the globalLock, giving either readers or a single writer access.

Listing 4.14 Implementation of the ReadUnlock() function

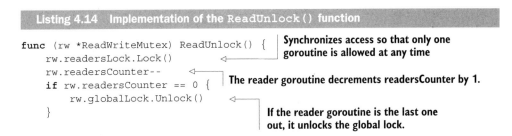

```
func (rw *ReadWriteMutex) ReadUnlock() {        Synchronizes access so that only one
    rw.readersLock.Lock()                       goroutine is allowed at any time
    rw.readersCounter--
    if rw.readersCounter == 0 {        The reader goroutine decrements readersCounter by 1.
        rw.globalLock.Unlock()
    }
                                       If the reader goroutine is the last one
                                       out, it unlocks the global lock.
```

```
        rw.readersLock.Unlock()        ◁─────┐
}                                             │  Synchronizes access so that only one
                                                 goroutine is allowed at any time
func (rw *ReadWriteMutex) WriteUnlock() {
        rw.globalLock.Unlock()         ◁─────┐
}                                             │  The writer goroutine, finishing its critical
                                                 section, releases the global lock.
```

NOTE This implementation of the readers–writer lock is *read-preferring*. This means that if we have a consistent number of readers' goroutines hogging the read part of the mutex, a writer goroutine would be unable to acquire the mutex. In technical terms, we say that the reader goroutines are *starving* the writer ones, not allowing them access to the shared resource. In the next chapter, we will improve this when we discuss condition variables.

4.3 Exercises

NOTE Visit http://github.com/cutajarj/ConcurrentProgrammingWithGo to see all the code solutions.

1 Listing 4.15 (originally from chapter 3) does not use any mutexes to protect access to its shared variable. This is bad practice. Change this program so that access to the shared `seconds` variable is protected by a mutex. Hint: you might need to copy a variable.

Listing 4.15 Goroutines sharing a variable without synchronization

```go
package main

import (
    "fmt"
    "time"
)

func countdown(seconds *int) {
    for *seconds > 0 {
        time.Sleep(1 * time.Second)
        *seconds -= 1
    }
}

func main() {
    count := 5
    go countdown(&count)
    for count > 0 {
        time.Sleep(500 * time.Millisecond)
        fmt.Println(count)
    }
}
```

2 Add a non-blocking `TryLock()` function to the implementation of the readers-writer mutex. The function should try to lock the writer's side of the lock. If the lock is acquired, it should return a `true` value; otherwise, the function should return immediately, without blocking, with a `false` return value.

3 Add a non-blocking `TryReadLock()` function to the implementation of the readers-writer lock. The function should try to lock the readers' side of the lock. Just like in exercise 2, the function should return immediately with `true` if it managed to obtain the lock and return `false` otherwise.

4 In the previous chapter, in exercise 3.1, we developed a program to output the frequencies of words from downloaded web pages. If you used a shared memory map to store the word frequencies, access to the shared map would need to be protected. Can you use a mutex to guarantee exclusive access to the map?

Summary

- Mutexes can be used to protect critical sections of our code from concurrent executions.
- We can protect critical sections using mutexes by calling the `Lock()` and `UnLock()` functions at the start and end of critical sections, respectively.
- Locking a mutex for too long can turn our concurrent code into sequential execution, reducing performance.
- We can test whether a mutex is already locked by calling `TryLock()`.
- Readers–writer mutexes can provide performance improvements for read-heavy applications.
- Readers–writer mutexes allow multiple readers' goroutines to execute critical sections concurrently and provide exclusive access to a single writer goroutine.
- We can build a read-preferred readers–writer mutex with a counter and two normal mutexes.

Condition variables and semaphores

This chapter covers

- Waiting on conditions with condition variables
- Implementing a write-preferring readers–writer lock
- Storing signals with counting semaphores

In the previous chapter, we saw how we can use mutexes to protect critical sections of our code and prevent multiple goroutines from executing at the same time. Mutexes are not the only synchronization tool that we have available: condition variables give us extra controls that complement exclusive locking. They give us the ability to wait for a certain condition to occur before unblocking the execution. Semaphores go one step further than mutexes in that they allow us to control how many concurrent goroutines can execute a certain section at the same time. In addition, semaphores can be used to store a signal (of an occurring event) for later access by an execution.

Apart from being useful in our concurrent applications, condition variables and semaphores are additional primitive building blocks that we can use to build more complex tools and abstractions. In this chapter, we will also re-examine our readers-writer lock, developed in the previous chapter, and improve it using condition variables.

5.1   *Condition variables*

Condition variables give us extra functionality on top of mutexes. We can use them in situations where a goroutine needs to block and wait for a particular condition to occur. Let's look at an example to understand how they're used.

5.1.1   *Combining mutexes with condition variables*

In previous chapters, we saw examples of two goroutines (Stingy and Spendy) sharing the same bank account. Stingy's and Spendy's goroutines would repeatedly earn and spend $10 respectively. What if we try to create an imbalance where Spendy is spending at a faster rate than Stingy is earning? Previously we had the total earnings and expenditure balanced at $10 million. In this example, we'll keep the same total amount balanced at $10 million, but we'll increase the rate of spending to $50 and reduce the total number of iterations to 200,000. In this way, the bank account will go into the negative very quickly (see figure 5.1) since we're now spending at a faster rate than we're earning. The bank might also have additional costs when we go into a negative balance. Ideally, we need a way to slow down the spending so that the balance doesn't go below zero.

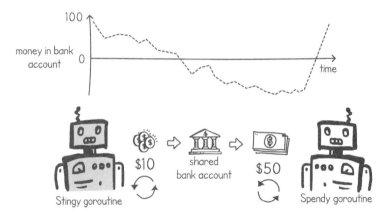

Figure 5.1   The Spendy goroutine spends the same amount as Stingy earns, but at a faster rate.

Listing 5.1 shows a modified `spendy()` function to show this scenario. In this listing, when the bank account goes negative, we print a message and exit the program. Notice that in both functions, the value earned and spent is the same. It's just that at the start, Spendy is spending at a faster rate than Stingy is earning. If we omit `os.Exit()`, the `spendy()` function will complete earlier, and then the `stingy()` function will eventually fill up the bank account to the original value.

```go
package main

import (
    "fmt"
    "os"
    "sync"
    "time"
)

func stingy(money *int, mutex *sync.Mutex) {
    for i := 0; i < 1000000; i++ {
        mutex.Lock()
        *money += 10
        mutex.Unlock()
    }
    fmt.Println("Stingy Done")
}

func spendy(money *int, mutex *sync.Mutex) {
    for i := 0; i < 200000; i++ {
        mutex.Lock()
        *money -= 50
        if *money < 0 {
            fmt.Println("Money is negative!")
            os.Exit(1)
        }
        mutex.Unlock()
    }
    fmt.Println("Spendy Done")
}
```

Spends 50 while earning 10

When the money variable goes negative, outputs message and terminates program

When we run listing 5.1 using the `main()` method from chapter 4, the balance goes into the negative quickly, and the program terminates:

```
$ go run stingyspendynegative.go
Money is negative!
exit status 1
```

Is there anything we can do to stop the balance from going into the negative? Ideally, we want a system that doesn't spend money we don't have. We can try to have the `spendy()` function check if there is enough money before it goes ahead and spends it. If there isn't enough, we can have the goroutine sleep for some time and then check again. This approach for the `spendy()` function is shown in the next listing.

Listing 5.2 Spendy function retrying when it runs out of money

```go
func spendy(money *int, mutex *sync.Mutex) {
    for i := 0; i < 200000; i++ {
        mutex.Lock()
        for *money < 50 {
            mutex.Unlock()
```

Keeps trying if there isn't enough money

Unlocks mutex, allowing the other goroutine access to the money variable

Sleeps for a short while ⟶
```
        time.Sleep(10 * time.Millisecond)
        mutex.Lock()       ⟵
    }
    *money -= 50
    if *money < 0 {
        fmt.Println("Money is negative!")
        os.Exit(1)
    }
    mutex.Unlock()
    }
    fmt.Println("Spendy Done")
}
```
Locks the mutex again to ensure we access the latest money value

This solution will work for our use case, but it's not ideal. In our example, we choose the arbitrary sleep value of 10 milliseconds, but what would be the optimal number to choose? At one extreme, we can choose not to sleep at all. This ends up wasting CPU resources, as the CPU would be cycling needlessly, checking the money variable even if it doesn't change. At the other extreme, if the goroutine sleeps for too long, we might waste time waiting for a change in the money variable that has already happened.

This is where condition variables come in. Condition variables work together with mutexes and give us the ability to suspend the current execution until we have a signal that a particular condition has changed. Figure 5.2 shows a common pattern for using a condition variable with a mutex.

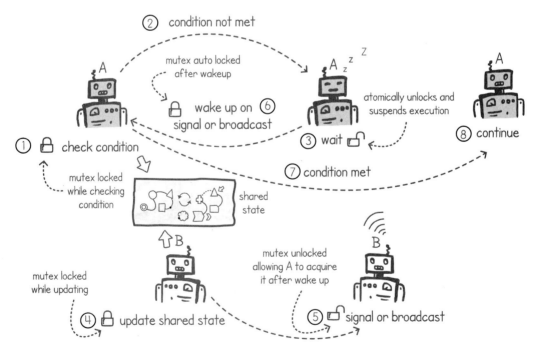

Figure 5.2 Common pattern for using a condition variable with a mutex

Let's go into the details of each step in figure 5.2 to understand this common pattern for using condition variables:

1. While holding a mutex, goroutine A checks for a particular condition on some shared state. In our example, the condition would be "Is there enough money in the shared bank account variable?"

2. If the condition is not met, goroutine A calls the `Wait()` function on the condition variable.

3. The `Wait()` function performs two operations *atomically* (defined after this list):

   a. It releases the mutex.

   b. It blocks the current execution, effectively putting the goroutine to sleep.

4. Since the mutex is now available, another goroutine (goroutine B) acquires it to update the shared state. For example, goroutine B increases the amount of funds available in the shared bank account variable.

5. After updating the shared state, goroutine B calls `Signal()` or `Broadcast()` on the condition variable and then unlocks the mutex.

6. Upon receiving `Signal()` or `Broadcast()`, goroutine A wakes up and automatically reacquires the mutex. Goroutine A can recheck the condition on the shared state, such as by checking whether there is enough money in the shared bank account before spending it. Steps 2 through 6 might repeat until the condition is met.

7. The condition is eventually met.

8. The goroutine continues executing its logic, such as by spending the money now available in the bank account.

NOTE The key to understanding condition variables is to grasp that the `Wait()` function releases the mutex and suspends the execution in an *atomic* manner. This means that another execution cannot come in between these two operations, acquire the lock, and call the `Signal()` function before the execution calling `Wait()` has been suspended.

An implementation of a condition variable in Go can be found in the `sync.Cond` type. If we look at the functions available on this type, we find the following:

```
type Cond
  func NewCond(l Locker) *Cond
  func (c *Cond) Broadcast()
  func (c *Cond) Signal()
  func (c *Cond) Wait()
```

Creating a new Go condition variable requires a `Locker`, which defines two functions:

```
type Locker interface {
    Lock()
    Unlock()
}
```

To use Go's condition variable, we need something that implements these two functions, and a mutex is one such type. The following listing shows a `main()` function that creates a mutex and then uses it in a condition variable. Later it passes the condition variable to the `stingy()` and `spendy()` goroutines.

Listing 5.3   `main()` function creating a condition variable with a mutex

```
package main

import (
    "fmt"
    "os"
    "sync"
    "time"
)

func main() {
    money := 100
    mutex := sync.Mutex{}
    cond := sync.NewCond(&mutex)
    go stingy(&money, cond)
    go spendy(&money, cond)
    time.Sleep(2 * time.Second)
    mutex.Lock()
    fmt.Println("Money in bank account: ", money)
    mutex.Unlock()
}
```

Creates a new mutex

Creates a new condition variable using a mutex

Passes the condition variable to both goroutines

We can use the pattern outlined previously in figure 5.2 in our `stingy()` and `spendy()` functions by using the functions available on the Go's `sync.Cond` type. Figure 5.3 shows the timings of a run with both goroutines using this pattern. If we have the Spendy goroutine check the condition before subtracting $50, we are protecting the balance

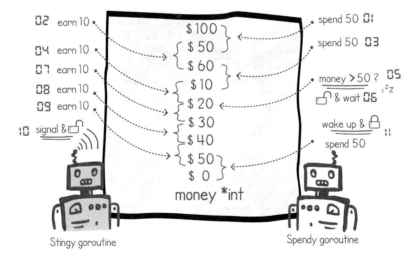

Figure 5.3   Stingy and Spendy using condition variables to prevent the balance from going negative

from ever going negative. If there aren't enough funds, the goroutine waits, suspending its execution until more money is available. When Stingy adds money, it sends a signal to resume any execution that is waiting for more funds.

Changing the Stingy goroutine is simpler because we only need to signal. Listing 5.4 shows our modifications to this goroutine. Every time we add money to our shared money variable, we send a signal by calling the Signal() function on the condition variable. The other change is that we're using the mutex present on the condition variable to protect access to our critical section.

Listing 5.4   Stingy function signaling that more funds are available

```
func stingy(money *int, cond *sync.Cond) {
    for i := 0; i < 1000000; i++ {
        cond.L.Lock()
        *money += 10
        cond.Signal()
        cond.L.Unlock()
    }
    fmt.Println("Stingy Done")
}
```

Uses mutex on the condition variable → (points to cond.L.Lock() and cond.L.Unlock())

Signals on the condition variable every time we add to the shared money variable → (points to cond.Signal())

Next, we can modify our spendy() function so that it waits until we have enough funds in our money variable. We can implement this condition-checking using a loop that calls Wait() every time the money amount is below the $50 mark. In listing 5.5, we use a for loop that continues to iterate as long as *money is less than $50. In each iteration, it calls Wait(). The function also now makes use of the mutexes contained on the condition variable type.

Listing 5.5   Spendy waiting for more funds to be available

```
func spendy(money *int, cond *sync.Cond) {
    for i := 0; i < 200000; i++ {
        cond.L.Lock()
        for *money < 50 {
            cond.Wait()
        }
        *money -= 50
        if *money < 0 {
            fmt.Println("Money is negative!")
            os.Exit(1)
        }
        cond.L.Unlock()
    }
    fmt.Println("Spendy Done")
}
```

Uses the mutex on the condition variable → (points to cond.L.Lock() and cond.L.Unlock())

Waits while we don't have enough money, releasing mutex and suspending execution → (points to for *money < 50 { cond.Wait() })

Returning from Wait(), reacquires the mutex and subtracts money once there is enough money → (points to *money -= 50 area)

NOTE   Whenever a waiting goroutine receives a signal or broadcast, it will try to reacquire the mutex. If another execution is holding on to the mutex, the goroutine will remain suspended until the mutex becomes available.

When we execute listings 5.3, 5.4, and 5.5 together, the program does not exit with a negative balance. Instead, we get the following output:

```
$ go run stingyspendycond.go
Stingy Done
Spendy Done
Money in bank account:  100
```

> **Monitors**
>
> Sometimes we hear the term *monitor* used in the context of condition variables and mutexes. A *monitor* is a synchronization pattern that has a mutex with an associated condition variable. We can use these to wait or signal other threads waiting on the condition, just as we have done in this section. Some languages, such as Java, have a monitor construct on every object instance. In Go, we use the monitor pattern every time we use a mutex with a condition variable.

5.1.2   *Missing the signal*

What happens if a goroutine calls `Signal()` or `Broadcast()` and there is no execution waiting for it? Will it be lost or stored for the next goroutine to call `Wait()`? The answer is shown in figure 5.4. If there is no goroutine in a waiting state, the `Signal()` or `Broadcast()` call will be missed. Let's look at this scenario by using condition variables to solve another problem—that of waiting for our goroutines to complete their tasks.

missed Signal()
or Broadcast()

busy goroutine
not on Wait()

doWork()

main()

Figure 5.4   Calling `Signal()` without `Wait()` will result in a missed signal.

So far, we have been using `time.Sleep()` in our `main()` function to wait for our goroutines to complete. This is not great, since we're only estimating how long the goroutines will take. If we run our code on a slower computer, we will have to increase the amount of time we have to sleep.

Instead of using sleep, we can have our `main()` function wait on a condition variable and then have the child goroutine send a signal when it's ready. The following listing shows an incorrect way of doing this.

Listing 5.6   Incorrect way of signaling

```
package main

import (
    "fmt"
    "sync"
)

func doWork(cond *sync.Cond) {
    fmt.Println("Work started")
    fmt.Println("Work finished")
    cond.Signal()                    ◁——————
}

func main() {
    cond := sync.NewCond(&sync.Mutex{})
    cond.L.Lock()
    for i := 0; i < 50000; i++ {
        go doWork(cond)              ◁——————
        fmt.Println("Waiting for child goroutine ")
        cond.Wait()                  ◁——————
        fmt.Println("Child goroutine finished")
    }
    cond.L.Unlock()
}
```

Repeats 50,000 times (for loop)

Goroutine signals that it has finished the work. (cond.Signal())

Starts a goroutine, simulating doing some work (go doWork(cond))

Waits for a finished signal from the goroutine (cond.Wait())

When we run listing 5.6, we get the following output:

```
$ go run signalbeforewait.go
Waiting for child goroutine
Work started
Work finished
Child goroutine finished
Waiting for child goroutine
Work started
Work finished
Child goroutine finished
. . .
Work started
Work finished
Waiting for child goroutine
fatal error: all goroutines are asleep - deadlock!

goroutine 1 [sync.Cond.Wait]:
sync.runtime_notifyListWait(0xc000024090, 0x9a9)
        sema.go:517 +0x152
sync.(*Cond).Wait(0xe4e1c4?)
        cond.go:70 +0x8c
main.main()
        signalbeforewait.go:19 +0xaf
exit status 2
```

TIP Listing 5.6 might behave differently depending on the hardware and operating system we run it on. To increase the chance of the preceding error happening, we can insert a `runtime.Gosched()` call just before `cond.Wait()` in the `main()` function. This gives the child goroutine more chances to execute before the `main()` goroutine is in a wait state.

The problem in the preceding output is that we might end up signaling when the `main()` goroutine is not waiting on the condition variable. When this happens, we miss the signal. Go's runtime detects that a goroutine is waiting in vain since there are no other goroutines that might call the signal function, and it throws a fatal error.

NOTE We need to ensure that when we call the signal or broadcast function, there is another goroutine waiting for it; otherwise, the signal or broadcast is not received by any goroutine, and it's missed.

To ensure that we don't miss any signals and broadcasts, we need to use them in conjunction with mutexes. That is, we should call these functions only when we're holding the associated mutex. In this way, we know for sure that the `main()` goroutine is in a waiting state because the mutex is only released when the goroutine calls `Wait()`. Figure 5.5 shows both scenarios: missing the signal and signaling with a mutex.

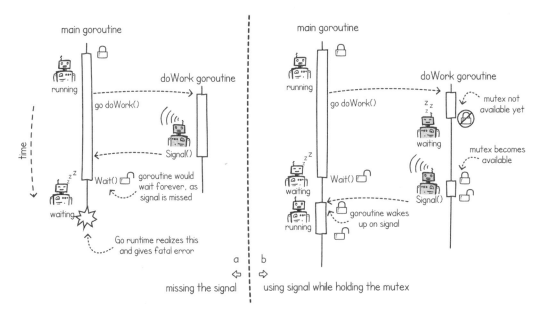

Figure 5.5 **(a) Missing the signal when no goroutine is waiting; (b) using a mutex in the `doWork()` goroutine and calling a signal when holding the mutex**

We can modify the `doWork()` function from listing 5.6 so that it locks the mutex before calling `signal()`, as shown on the right side of figure 5.5. This ensures that the `main()` goroutine is in a waiting state, as shown in the next listing.

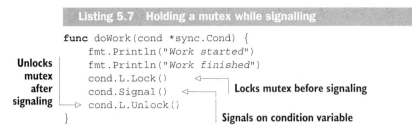

TIP Always use `Signal()`, `Broadcast()`, and `Wait()` when holding the mutex lock to avoid synchronization problems.

5.1.3 Synchronizing multiple goroutines with waits and broadcasts

We have only looked at examples using `Signal()` instead of `Broadcast()` so far. When we have multiple goroutines suspended on a condition variable's `Wait()`, `Signal()` will arbitrarily wake up one of these goroutines. The `Broadcast()` call, on the other hand, will wake up all goroutines that are suspended on a `Wait()`.

NOTE When a group of goroutines is suspended on `Wait()` and we call `Signal()`, we only wake up one of the goroutines. We have no control over which goroutine the system will resume, and we should assume that it can be any goroutine blocked on the condition variable's `Wait()`. Using `Broadcast()`, we ensure that all suspended goroutines on the condition variable are resumed.

Let's now demonstrate the `Broadcast()` functionality with an example. Figure 5.6 shows a game that has players waiting for everyone to join before the game begins. This is a common scenario in both online multiplayer gaming and game consoles. Let's imagine our program has a goroutine handling interactions with each player. How can we write our code to suspend execution to each goroutine until all the players have joined the game?

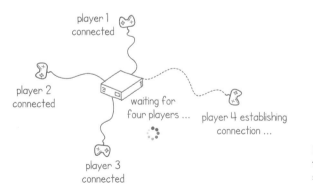

Figure 5.6 Server waiting for four players to join before starting game play

To simulate the goroutines handling four players, with each player connecting to the game at a different time, we can have a `main()` function creating each of the goroutines at a time interval (see listing 5.8). In our `main()` function, we are also sharing a playersInGame variable. This tells the goroutines how many players are participating in the game. Each goroutine executes a playerHandler() function, which we'll implement later.

Listing 5.8 main() function starting player handlers with a time interval

```
package main

import (
    "fmt"
    "sync"
    "time"
)

func main() {
    cond := sync.NewCond(&sync.Mutex{})          Creates a new condition variable
    playersInGame := 4                            Initializes the total number of players to be 4
    for playerId := 0; playerId < 4; playerId++ {
        go playerHandler(cond, &playersInGame, playerId)    Starts goroutine sharing a condition variable, players in game, and player ID
        time.Sleep(1 * time.Second)               Sleeps for a 1-second interval before the next player connects
    }
}
```

We can make use of condition variables by having more than one goroutine wait on the same condition. Since we have a goroutine handling each player, we can have each one wait on a condition that tells us when all the players have connected. We can then use the same condition variable to check if all the players are connected, and if not, we call Wait(). Each time a new goroutine connects to a new player, we reduce this shared variable by 1. When it reaches a count of 0, we can wake up all the suspended threads by calling Broadcast().

Figure 5.7 shows the four different goroutines checking a playersRemaining variable and waiting until the last player connects and its goroutine calls Broadcast(). The last goroutine knows that it's the last one since the playersRemaining shared variable has a value of 0.

The player handler goroutine is shown in listing 5.9. Each goroutine follows the same condition variable pattern. We hold the mutex lock while subtracting a count from the playersRemaining variable and checking to see if more players need to connect. We also release this mutex atomically when we call Wait(). The difference here is that a goroutine will call Broadcast() if it finds out that there are no more players remaining to connect. The goroutine knows that there are no more players to connect because the playersRemaining variable is 0.

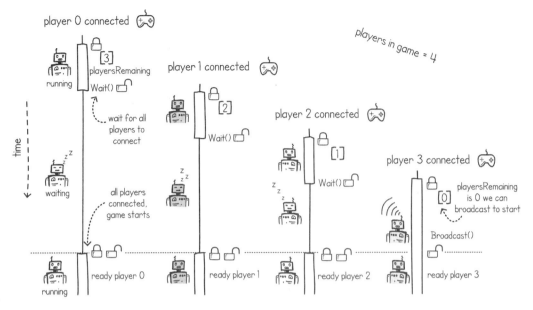

Figure 5.7 Using the `Wait()` and `Broadcast()` pattern to wait for four players to connect

When all the other goroutines unblock from the `Wait()`, as a result of the `Broadcast()`, they exit the condition-checking loop and release the mutex. From this point onward, if this were a real multiplayer game, we would have code that handles game play.

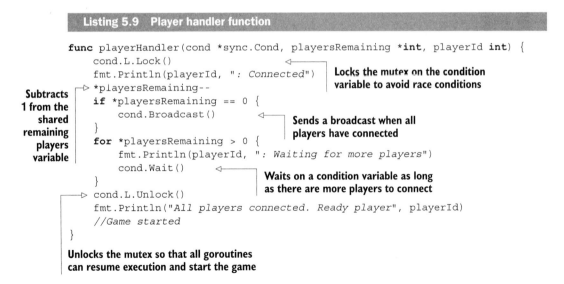

Listing 5.9 Player handler function

```
func playerHandler(cond *sync.Cond, playersRemaining *int, playerId int) {
    cond.L.Lock()
    fmt.Println(playerId, ": Connected")          ← Locks the mutex on the condition
    *playersRemaining--                              variable to avoid race conditions
    if *playersRemaining == 0 {
        cond.Broadcast()                          ← Sends a broadcast when all
    }                                               players have connected
    for *playersRemaining > 0 {
        fmt.Println(playerId, ": Waiting for more players")
        cond.Wait()                               ← Waits on a condition variable as long
    }                                               as there are more players to connect
    cond.L.Unlock()
    fmt.Println("All players connected. Ready player", playerId)
    //Game started
}
```

Subtracts 1 from the shared remaining players variable — `*playersRemaining--`

Unlocks the mutex so that all goroutines can resume execution and start the game

When we run the code in listings 5.8 and 5.9 together, each goroutine waits for all the players to join until the last goroutine sends the broadcast and unblocks all the goroutines. Here is the output:

```
$ go run gamesync.go
0 : Connected
0 : Waiting for more players
1 : Connected
1 : Waiting for more players
2 : Connected
2 : Waiting for more players
3 : Connected
All players connected. Ready player 3
All players connected. Ready player 2
All players connected. Ready player 1
All players connected. Ready player 0
```

5.1.4   *Revisiting readers–writer locks using condition variables*

In the previous chapter, we used mutexes to develop our own implementation of a
readers–writer lock. That implementation was read-preferring, meaning that as long
as we have at least one reader goroutine holding the lock, the writer goroutine can't
access the resource in its critical section. A writer goroutine can only acquire the lock
if all the readers have released their locks. If we don't have a readers' free window, the
writer will be left out. Figure 5.8 shows a scenario where two goroutines take turns
holding the reader's lock, blocking the writer from acquiring a lock.

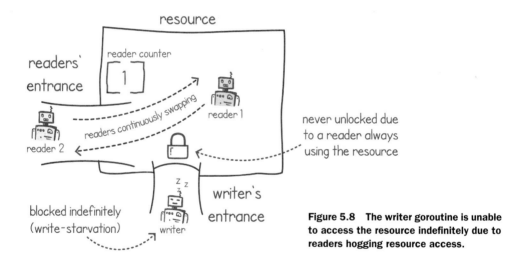

Figure 5.8   **The writer goroutine is unable
to access the resource indefinitely due to
readers hogging resource access.**

In technical-speak, we call this scenario *write-starvation*—we can't update our shared
data structures because the reader parts of the execution are continuously accessing
them, blocking access to the writer. The following listing simulates this scenario.

Listing 5.10   Reader goroutines hogging the reader's lock, blocking write access

```
package main

import (
```

```
    "fmt"
    "github.com/cutajarj/ConcurrentProgrammingWithGo/chapter4/listing4.12"
    "time"
)

func main() {                                          Uses readers–writer mutex
    rwMutex := listing4_12.ReadWriteMutex{}            developed in chapter 4
    for i := 0; i < 2; i++ {
        go func() {
            for {
                rwMutex.ReadLock()
                time.Sleep(1 * time.Second)            Sleeps for 1 second while
                fmt.Println("Read done")               holding the reader lock
                rwMutex.ReadUnlock()
            }
        }()
    }
    time.Sleep(1 * time.Second)
    rwMutex.WriteLock()
    fmt.Println("Write finished")
}
```

Starts two goroutines

Repeats forever

Tries to acquire the writer's lock from the main() goroutine

After the writer's lock is acquired, outputs message and terminates

Even though we have an infinite loop in our goroutines, we expect that eventually the main() goroutine will acquire a hold on the writer's lock, output the message Write finished, and terminate. This should happen because in Go, whenever the main() goroutine terminates, the entire process exits. However, when we run listing 5.10, this is what happens:

```
$ go run writestarvation.go
Read done
Read done
Read done
Read done
Read done
Read done
Read done
Read done
. . . continues indefinitely
```

Our two goroutines constantly hold the reader part of our mutex, which prevents our main() goroutine from ever acquiring the writer's part of the lock. If we are lucky, the readers might release the readers´ lock at the same time, enabling the writer goroutine to acquire it. However, in practice, it is unlikely that both reader threads will release the lock at the same time. This leads to the writer-starvation of our main() goroutine.

DEFINITION *Starvation* is a situation where an execution is blocked from gaining access to a shared resource because the resource is made unavailable for a long time (or indefinitely) by other greedy executions.

We need a different design for a readers–writer lock that is not read-preferred—one that doesn't starve our writer goroutines. We could block new readers from acquiring the read lock as soon as a writer calls the `WriteLock()` function. To achieve this, instead of having the goroutines block on a mutex, we could have them suspended using a condition variable. With a condition variable, we can have different conditions on when to block readers and writers. To design a write-preferred lock, we need a few properties:

- *Readers' counter*—Initially set to `0`, this tells us how many reader goroutines are actively accessing the shared resources.
- *Writers' waiting counter*—Initially set to `0`, this tells us how many writer goroutines are suspended waiting to access the shared resource.
- *Writer active indicator*—Initially set to `false`, this flag tells us if the resource is currently being updated by a writer goroutine.
- *Condition variable with mutex*—This allows us to set various conditions on the preceding properties, suspending execution when the conditions aren't met.

> ### Go's `RWMutex`
>
> The `RWMutex` bundled with Go is write-preferring. This is highlighted in Go's documentation (from https://pkg.go.dev/sync#RWMutex; calling `Lock()` acquires the writer's part of the mutex):
>
> *If a goroutine holds a RWMutex for reading and another goroutine might call Lock, no goroutine should expect to be able to acquire a read lock until the initial read lock is released. In particular, this prohibits recursive read locking. This is to ensure that the lock eventually becomes available; a blocked Lock call excludes new readers from acquiring the lock.*

Let's look at different scenarios to help us understand the implementation. The first scenario is when nothing is accessing the critical sections and no goroutines are requesting write access. In this case, we allow reader goroutines to acquire the read part of the lock and access the shared resource. This scenario is shown on the left side of figure 5.9.

We know that there are no writers using the resource because the writer active indicator is off. We can implement the writer active indicator as a Boolean flag that is set to `true` when the writer acquires access to the lock. We also know that no writers are waiting to acquire the lock because the writers' waiting counter is set to `0`. This waiting counter can be implemented as an integer data type.

The second scenario, shown on the right side of figure 5.9, is when readers acquire the lock. When this happens, they must increment the readers' counter. This indicates to any writers wanting to acquire the writer's lock that the resource is busy being read. If a writer tries to acquire the lock at this time, it must wait on a condition variable as long as readers are using the resource. It must also update the writers' waiting counter by incrementing it.

The writers' waiting counter ensures that any newcomer reader will know there are waiting writers. The reader will then give priority to the writer by blocking until the

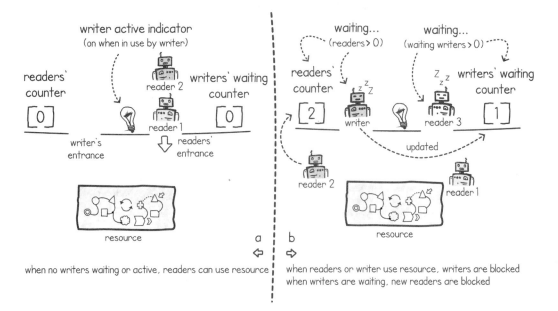

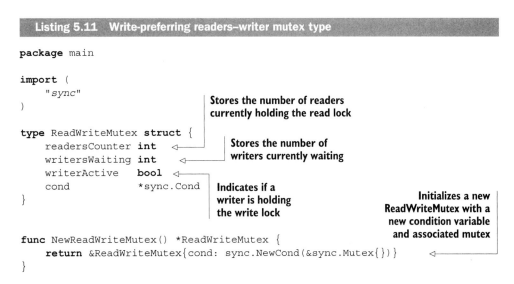

Figure 5.9 **(a) Readers can access the shared resource when no writers are active or waiting. (b) We block writers from accessing the shared resource when readers or a writer are using it. We also block new readers when writers are waiting.**

writers' waiting counter is back to 0. This is what makes our readers–writer mutex write-preferring.

To implement these two scenarios, we first need to create the properties we have outlined. In the following listing, we set up a new struct with the required properties and a function that initializes the condition variable and mutex.

Listing 5.11 Write-preferring readers–writer mutex type

```go
package main

import (
    "sync"
)

type ReadWriteMutex struct {
    readersCounter int      ◁──── Stores the number of readers currently holding the read lock
    writersWaiting int      ◁──── Stores the number of writers currently waiting
    writerActive   bool     ◁──── Indicates if a writer is holding the write lock
    cond           *sync.Cond
}

func NewReadWriteMutex() *ReadWriteMutex {
    return &ReadWriteMutex{cond: sync.NewCond(&sync.Mutex{})}   ◁──── Initializes a new ReadWriteMutex with a new condition variable and associated mutex
}
```

Listing 5.12 shows the implementation of the read-locking function. When acquiring the readers' lock, the ReadLock() function uses the mutex on the condition variable and then conditionally waits as long as there are writers waiting or active. Waiting for the writersWaiting count to be 0 ensures we give priority to writer goroutines. Once the reader checks these two conditions, the readersCounter is incremented and the mutex is released.

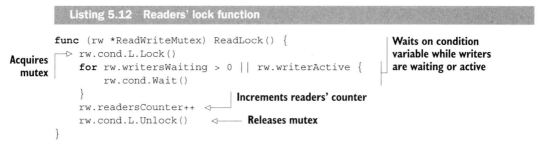

Listing 5.12 Readers' lock function

```
func (rw *ReadWriteMutex) ReadLock() {
    rw.cond.L.Lock()
    for rw.writersWaiting > 0 || rw.writerActive {
        rw.cond.Wait()
    }
    rw.readersCounter++
    rw.cond.L.Unlock()
}
```

Acquires mutex

Waits on condition variable while writers are waiting or active

Increments readers' counter

Releases mutex

In the WriteLock() function, shown in listing 5.13, we use the same mutex and condition variable to wait as long as readers or a writer are active. In addition, the function increments the writers' waiting counter variable to indicate that it's waiting for the lock to become available. Once we can acquire the writer's lock, we decrement the writers' waiting counter by 1 and set the writeActive flag to true.

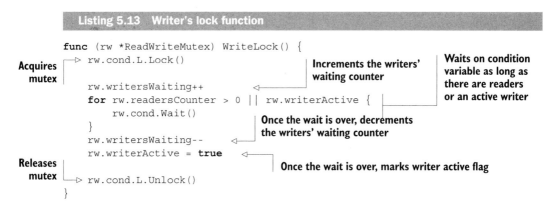

Listing 5.13 Writer's lock function

```
func (rw *ReadWriteMutex) WriteLock() {
    rw.cond.L.Lock()

    rw.writersWaiting++
    for rw.readersCounter > 0 || rw.writerActive {
        rw.cond.Wait()
    }
    rw.writersWaiting--
    rw.writerActive = true

    rw.cond.L.Unlock()
}
```

Acquires mutex

Releases mutex

Increments the writers' waiting counter

Waits on condition variable as long as there are readers or an active writer

Once the wait is over, decrements the writers' waiting counter

Once the wait is over, marks writer active flag

The goroutine calling the WriteLock() function sets the writeActive flag to true so that no other goroutine tries to access the lock at the same time. A writeActive flag set to true will block both readers' and writers' goroutines from acquiring the lock. This scenario is shown on the left side of figure 5.10.

The last scenario is what we do when our goroutines release the lock. When the last reader releases the lock, we can notify any suspended writer by broadcasting on the conditional variable. A goroutine knows that it's the last reader because the readers'

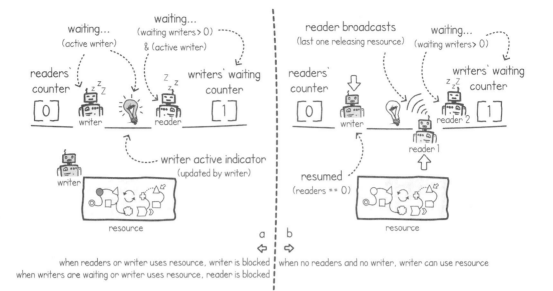

Figure 5.10 (a) Readers and writers blocked when writer has access; (b) last reader broadcasts to resume any writer so that it can have access

counter will be 0 after it decrements it. This scenario is shown on the right side of figure 5.10. The `ReadUnlock()` function is shown in the following listing.

Listing 5.14 Readers' unlock function

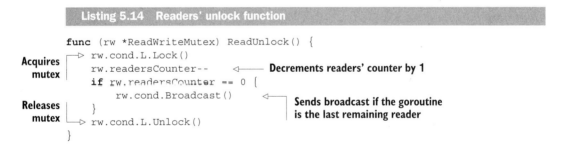

```go
func (rw *ReadWriteMutex) ReadUnlock() {
    rw.cond.L.Lock()
    rw.readersCounter--          ⟵── Decrements readers' counter by 1
    if rw.readersCounter == 0 {
        rw.cond.Broadcast()      ⟵┐  Sends broadcast if the goroutine
    }                            └  is the last remaining reader
    rw.cond.L.Unlock()
}
```

Acquires mutex (left bracket on `rw.cond.L.Lock()` / `rw.readersCounter--`)
Releases mutex (left bracket on `}` / `rw.cond.L.Unlock()`)

The writer's unlock function is simpler. Since there can only ever be one writer active at any point in time, we can send a broadcast every time we unlock. This will wake up any writers or readers that are currently waiting on the condition variable. If there are both readers and writers waiting, a writer will be preferred since the readers will go back into suspension when the writers' waiting counter is above 0. The `WriteUnlock()` function is shown in the following listing.

Listing 5.15 Writer's unlock function

```go
func (rw *ReadWriteMutex) WriteUnlock() {
    rw.cond.L.Lock()
    rw.writerActive = false      ⟵── Unmarks writer active flag
```

Acquires mutex

```
    rw.cond.Broadcast()      ⟵——— Sends a broadcast
    rw.cond.L.Unlock()       ⟵——┐
}                                 │ Releases mutex
```

With this new writer-preferred implementation, we can rerun our code from listing 5.10 to confirm that we don't get writer starvation. As expected, as soon as we have a goroutine asking for write access, the reader goroutines wait and give way to the writer. Our main() goroutine then completes, and the process terminates:

```
$ go run readwritewpref.go
Read done
Read done
Write finished
$
```

5.2   Counting semaphores

In the previous chapter, we saw how mutexes allow only one goroutine to have access to a shared resource, while a readers–writer mutex allows us to specify multiple concurrent reads but exclusive writes. Semaphores give us a different type of concurrency control, in that we can specify the number of concurrent executions that are permitted. Semaphores can also be used as building blocks for developing more complex concurrency tools, as we shall see in the following chapters.

5.2.1   What's a semaphore?

Mutexes give us a way to allow only one execution to happen at a time. What if we need to allow a variable number of executions to happen concurrently? Is there a mechanism that can allow us to specify how many goroutines can access our resource? A mechanism that allows us to limit concurrency would enable us to limit the load on a system. Think, for example, about a slow database that only accepts a certain number of simultaneous connections. We could limit the number of interactions by allowing a fixed number of goroutines to access the database. Once the limit is reached, we can either make the goroutines wait or return an error message to the client saying the system is at capacity.

This is where *semaphores* come in handy. They allow a fixed number of permits that enable concurrent executions to access shared resources. Once all the permits are used, further requests for access will have to wait until a permit is freed again (see figure 5.11).

To better understand semaphores, let's compare them to mutexes. A mutex ensures that only a single goroutine has exclusive access, whereas a semaphore ensures that at most N goroutines have access. In fact, a mutex gives the same functionality as a semaphore where N has a value of 1. A counting semaphore allows us the flexibility to choose any value of N.

> **DEFINITION**   A semaphore with only one permit is sometimes called a *binary semaphore*.

Figure 5.11 A fixed number of goroutines are allowed to have access.

NOTE Although a mutex is a special case of a semaphore with one permit, there is a slight difference in how they are expected to be used. When using mutexes, the execution that is holding a mutex should also be the one to release it. When using semaphores, this is not always the case.

To understand how we can use semaphores, let's first have a look at the three functions it provides:

- *New semaphore function*—Creates a new semaphore with *X* permits.
- *Acquire permit function*—A goroutine will take one permit from the semaphore. If none are available, the goroutine will suspend and wait until one becomes available.
- *Release permit function*—Releases one permit so a goroutine can use it again with the acquire function.

5.2.2 Building a semaphore

In this section, we will implement our own semaphore so that we can better understand how they work. Go does not come with a semaphore type in its bundled libraries, but there is an extension `sync` package at https://pkg.go.dev/golang.org/x/sync containing an implementation of a semaphore. This package is part of the Go project, but it is developed under looser compatibility requirements than the core packages.

To build a semaphore, we need to record how many permits we have left, and we can also use a condition variable to help us wait when we don't have enough permits. The following listing shows the type structure of our semaphore, containing the permit counter and the condition variable. There is also a create semaphore function that accepts the initial number of permits contained on the semaphore.

Listing 5.16 The `Semaphore` type

```go
package listing5_16

import (
    "sync"
)
```

```
type Semaphore struct {
    permits int          ◁──────┐   Permits remaining on the semaphore
    cond *sync.Cond      ◁───┐
}                                │   Condition variable used for waiting
                                 │   when there are not enough permits
func NewSemaphore(n int) *Semaphore {
    return &Semaphore{
        permits: n,      ◁──────┐   Initial number of permits on the new semaphore
        cond: sync.NewCond(&sync.Mutex{}),  ◁──┐
    }                                            │   Initializes a new condition variable and
}                                                │   associated mutex on the new semaphore
}
```

To implement the `Acquire()` function, we need to call `wait()` on a condition variable whenever the permits are 0 (or less). If there are enough permits, we simply subtract 1 from the permit count. The `Release()` function does the opposite: it increases the permit count by 1 and signals that a new permit is available. We use the `Signal()` function instead of `Broadcast()` since only one permit is released and we only want one goroutine to be unblocked.

Listing 5.17   `Acquire()` and `Release()` functions

```
func (rw *Semaphore) Acquire() {
    rw.cond.L.Lock()            ◁────── Acquires mutex to protect permits variable
    for rw.permits <= 0 {
        rw.cond.Wait()          ◁────── Waits until there is an available permit
    }
    rw.permits--                ◁────── Decreases the number of available permits by 1
    rw.cond.L.Unlock()
}
```
Releases mutex

```
func (rw *Semaphore) Release() {
    rw.cond.L.Lock()            ◁────── Acquires mutex to protect permits variable

    rw.permits++                ◁────── Increases the number of available permits by 1
    rw.cond.Signal()            ◁───┐
    rw.cond.L.Unlock()              │   Signals condition variable that one more permit is available
}
```
Releases mutex

5.2.3   *Never miss a signal with semaphores*

Looking at semaphores from another perspective, they provide similar functionality to the wait and signal of a condition variable, with the added benefit of recording a signal even if no goroutine is waiting.

What's in a name?

Semaphores were invented by the Dutch computer scientist Edsger Dijkstra in his unpublished 1962 paper "Over Seinpalen" ("About Semaphores"). The name takes inspiration from an early railway signaling system, which used a pivot arm to signal train drivers. The signal had different meanings depending on the angle of inclination of the pivoted arm.

In listing 5.6, we saw an example of using condition variables to wait for a goroutine to finish its task. The problem we had was that we could end up calling the `Signal()` function before the `main()` goroutine had called `Wait()`, resulting in a missed signal.

We can solve this problem by using a semaphore initialized with `0` permits. This gives us a system in which calling the `Release()` function acts as our signal of work complete. The `Acquire()` function then acts as our `Wait()`. In this system, it doesn't matter if we call `Acquire()` before or after the work is complete, as the semaphore keeps a record of how many times the `Release()` has been called by using the permits count. If we call it before, the goroutine will block and wait for the `Release()` signal. If we call it after, the goroutine will return immediately since there is an available permit.

Figure 5.12 shows an example of using semaphores to wait for a concurrent task to complete. It shows a goroutine executing a `doWork()` function, which calls `Release()` after it finishes its task. Our goroutine executing `main()` wants to know if this task is complete, but it's still busy and hasn't yet stopped to wait and check. Since we're using semaphores, this release call is recorded as a permit. Later, when the `main()` goroutine calls `Acquire()`, the function will return immediately, indicating that the `doWork()` goroutine has completed its assigned work.

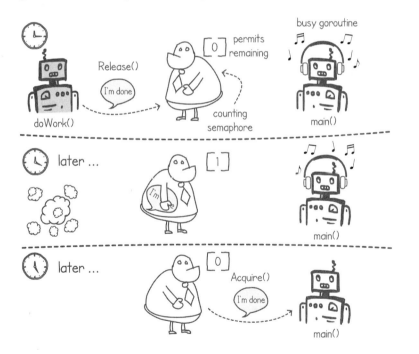

Figure 5.12   Using a semaphore to know when a goroutine is done

Listing 5.18 shows the implementation of this. When we start the `doWork()` goroutine, we pass a reference to our semaphore, which is used as shown in figure 5.11. In this function, we are simulating the goroutine doing some concurrent quick task. When the goroutine finishes its task, it calls `Release()` to signal that it's finished. In the `main()` function, we create many of these goroutines, and after each creation, we wait for it to complete by calling `Acquire()` on the semaphore.

Listing 5.18   Using semaphores to signal completion of a task

```
package main

import (
    "fmt"
    "github.com/cutajarj/ConcurrentProgrammingWithGo/chapter5/listing5.16"
)

func main() {
    semaphore := listing5_16.NewSemaphore(0)     ◁———  Creates a new semaphore using
                                                        the previous implementation
    for i := 0; i < 50000; i++ {
        go doWork(semaphore)                     ◁———  Starts the goroutine passing a
        fmt.Println("Waiting for child goroutine ")     reference to the semaphore
        semaphore.Acquire()                      ◁———  Waits for an available permit on
        fmt.Println("Child goroutine finished")         the semaphore indicating the task
    }                                                   is complete
}

func doWork(semaphore *listing5_16.Semaphore) {
    fmt.Println("Work started")
    fmt.Println("Work finished")                 ┐ When the goroutine finishes, it releases
    semaphore.Release()                      ◁———┘ a permit to notify the main() goroutine
}
```

Repeats 50,000 times

If `Release()` is called first, the semaphore stores this release permit, and when the `main()` goroutine calls the `Acquire()` function, it will immediately return without blocking. If we were using a condition variable without mutex locking, this would have resulted in our `main()` goroutine missing the signal.

5.3   Exercises

NOTE You can see all code solutions at https://github.com/cutajarj/ ConcurrentProgrammingWithGo.

1 In listing 5.4, Stingy's goroutine is signaling on the condition variable every time we add money to the bank account. Can you change the function so that it signals only when there is $50 or more in the account?

2 Change the game-sync listings 5.8 and 5.9 so that, still using condition variables, the players wait for a fixed number of seconds. If the players haven't all joined within this time, the goroutines should stop waiting and let the game start without all the players. Hint: try using another goroutine with an expiry timer.

3 A *weighted semaphore* is a variation on a semaphore that allows you to acquire and release more than one permit at the same time. The function signatures for a weighted semaphore are as follows:

```
func (rw *WeightedSemaphore) Acquire(permits int)
func (rw *WeightedSemaphore) Release(permits int)
```

Use these function signatures to implement a weighted semaphore with a similar functionality to a counting semaphore. It should allow you to acquire or release more than one permit.

Summary

- An execution can be suspended, waiting until a condition is met, by using a condition variable together with a mutex.
- Calling `Wait()` on a condition variable atomically unlocks the mutex and suspends the current execution.
- Calling `Signal()` resumes the execution of one suspended goroutine that has called `Wait()`.
- Calling `Broadcast()` resumes the execution of all suspended goroutines that have called `Wait()`.
- If we call `Signal()` or `Broadcast()` and no goroutines are suspended on a `Wait()` call, the signal or broadcast is missed.
- We can use condition variables and mutexes as building blocks to build more complex concurrency tools, such as semaphores and write-preferring readers–writer locks.
- Starvation occurs when an execution is blocked from a shared resource because the resource is made unavailable for a long time by other executions.
- Write-preferring readers–writer mutexes solve the problem of write starvation.
- Semaphores give us the ability to limit concurrency on a shared resource to a fixed number of concurrent executions.
- Like condition variables, semaphores can be used to send a signal to another execution.
- When used to signal, semaphores have the added advantage that the signal is stored if the execution is not yet waiting for it.

Synchronizing with
waitgroups and barriers

6

This chapter covers

- Waiting for completed tasks with waitgroups
- Building waitgroups with semaphores
- Implementing waitgroups using condition variables
- Synchronizing concurrent work using barriers

Waitgroups and barriers are two synchronization abstractions that work on groups of executions (such as goroutines). We typically use *waitgroups* to wait for a group of tasks to complete. We use *barriers* to synchronize many executions at a common point.

We'll start this chapter by examining Go's bundled waitgroups using a couple of applications. Later, we'll investigate two implementations of waitgroups: one built using semaphores and a more functionally complete one using condition variables.

Go does not bundle barriers in its libraries, so we'll build our own barrier type. Then we'll employ this barrier type in a simple concurrent matrix multiplication algorithm.

6.1 Waitgroups in Go

With waitgroups, we can have a goroutine wait for a set of concurrent tasks to complete. We can think of a waitgroup as a project manager managing a set of tasks given to different workers. Once the tasks are all complete, the project manager notifies us.

6.1.1 Waiting for tasks to complete with waitgroups

In previous chapters, we saw a concurrency pattern where a main goroutine splits a problem into multiple tasks and passes each task to a separate goroutine. The goroutines then complete these tasks concurrently. For example, in chapter 3, we saw this pattern when we were developing the letter-frequency program. The main goroutine created many goroutines, each of which downloaded and processed a separate web page. In our first implementation, we used a `sleep()` function to wait for some seconds until all the goroutines completed their downloads. Using a waitgroup will make it easier to wait for all the goroutines to complete their tasks.

Figure 6.1 shows a typical pattern of using a waitgroup. We set the size of the waitgroup and then use the two operations `Wait()` and `Done()`d. In this pattern, we typically have multiple goroutines that need to complete a few tasks concurrently. We can create a waitgroup and set its size to be equal to the number of assigned tasks. The main goroutine will hand over the tasks to the newly created goroutines, and its execution will be suspended after it calls the `Wait()` operation. Once a goroutine finishes its task, it calls the `Done()` operation on the waitgroup (see the left side of figure 6.1). When all the goroutines have called the `Done()` operation for all their assigned tasks, the main goroutine will unblock. At this point, the main goroutine knows that all the tasks have been completed (see the right side of figure 6.1).

Go comes bundled with a `WaitGroup` implementation in its `sync` package. It contains the three functions that allow us to use the pattern described in figure 6.1:

- `Done()`—Decrements the waitgroup size counter by `1`
- `Wait()`—Blocks until the waitgroup size counter is `0`
- `Add(delta int)`—Increments the waitgroup size counter by delta

Listing 6.1 shows a simple example of how we can use these three operations. We have a `doWork()` function that simulates completing a task by sleeping for a random length of time. Once it finishes, it prints out a message and calls the `Done()` function on the waitgroup. The `main()` function calls the `Add(4)` function, creates four of these `doWork()` goroutines, and calls `Wait()` on the waitgroup.

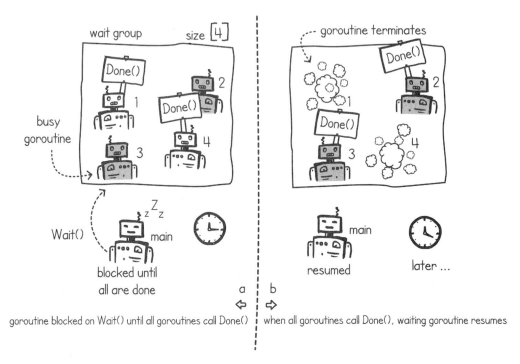

Figure 6.1   Typical use of a waitgroup

Once all the goroutines have signaled that they're finished, the `Wait()` unblocks, and the `main()` function resumes.

Listing 6.1   Simple use of a waitgroup

```
package main

import (
    "fmt"
    "math/rand"
    "sync"
    "time"
)

func main() {
    wg := sync.WaitGroup{}
    wg.Add(4)
    for i := 1; i <= 4; i++ {
        go doWork(i, &wg)
    }
    wg.Wait()
    fmt.Println("All complete")
}

func doWork(id int, wg *sync.WaitGroup) {
```

Adds 4 to the waitgroup since we have four pieces of work

Creates a new waitgroup

Creates four goroutines, passing a reference to the waitgroup

Waits for the work to be complete

```
i := rand.Intn(5)
time.Sleep(time.Duration(i) * time.Second)          ◁——  Sleeps for a random
fmt.println(id, "Done working after", i, "seconds")       time (up to 5 seconds)
wg.Done()   ◁——
}                    Signals that the goroutine
                     has completed its task
```

When we run listing 6.1, all the goroutines complete after sleeping for slightly different times. They call `Done()` on the waitgroup, and the `main()` goroutine unblocks, giving us the following output:

```
$ go run waitforgroup.go
1 Done working after 1 seconds
4 Done working after 2 seconds
2 Done working after 2 seconds
3 Done working after 4 seconds
All complete
```

Now that we have this extra tool at our disposal, let's fix the letter-frequency program (from listing 4.5) so that it uses waitgroups. In the `main()` goroutine, instead of calling the `sleep()` function for 10 seconds, we can create a goroutine that calls our existing `CountLetters()` function and then calls `Done()` on the waitgroup, as shown in the following listing. Notice that we didn't need to modify the `CountLetters()` function to call `Done()`; instead, we use an anonymous function running in a separate goroutine, calling both functions.

Listing 6.2 Count frequency using waitgroups

```
package main

import (
    "fmt"
    "github.com/cutajarj/ConcurrentProgrammingWithGo/chapter4/listing4.5"
    "sync"
)

func main() {
    wg := sync.WaitGroup{}                                      Adds a delta of 31—one
    wg.Add(31)   ◁——                                           for each web page to be
    mutex := sync.Mutex{}                                      downloaded concurrently
    var frequency = make([]int, 26)
    for i := 1000; i <= 1030; i++ {
        url := fmt.Sprintf("https://rfc-editor.org/rfc/rfc%d.txt", i)
        go func() {                                            ◁——
            listing4_5.CountLetters(url, frequency, &mutex)         Creates a goroutine
            wg.Done()   ◁——                                        with an anonymous
        }()                      Calls Done() after it              function
    }                            finishes counting letters
    wg.Wait()
    mutex.Lock()
    for i, c := range listing4_5.AllLetters {
```

Creates a new waitgroup → (points to `wg := sync.WaitGroup{}`)

Waits until all goroutines are complete → (points to `wg.Wait()`)

```
        fmt.Printf("%c-%d ", c, frequency[i])
    }
    mutex.Unlock()
}
```

When we run listing 6.2, instead of having to wait a fixed time for all the goroutines to complete, the `main()` function will output the result as soon as the waitgroup unblocks.

6.1.2   *Creating a waitgroup type using semaphores*

Let's now take a look at how we can implement a waitgroup ourselves instead of using the implementation bundled with Go. We can create a simple version of a waitgroup just by building on top of the semaphore type that we developed in the previous chapter.

We can include logic in the `Wait()` function to call the semaphore's `Acquire()` function. In a semaphore, the `Acquire()` call will suspend the execution of the goroutine if the permits available are 0 or less. We can use a trick and initialize a semaphore with the number of permits equal to 1 - n to act as our waitgroup of size n. This means that our `Wait()` function will block until the number of permits is increased n times, from 1 - n up to 1. Figure 6.2 shows an example of a waitgroup of size 3. For a group of size 3, we can use a semaphore of size -2.

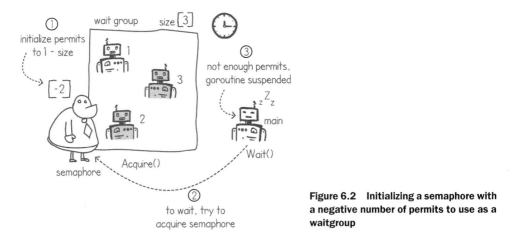

Figure 6.2   **Initializing a semaphore with a negative number of permits to use as a waitgroup**

Every time a goroutine calls `Done()` on the waitgroup, we can call the `Release()` operation on the semaphore. This will increment the number of permits available on the semaphore by 1 each time. Once all the goroutines finish their task and have all called `Done()`, the number of permits in the semaphore will end up being 1. This process is shown in figure 6.3.

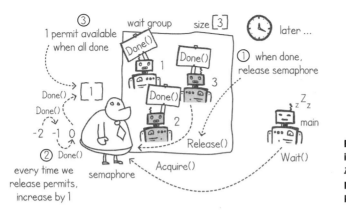

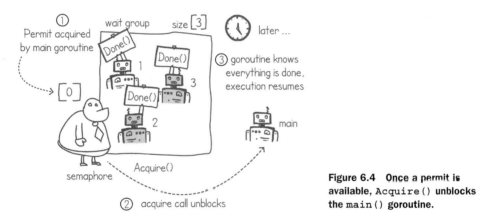

Figure 6.3 **When a goroutine is done, it results in an `Acquire()`, increasing the permits by 1 and leaving 1 permit available in the end.**

When the number of permits is greater than `0`, the `Acquire()` call unblocks, releasing our suspended goroutine. In figure 6.4, the permit is acquired by the `main()` goroutine, and the number of permits goes back down to `0`. In this way, the `main()` goroutine is resumed, and it knows that all goroutines have completed their assigned tasks.

Figure 6.4 **Once a permit is available, `Acquire()` unblocks the `main()` goroutine.**

Listing 6.3 shows an implementation of a waitgroup using a semaphore. In this listing, we're using the implementation of semaphores from chapter 5. As discussed previously, when we create the waitgroup, we initialize a semaphore of `1 - size` permits. We try to acquire one permit when we call the `Wait()` function and release one permit when we call `Done()`.

Listing 6.3   Waitgroup implementation using a semaphore

```go
package listing6_3

import (
    "github.com/cutajarj/ConcurrentProgrammingWithGo/chapter5/listing5.16"
)
```

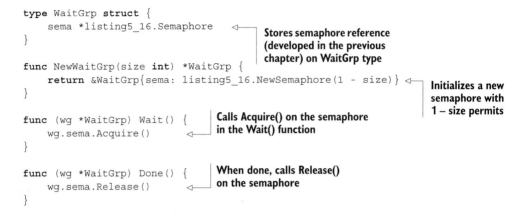

```
type WaitGrp struct {
    sema *listing5_16.Semaphore
}
```
Stores semaphore reference (developed in the previous chapter) on WaitGrp type

```
func NewWaitGrp(size int) *WaitGrp {
    return &WaitGrp{sema: listing5_16.NewSemaphore(1 - size)}
}
```
Initializes a new semaphore with 1 – size permits

```
func (wg *WaitGrp) Wait() {
    wg.sema.Acquire()
}
```
Calls Acquire() on the semaphore in the Wait() function

```
func (wg *WaitGrp) Done() {
    wg.sema.Release()
}
```
When done, calls Release() on the semaphore

Listing 6.4 shows a simple use of our semaphore waitgroup. The main difference between Go's bundled waitgroup and our implementation is that we need to specify the size of the waitgroup at the start before we use it. In the waitgroup in Go's `sync` package, we can increase the size of the group at any point—even when we have goroutines waiting on the work to be completed.

Listing 6.4 Simple use of the semaphore waitgroup

```
package main

import (
    "fmt"
    "github.com/cutajarj/ConcurrentProgrammingWithGo/chapter6/listing6.3"
)

func doWork(id int, wg *listing6_3.WaitGrp) {
    fmt.Println(id, "Done working ")
    wg.Done()
}
```
When the goroutine is complete, it calls Done() on the waitgroup.

```
func main() {
    wg := listing6_3.NewWaitGrp(4)
    for i := 1; i <= 4; i++ {
        go doWork(i, wg)
    }
    wg.Wait()
    fmt.Println("All complete")
}
```
Creates new waitgroup of size 4

Creates a goroutine, passing a reference to the waitgroup

Waits on the waitgroup for work to be complete

6.1.3   *Changing the size of our waitgroup while waiting*

Our waitgroup implementation using semaphores is limited because we must specify the size of the waitgroup at the start. This means we cannot change the size after we create our waitgroup. To better understand this limitation, let's look at an application in which we need to resize the waitgroup after creation.

Imagine we are writing a filename search program using multiple goroutines. The program will search recursively for a filename string starting from an input directory. We want the program to accept the input directory and the filename string as two input arguments. It should output a list of matches with a full path:

```
$ go run filesearch.go /home cat
/home/photos/holiday/cat.jpg
/home/art/cat.png
/home/sketches/cat.svg
. . .
```

Using multiple goroutines would help us find files quicker, especially when we are searching across multiple drives. We can take the approach of creating a separate goroutine for each directory that we encounter in our search. Figure 6.5 shows the concept.

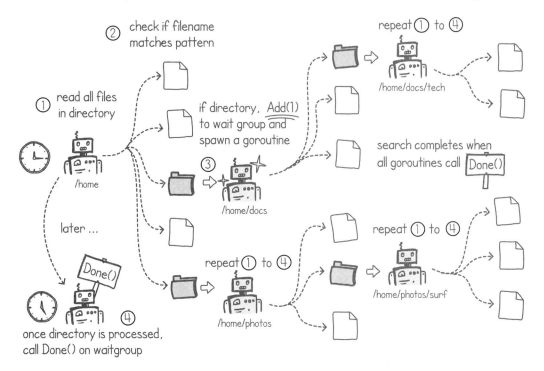

Figure 6.5   Recursive concurrent filename search

The idea here is to have a goroutine find files that match the input string. If this goroutine encounters a directory, it adds 1 to a global waitgroup and spawns a new goroutine that runs the same exact logic for that directory. The search ends after every goroutine calls Done() on the waitgroup. This means that we have explored every single subdirectory of our first input directory. The following listing implements this recursive search function.

Listing 6.5   Recursive search function (error handling omitted for brevity)

```
package main

import (
    "fmt"
    "os"
    "path/filepath"
    "strings"
    "sync"
)

func fileSearch(dir string, filename string, wg *sync.WaitGroup) {
    files, _ := os.ReadDir(dir)
    for _, file := range files {
        fpath := filepath.Join(dir, file.Name())
        if strings.Contains(file.Name(), filename) {
            fmt.Println(fpath)
        }
        if file.IsDir() {
            wg.Add(1)
            go fileSearch(fpath, filename, wg)
        }
    }
    wg.Done()
}
```

Reads all files from the directory given to the function

Joins each file to the directory: 'cat.jpg' becomes '/home/pics/cat.jpg'

If there is a match, prints path on console

If it is a directory, adds 1 to the waitgroup before starting a new goroutine

Creates goroutine recursively, searching in the new directory

Marks Done() on the waitgroup after processing all files

Now we just need a `main()` function that creates a waitgroup, adds 1 to it, and then starts a goroutine that calls our `fileSearch()` function. The `main()` function can just wait on the waitgroup for the search to complete, as shown in the following listing. In this listing, we are using command-line arguments to read the search directory and the filename string to be matched.

Listing 6.6   `main()` function calling the file search function and waiting on the waitgroup

```
func main() {
    wg := sync.WaitGroup{}
    wg.Add(1)
    go fileSearch(os.Args[1], os.Args[2], &wg)
    wg.Wait()
}
```

Creates a new, empty waitgroup

Adds a delta of 1 to the waitgroup

Creates a new goroutine, performing the file search and passing a reference to the waitgroup

Waits for the search to complete

6.1.4   *Building a more flexible waitgroup*

The file search program shows us the advantage of using Go's bundled waitgroup over our own semaphore waitgroup implementation. Not knowing how many goroutines we are going to create at the start forces us to resize our waitgroup as we go along. In addition, our semaphore waitgroup implementation had the limitation that only one goroutine could wait on the waitgroup. If we had multiple goroutines calling the `Wait()` function, only one would be resumed because we only incremented the permit count on the semaphore to 1. Can we change our implementation to match the functionality of Go's bundled waitgroup?

We can use condition variables to implement a more complete waitgroup. Figure 6.6 shows us how we can implement both the Add(delta) and Wait() functions with a condition variable. The Add() function simply adds to a waitgroup's size variable. We can protect this variable with a mutex so that we don't modify it at the same time as another goroutine (see the left side of figure 6.6). To implement the Wait() operation, we can have a condition variable that waits while the size of the waitgroup is bigger than 0 (see the right side of figure 6.6).

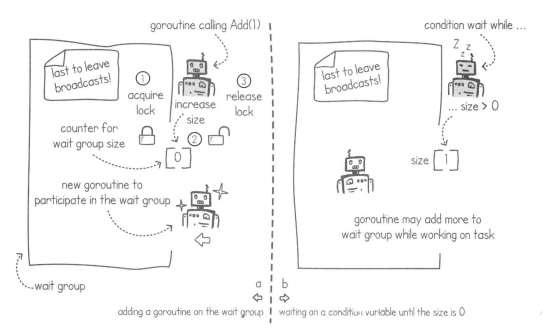

Figure 6.6 (a) An Add() operation on a waitgroup; (b) a Wait() operation results in waiting on a condition variable.

The next listing implements a WaitGrp type containing this waitgroup size variable and a condition variable. Go initializes the group size to the value of 0 by default. The listing also shows a function that initializes the condition variable with its mutex.

Listing 6.7 Initializing a waitgroup using condition variables

```
package listing6_7

import (
    "sync"
)

type WaitGrp struct {
```

```
    groupSize int      ◁──── The waitgroup size property, initialized to 0 by default
    cond      *sync.Cond   ◁────┐
}                              │ The condition variable to be used in the waitgroup

func NewWaitGrp() *WaitGrp {
    return &WaitGrp{                          Initializes the condition
        cond: sync.NewCond(&sync.Mutex{}),  ◁─┘ variable with a new mutex
    }
}
```

To write our `Add(delta)` function, we need to acquire the mutex on the condition variable, add the delta to the `groupSize` variable, and then finally release the mutex. In the `Done()` operation, we again need to protect the `groupSize` variable with a mutex `Lock()` and `Unlock()`. We also perform a condition wait while the group size is larger than `0`. This logic is shown in the following listing.

Listing 6.8   `Add(delta)` and `Wait()` operations for the waitgroup

```
             func (wg *WaitGrp) Add(delta int) {
Increases        wg.cond.L.Lock()            ◁───┐
groupSize   ┌──▷ wg.groupSize += delta            Protects the update to groupSize with
by delta    │    wg.cond.L.Unlock()          ◁─── a mutex lock on the condition variable
            │}

             func (wg *WaitGrp) Wait() {
       ┌───▷     wg.cond.L.Lock()
       │         for wg.groupSize > 0 {          Waits and atomically releases the mutex
       │             wg.cond.Wait()      ◁─────  while groupSize is greater than 0
       │         }
       └───▷     wg.cond.L.Unlock()
       │}
```

Protects the read of the groupSize variable
with a mutex lock on the condition variable

A goroutine calls the `Done()` function when it wants to signal that it has completed its task. When this happens, inside the waitgroup's `Done()` function, we can reduce the group size by 1. We also need to add logic so that the last goroutine to call the `Done()` function in the waitgroup broadcasts to any other goroutines currently suspended on the `Wait()` operation. The goroutine knows that it's the last goroutine because the group size will be `0` after it decrements the group size.

The left side of figure 6.7 shows how a goroutine acquires the mutex lock, reduces the value of the group size, and then releases the mutex lock. The right side of figure 6.7 shows that when the group size reaches `0`, the goroutine knows that it's the last one, and it broadcasts on the condition variable so that any suspended goroutines are resumed. In this way, we're indicating that all the work done by the waitgroup is complete. We use a broadcast call instead of a signal since there might be more than one goroutine suspended on the `Wait()` operation.

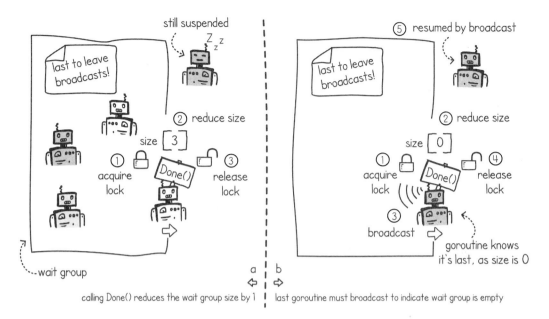

Figure 6.7   (a) The `Done()` operation decrements group size; (b) last `Done()` operation results in a broadcast.

Listing 6.9 implements the `Done()` operation of our waitgroup. As usual, we protect the `groupSize` variable by using a mutex. Afterward, we reduce this variable by 1. Finally, we check to see whether we're the last goroutine in the waitgroup by checking whether the value is 0. If it is 0, we call the `Broadcast()` operation on the condition variable to resume any suspended goroutines.

Listing 6.9   `Done()` operation for the waitgroup using condition variables

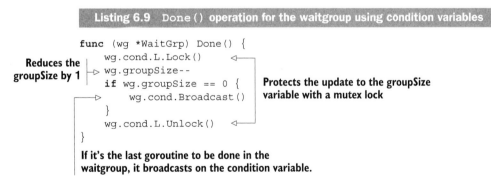

```
func (wg *WaitGrp) Done() {
    wg.cond.L.Lock()
    wg.groupSize--
    if wg.groupSize == 0 {
        wg.cond.Broadcast()
    }
    wg.cond.L.Unlock()
}
```

Reduces the groupSize by 1

Protects the update to the groupSize variable with a mutex lock

If it's the last goroutine to be done in the waitgroup, it broadcasts on the condition variable.

This new implementation satisfies both our initial requirements. We can change the size of the waitgroup after creating the waitgroup, and we can unblock more than one goroutine suspended on the `Wait()` operation.

6.2   *Barriers*

Waitgroups are great for synchronizing after a task has been completed. But what if we need to coordinate our goroutines before we start a task? We might also need to align different executions at different points in time. Barriers give us the ability to synchronize groups of goroutines at specific points in our code.

Let's look at a simple analogy to help us compare waitgroups and barriers. A private plane will only leave when all the passengers arrive at the departure terminal. This represents a barrier. Everyone has to wait until every passenger arrives at this barrier (the airport terminal). When everyone has finally arrived, the passengers can proceed and board the plane.

For the same flight, the pilot must wait for a number of tasks to be complete before departing, such as refueling, stowing luggage, and loading passengers. In our analogy, this represents the waitgroup. The pilot is waiting for these concurrent tasks to be complete before the plane can depart.

6.2.1   *What is a barrier?*

To understand program barriers, think about a set of goroutines, all working together on different parts of the same computation. Before the goroutines start, they all need to wait for their input data. Once they have completed, they again need to wait for another execution to collect and merge the results of their computations. The cycle might repeat multiple times, as long as there is more input data that needs to be computed. Figure 6.8 illustrates this concept.

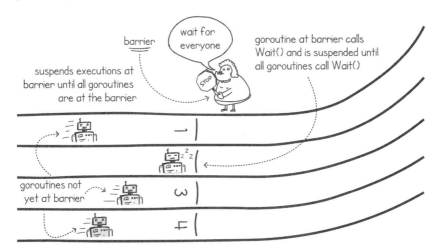

Figure 6.8   Barriers suspend executions until all goroutines catch up.

When thinking about barriers, we can visualize our goroutines as being in one of two possible states: either executing their task or suspended and waiting for others to catch up. For example, a goroutine might perform some computation and then wait (by calling a `Wait()` function) for the other goroutines to finish their computations. This `Wait()` function would suspend the goroutine's execution until all the other goroutines participating in this barrier group catch up by also calling `Wait()` themselves. At this point, the barrier releases all the suspended goroutines together (see figure 6.9) so that they can continue or restart their execution.

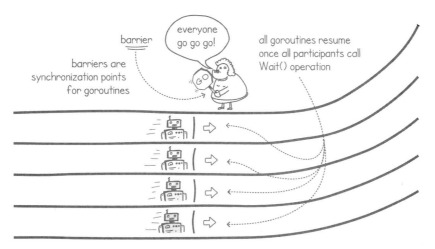

Figure 6.9 Goroutines resume execution after they all call the `Wait()` operation.

Barriers are different from waitgroups in that they combine the waitgroup's `Done()` and `Wait()` operations together into one atomic call. The other difference is that depending on the implementation, barriers can be reused multiple times.

DEFINITION   A barrier that can be reused is sometimes called a *cyclic barrier*.

6.2.2 Implementing a barrier in Go

Unfortunately, Go does not come with a bundled implementation of a barrier, so if we want to use one, we need to implement it ourselves. As with waitgroups, we can use a condition variable to implement our barrier.

To start with, we need to know the size of the group of executions that will be using this barrier. In the implementation, we'll call this the *barrier size*. We can use this size to know when enough goroutines are at the barrier.

In the barrier implementation, we'll only need to worry about the `Wait()` operation. Figure 6.10 shows the two scenarios of calling this function. The first scenario is when a goroutine calls this function and not all executions are at the barrier (shown on the left side of figure 6.10). In this scenario, calling the `Wait()` function results in an increment of the wait counter, which tells us how many goroutines are currently waiting on the barrier to be released. When the number of goroutines waiting is less than the size of the barrier, we suspend the goroutine by waiting on a condition variable.

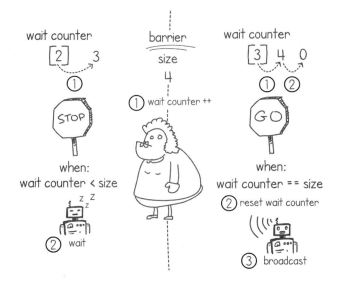

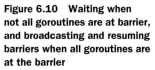

Figure 6.10   Waiting when not all goroutines are at barrier, and broadcasting and resuming barriers when all goroutines are at the barrier

When the wait counter reaches the size of the barrier (on the right side of figure 6.10), we need to reset the counter to 0 and broadcast on the condition variable to wake up any suspended goroutines. In this way, any goroutines that were waiting on the barrier become unblocked and can resume their execution.

In listing 6.10, we implement the struct type and `NewBarrier(size)` construct function for the barrier. The Go struct contains the size of the barrier, a wait counter, and a reference to the condition variable. In the constructor, we then initialize the wait counter to 0, create a new condition variable, and set the barrier size to be the same value as the input parameter in the function.

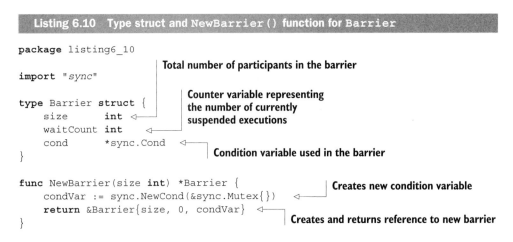

Listing 6.10   Type struct and `NewBarrier()` function for `Barrier`

```
package listing6_10

import "sync"                          Total number of participants in the barrier

type Barrier struct {                  Counter variable representing
    size      int   <──                the number of currently
    waitCount int   <──                suspended executions
    cond      *sync.Cond  <──
}                                      Condition variable used in the barrier

func NewBarrier(size int) *Barrier {
    condVar := sync.NewCond(&sync.Mutex{})   <──  Creates new condition variable
    return &Barrier{size, 0, condVar}  <──
}                                      Creates and returns reference to new barrier
```

Listing 6.11 implements the `Wait()` function with its two scenarios. In the function, we immediately acquire the mutex lock on the condition variable and then increment the wait count. If the wait counter hasn't yet reached the size of the barrier, we suspend the goroutine's execution by calling the `Wait()` function on the condition variable. This second part of our `if` statement represents the left side of figure 6.10, where the counter reaches the barrier's size. In this case, we simply reset the counter to `0` and broadcast on the condition variable. This will wake up all of the suspended goroutines waiting on the barrier.

Listing 6.11   `Wait()` function for barrier

```
func (b *Barrier) Wait() {
    b.cond.L.Lock()         ◁——————  Protects access to the waitCount
    b.waitCount += 1                  variable by using a mutex

    if b.waitCount == b.size {        If waitCount has reached the barrier
        b.waitCount = 0               size, resets waitCount and broadcasts
        b.cond.Broadcast()            on the condition variable
    } else {
        b.cond.Wait()       ◁——————  If waitCount hasn't reached the barrier
    }                                 size, waits on the condition variable

    b.cond.L.Unlock()       ◁——————  Protects access to the waitCount
}                                     variable by using a mutex
```

Increments the count variable by 1

We can test our barrier by having two goroutines simulate executing for different periods of time. In listing 6.12, we have a `workAndWait()` function that simulates doing work for a period of time and then goes to wait on a barrier. As usual, we simulate doing work by using the `time.Sleep()` function. After the goroutine is unblocked from the barrier, it goes back to work for the same amount of time. At each stage, the function prints the time in seconds from the start of the goroutine.

Listing 6.12   Simple use of a barrier

```
package main

import (
    "fmt"
    "github.com/cutajarj/ConcurrentProgrammingWithGo/chapter6/listing6.10"
    "time"
)

func workAndWait(name string, timeToWork int, barrier *listing6_10.Barrier) {
    start := time.Now()
    for {
        fmt.Println(time.Since(start), name,"is running")
        time.Sleep(time.Duration(timeToWork) * time.Second)    ◁——  Simulates doing
        fmt.Println(time.Since(start), name,"is waiting on barrier")    work for a number
        barrier.Wait()      ◁——┐                                       of seconds
    }                          Waits for other goroutines to catch up
}
```

We can now start two goroutines that use the `workAndWait()` function, each with a different `timeToWork`. In this way, the goroutine that completes the work earlier will have its execution suspended by the barrier, and it will wait for the slower goroutine before starting work again. In the next listing, we create a barrier and start two goroutines, passing a reference to both. We call the two goroutines `Red` and `Blue`, giving them 4 and 10 seconds to work, respectively.

Listing 6.13   Starting slow and fast goroutines and sharing a barrier

```
func main() {
    barrier := listing6_10.NewBarrier(2)          Creates a new barrier with two participants
                                                  using the implementation from listing 6.10

    go workAndWait("Red", 4, barrier)             Starts goroutine with the name
                                                  Red and a timeToWork of 4

    go workAndWait("Blue", 10, barrier)
                                                  Starts goroutine with the name
    time.Sleep(100 * time.Second)                 Blue and a timeToWork of 10
}
```

Waits for 100 seconds

When we run listings 6.12 and 6.13 together, the program runs for 100 seconds, after which the `main()` goroutine terminates. As expected, the fast 4-second goroutine, called `Red`, finishes early and waits for the slower one, called `Blue`, which takes 10 seconds. We can see this reflected in the output timestamps:

```
$ go run simplebarrierexample.go
0s Blue is running
0s Red is running
4.0104152s Red is waiting on barrier
10.0071386s Blue is waiting on barrier
10.0076689s Blue is running
10.0076689s Red is running
14.0145434s Red is waiting on barrier
20.0096403s Blue is waiting on barrier
20.010348s Blue is running
20.010348s Red is running
. . .
```

Let's now look at a real-world application that uses barriers to synchronize multiple executions.

6.2.3   *Concurrent matrix multiplication using barriers*

Matrix multiplication is a fundamental operation from linear algebra that is used in various computer science fields. Many algorithms in graph theory, artificial intelligence, and computer graphics adopt matrix multiplication in their algorithms. Unfortunately, computing this linear algebra operation is a time-consuming process.

Multiplying two $n \times n$ matrices together using the simple iterative approach gives us a runtime complexity of $O(n^3)$. This means that the time spent on computing the result will grow cubically with regard to the matrix size n. For example, if it takes us 10 seconds to compute the multiplication of two 100×100 matrices, then when we double the size of the matrices to 200×200, it will take us 80 seconds to compute the result. Doubling the input size results in scaling the time taken by 2^3.

Faster matrix multiplication algorithms

There are matrix multiplication algorithms with a better runtime complexity than $O(n^3)$. In 1969, Volker Strassen, a German mathematician, devised a faster algorithm with a runtime complexity of $O(n^{2.807})$. Although this is a big improvement over the simple approach, the speedup is significant only when the size of the matrices is very large. For smaller matrix sizes, the simple approach seems to work best.

Other more recent algorithms have even better runtime complexities. However, these algorithms are not used in practice because they perform faster only if the input size of the matrices is extremely large—so large, in fact, that they wouldn't fit in the memory of today's computers. These solutions belong to a class of algorithms called *galactic algorithms*, where the algorithms outperform other algorithms for inputs that are too big to be used in practice.

How can we use parallel computing and build a concurrent version of the matrix multiplication algorithm to help speed up this operation? Let's start by reminding ourselves how matrix multiplication works. To keep the implementation simple, we'll consider only square matrices ($n \times n$) in this section. For example, when computing the multiplication of matrix A by matrix B, the result of the first cell (row 0, col 0) is the result of multiplying row 0 from A with column 0 from B. An example of a 3×3 matrix multiplication is shown in figure 6.11. To compute the second cell (row 0, col 1), we need to multiply row 0 from A with column 1 from B, and so on.

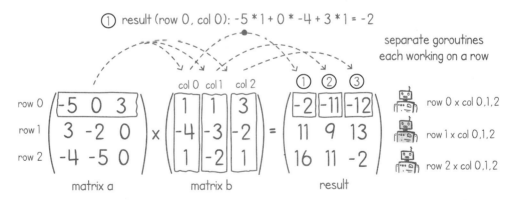

Figure 6.11 Parallel matrix multiplication using a separate goroutine on each result row

The following listing shows a function that does this multiplication in a single goroutine. The function uses three nested loops iterating first over the rows, then over the columns, and multiplying and adding each together in the final loop.

Listing 6.14   A simple matrix multiplication function

```
package main

const matrixSize = 3

func matrixMultiply(matrixA, matrixB, result *[matrixSize][matrixSize]int) {
    for row := 0; row < matrixSize; row++ {
        for col := 0; col < matrixSize; col++ {
            sum := 0
            for i := 0; i < matrixSize; i++ {
                sum += matrixA[row][i] * matrixB[i][col]
            }
            result[row][col] = sum
        }
    }
}
```

Iterates over every row

Iterates over every column

Sums up each value of the row from A multiplied by each value of the column from B

Updates the result matrix with the sum

One way to convert our algorithm to be executed in parallel by multiple processors is to break down the matrix multiplication into different parts and let each part be computed by a goroutine. Figure 6.11 shows how we can compute the result of each row separately, using a goroutine for each row. For an $n \times n$ result matrix, we can create n goroutines and assign one goroutine to each row. Each goroutine would then be responsible for computing the result for its row.

To make our matrix multiplication application more realistic, we can make it go through three steps and then have these three steps repeat, simulating a long-running computation:

1 Load the inputs of matrices A and B.
2 Compute the result of A × B concurrently, using one goroutine per row.
3 Output the result on the console.

For step 1, loading the input matrices, we can just generate them using random integers. In a real-world application, we would read these inputs from a source, such as a network connection or a file. The following listing shows a function we can use to populate a matrix with random integers.

Listing 6.15   Generate a matrix using random integers

```
package main

import (
    "math/rand"
)

const matrixSize = 3

func generateRandMatrix(matrix *[matrixSize][matrixSize]int) {
    for row := 0; row < matrixSize; row++ {
        for col := 0; col < matrixSize; col++ {
```

```
matrix[row][col] = rand.Intn(10) - 5
      }
   }
}
```

For every row and column, assigns a random number between –5 and 4

To compute the concurrent multiplication (step 2), we need a function that evaluates the multiplication for a single row in our result matrix. The idea is that we run this function from multiple goroutines, one per row. Once the goroutines compute all the rows of our result matrix, we can output the resulting matrix on the console (step 3).

If we are going to perform steps 1 through 3 multiple times, we also need a mechanism to coordinate the steps. For example, we cannot perform the multiplication before loading up the input matrices. Nor should we output the result before our goroutines are finished computing all the rows.

This is where the barrier utility that we developed in the previous section comes in handy. We can ensure proper synchronization between the various steps by using our barrier so that we don't start one step before finishing the other. Figure 6.12 shows how we can do this. The figure shows that for a 3 × 3 matrix, we can use a barrier with a size of 4 (total number of rows + 1). This is the total number of goroutines in our Go program when we include the main() goroutine.

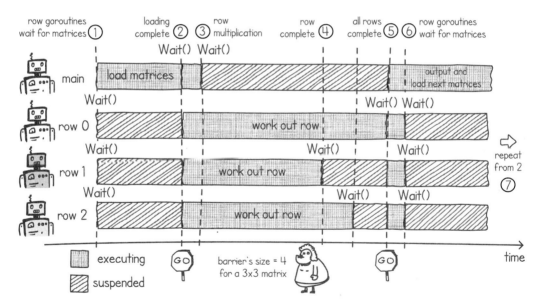

Figure 6.12   Synchronization using a barrier during matrix multiplication

Let's walk through the various steps of the concurrent matrix multiplication program, shown in figure 6.12:

1 Initially, the `main()` goroutine loads up the input matrices while the row goroutines wait on a barrier. In our application, we will be randomly generating the matrices using the function developed in listing 6.15.

2 Once the loading is complete, the `main()` goroutine calls the final `Wait()` operation, releasing all the goroutines.

3 It is now the `main()` goroutine's turn to wait on the barrier for the goroutines to complete their row multiplication.

4 Once a goroutine calculates its result on its row, it will call another `Wait()` on the barrier.

5 Once all goroutines finish and call `Wait()` on the barrier, all goroutines will unblock, and the `main()` goroutine will output the results and load the next input matrices.

6 Each row goroutine will wait by calling `Wait()` on the barrier until the loading from the `main()` goroutine is complete.

7 Repeat from step 2 as long as we have more matrices to multiply.

Listing 6.16 shows how we can implement the single row multiplication. The function accepts two input matrices, a space where the resulting matrix can be put, a barrier, and a row number representing which row it is supposed to work out. Instead of iterating over every row, it will only work on the row number passed in as a parameter. It has the same implementation as listing 6.14, but it's missing the outer row loop. In terms of parallelism, depending on how many free processors we have, Go's runtime should be able to balance the row computations on the available CPU resources. In an ideal scenario, we would have one CPU available for each goroutine executing each row calculation.

Listing 6.16   A matrix single-row multiplication function for separate goroutines

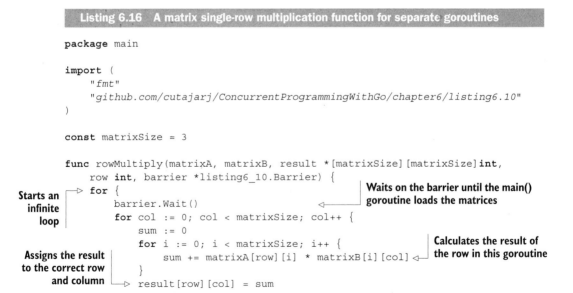

```go
package main

import (
    "fmt"
    "github.com/cutajarj/ConcurrentProgrammingWithGo/chapter6/listing6.10"
)

const matrixSize = 3

func rowMultiply(matrixA, matrixB, result *[matrixSize][matrixSize]int,
    row int, barrier *listing6_10.Barrier) {
    for {
        barrier.Wait()
        for col := 0; col < matrixSize; col++ {
            sum := 0
            for i := 0; i < matrixSize; i++ {
                sum += matrixA[row][i] * matrixB[i][col]
            }
            result[row][col] = sum
```

Starts an infinite loop

Waits on the barrier until the main() goroutine loads the matrices

Calculates the result of the row in this goroutine

Assigns the result to the correct row and column

```
        }
        barrier.Wait()    ◁────┐ Waits on the barrier until every
    }                          │ other row has been computed
}
```

The `rowMultiply()` function from listing 6.16 uses the barrier twice. The first time is to wait until the `main()` goroutine loads up the two input matrices. The second time, at the end of the loop, it waits for all the other goroutines to finish working out their own respective rows. In this way, it can stay synchronized with the main and other goroutines.

Now we can write our `main()` function, which will perform the loading of the matrices, wait on the barrier, and output the results. The `main()` function also initializes the barrier of size `matrixSize + 1` and starts up the goroutines at the beginning, as the following listing shows.

Listing 6.17 `main()` **function for matrix multiplication**

```
func main() {
    var matrixA, matrixB, result [matrixSize][matrixSize]int
    barrier := listing6_10.NewBarrier(matrixSize + 1)    ◁──────  Creates a new barrier with size of row goroutines + main() goroutine
    for row := 0; row < matrixSize; row++ {
        go rowMultiply(&matrixA, &matrixB, &result, row, barrier)    ◁────
    }
                                                       Creates a goroutine per row,
                                                       assigning the correct row numbers
    for i := 0; i < 4; i++ {
        generateRandMatrix(&matrixA)
        generateRandMatrix(&matrixB)    ┐ Loads up both matrices by
                                        ┘ randomly generating them
        barrier.Wait()    ◁────
                              Releases the barrier so the goroutines
          ┌▷ barrier.Wait()   can start their computations
 Waits    │
 until the│
goroutines│  for i := 0; i < matrixSize; i++ {
finish    │      fmt.Println(matrixA[i], matrixB[i], result[i])    ◁────
their     │  }                                                         Ouputs results
computations fmt.Println()                                             to console
          }
}
```

Running listings 6.15, 6.16, and 6.17 together, we get the following results on the console:

```
$ go run matrixmultiplysimple.go
[-4 2 2] [-5 -1 -4] [12 4 22]
[4 -4 3] [-3 4 3] [-11 -32 -28]
[0 -5 1] [-1 -4 0] [14 -24 -15]
. . .
[-5 0 3] [1 1 3] [-2 -11 -12]
[3 -2 0] [-4 -3 -2] [11 9 13]
[-4 -5 0] [1 -2 1] [16 11 -2]
```

Barriers or no barriers?

Barriers are useful concurrency tools that let us synchronize executions at certain points in our code, as we saw in the matrix multiplication application. This pattern of loading work, waiting for it to complete, and collecting the results is a typical application for barriers. However, it is mostly useful when creating new executions is a fairly expensive operation, such as when we use kernel-level threads. Using this pattern, you save the time taken to create new threads on every load cycle.

In Go, creating goroutines is cheap and fast, so using a barrier for this pattern does not bring huge performance improvements. It is usually easier to just load work, create your worker goroutines, wait for their completion using a waitgroup, and then collect the results. Nonetheless, barriers might still have performance benefits in scenarios when you need to synchronize large numbers of goroutines.

6.3   *Exercises*

1   In listings 6.5 and 6.6, we developed a recursive concurrent file search. When a goroutine finds a file match, it outputs it on the console. Can you change the implementation of this file search so that it prints all the file matches, sorted into alphabetical order, after the search completes? Hint: try collecting the results in a shared data structure instead of printing them on the console from the goroutine.

2   In previous chapters, we saw the `TryLock()` operation on mutexes. This is a non-blocking call that returns immediately without waiting. If the lock is not available, the function returns `false`; otherwise, it locks the mutex and returns `true`. Can you write a similar non-blocking function called `TryWait()` on our implementation of a waitgroup from listing 6.8? This function will return immediately with `false` if the waitgroup is not done; otherwise, it returns `true`.

3   In listings 6.14 and 6.15 and again in 6.16 and 6.17, we implemented single- and multi-threaded matrix multiplication programs. Can you measure the time it takes to compute the multiplication for large matrices of size 1000×1000 or larger? For the time measurement to be accurate, you should remove the `Println()` calls because large matrices will take a long time to be printed on the console. You might notice a difference only if your system has multiple cores.

4   In listings 6.16 and 6.17, the concurrent matrix multiplication, we used a barrier to reuse the goroutines when they needed to start working on a new row. Since in Go it's cheap and quick to create new threads, can you change this implementation so that it doesn't use barriers? Instead, you can create a set of goroutines (one per row) every time you generate a new matrix. Hint: you still need a way to notify the `main()` goroutine that all the rows have been calculated.

Summary

- Waitgroups allow us to wait for a set of goroutines to finish their work.
- When using a waitgroup, a goroutine calls `Done()` after it finishes a task.
- To wait for all tasks to complete using a waitgroup, we call the `Wait()` function.
- We can use a semaphore initialized to a negative permit number to implement a fixed-size waitgroup.
- Go's bundled waitgroup allows us to resize the group dynamically after we create the waitgroup by using the `Add()` function.
- We can use condition variables to implement a dynamically sized waitgroup.
- Barriers allow us to synchronize our goroutines at specific points in their executions.
- Barriers suspend the execution when a goroutine calls `Wait()` until all the goroutines participating in the barrier also call `Wait()`.
- When all the goroutines participating in the barrier call `Wait()`, all the suspended executions on the barrier are resumed.
- Barriers can be reused multiple times.
- We can also implement barriers using condition variables.

Part 2

Message passing

In the first part of the book, we talked about how to use memory sharing to enable communication between threads of execution. In this second part, we'll explore message passing, which is a different way for executions to communicate. In message passing, threads of executions pass copies of messages to each other whenever they need to communicate. Since these executions are not sharing memory, we eliminate the risks of many types of race conditions.

Go takes inspiration from a concurrency model called communicating sequential processes (CSP), which is a formal language for describing interactions of concurrent programs. In this model, processes connect to each other by communicating via synchronous message passing. In the same fashion, Go provides us with the concept of the channel, which enables goroutines to connect, synchronize, and share messages with one another.

In this part of the book, we'll explore message passing and the various tools and programming patterns we can use to manage this form of communication.

Communication
using message passing

7

This chapter covers

- Exchanging messages for thread communication
- Adopting Go's channels for message passing
- Collecting asynchronous results using channels
- Building our own channels

So far, we have talked about having our goroutines solve problems by sharing memory and using synchronization controls to prevent them from stepping over each other. Message passing is another way to enable *inter-thread communication* (ITC), which is when goroutines send messages to or wait for messages from other goroutines.

In this chapter, we will explore using Go's channels to send and receive messages among our goroutines. This chapter will serve as an introduction to programming concurrency using an abstraction that takes ideas from a formal language called communicating sequential processes (CSP). We'll go into more detail about CSP in the following chapters.

7.1 *Passing messages*

Whenever we converse or communicate with friends, family, or colleagues, we do so by passing messages to each other. In speech, we say something and usually expect a reply or a reaction from whomever we're speaking to. This expectation is also valid when we're communicating by letter, email, or phone. Message passing between goroutines is similar. In Go, we can open a channel between two or more goroutines and then program the goroutines to send and receive messages among themselves (see figure 7.1).

Figure 7.1   Goroutines passing messages to each other

Message passing and distributed systems

When we have distributed applications running on multiple machines, message passing is the main way they can communicate. Since the applications are running on separate machines and are not sharing any memory, they share information by sending messages via common protocols, such as HTTP.

The advantage of using message passing is that we greatly reduce the risk of causing race conditions with our bad programming. Since we're not modifying the contents of any shared memory, goroutines cannot step over each other in memory. Using message passing, each goroutine just works with its own isolated memory.

7.1.1 *Passing messages with channels*

A Go channel lets two or more goroutines exchange messages. Conceptually, we can think of a channel as being a direct line between our goroutines, as shown in figure 7.2. The goroutines can use the ends of the channel to send or receive messages.

To use a channel, we first create one by using the `make()` built-in function. We can then pass it onward as an argument whenever we create goroutines. To send messages, we use the `<-` operator. In listing 7.1, we are initializing a channel of type `string`. The

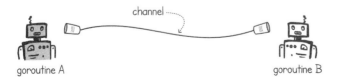

Figure 7.2   A channel is a direct line between goroutines.

specified type of the channel allows us to send messages of the same type. As shown in this example, we can only send strings over this channel. After we create this channel, we pass it to a newly created goroutine called `receiver()`. We then send three string messages over the channel.

Listing 7.1   Creating and using a channel

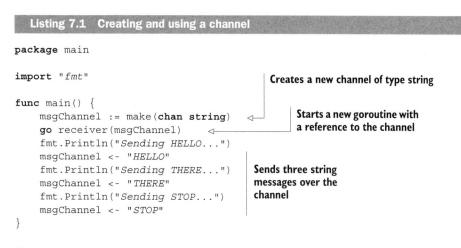

```
package main

import "fmt"

func main() {
    msgChannel := make(chan string)
    go receiver(msgChannel)
    fmt.Println("Sending HELLO...")
    msgChannel <- "HELLO"
    fmt.Println("Sending THERE...")
    msgChannel <- "THERE"
    fmt.Println("Sending STOP...")
    msgChannel <- "STOP"
}
```

Creates a new channel of type string

Starts a new goroutine with a reference to the channel

Sends three string messages over the channel

To consume a message from a channel, we use the same `<-` operator. However, we put the channel to the right of the operator instead of to the left. This is shown in the following implementation of the `receiver ()` goroutine, which reads messages from the channel until it receives the message `STOP`.

Listing 7.2   Reading messages from a channel

```
func receiver(messages chan string) {
    msg := ""
    for msg != "STOP" {
        msg = <-messages
        fmt.Println("Received:", msg)
    }
}
```

Continues while the message received is not STOP

Reads the next message from the channel

Outputs the message on the console

Putting listings 7.1 and 7.2 together results in the `main()` goroutine pushing messages on the common channel and the `receiver` goroutine consuming them. Once the `main()` goroutine sends the stop message, the receiver will exit the `for` loop and terminate. Here is the output:

```
$ go run messagepassing.go
Sending HELLO...
Sending THERE...
Received: HELLO
Received: THERE
Sending STOP...
```

Notice how on the output, we're missing the final STOP message from the receiver. This is because the `main()` goroutine sends the stop message and then terminates. Once the `main` goroutine terminates, the entire process exits, and we never get to see the stop message printed on the console.

What would happen if a goroutine were to push a message on a channel without there being another goroutine to read that message? Go's channels are synchronous by default, meaning that the sender goroutine will block until there is a receiver goroutine ready to consume the message. Figure 7.3 shows a goroutine sender blocked without a receiver.

blocked sender   no receiver

Figure 7.3 Sending a message on a channel with no receiver

We can try this out by changing the receiver from listing 7.2 to the following. In this receiver, we wait for 5 seconds before terminating instead of consuming any messages from the channel.

Listing 7.3 Receiver not consuming any messages

```
func receiver(messages chan string) {
    time.Sleep(5 * time.Second)          ◁——  Waits for 5 seconds instead of reading
    fmt.Println("Receiver slept for 5 seconds")   messages from the channel
}
```

When we run listing 7.3 with the `main()` function from listing 7.1, the `main()` goroutine blocks for 5 seconds. This is because there is nothing to consume the message that the `main()` goroutine is trying to place on the channel:

```
$ go run noreceiver.go
Sending HELLO...
Receiver slept for 5 seconds
fatal error: all goroutines are asleep - deadlock!

goroutine 1 [chan send]:
main.main()
        /chapter7/listing7.3/noreceiver.go:12 +0xb9
exit status 2
```

Since our `receiver()` goroutine terminates after 5 seconds, no other goroutine is available to consume messages from the channel. Go's runtime realizes this and raises the fatal error. Without this error, our program would stay blocked until we manually terminate it. The error message mentions that we have encountered a deadlock—we'll explore how to deal with deadlocks in chapter 11.

The same situation occurs if we have a receiver waiting for a message and no sender is available. The receiver's goroutine will be suspended until a message is available (see figure 7.4).

no sender   blocked receiver

Figure 7.4   A receiver is blocked until a message is available.

In the following listing, we have a `sender()` goroutine that, rather than write messages to the channel, sleeps for 5 seconds. The `main()` goroutine tries to consume a message from the same channel, but it will be blocked since nothing is sending messages.

> **Listing 7.4   Receiver blocked because sender is not sending any messages**

```
package main

import (
    "fmt"
    "time"
)

func main() {
    msgChannel := make(chan string)          Creates a new channel
    go sender(msgChannel)                     of type string
    fmt.Println("Reading message from channel...")
    msg := <-msgChannel
    fmt.Println("Received:", msg)             Reads a message from channel
}

func sender(messages chan string) {          Sleeps for 5 seconds instead
    time.Sleep(5 * time.Second)               of sending any message
    fmt.Println("Sender slept for 5 seconds")
}
```

Running listing 7.4 produces results similar to listing 7.3. We get a receiver waiting for messages, and when the `sender ()` goroutine terminates, Go's runtime outputs an error. Here's the console output:

```
$ go run nosender.go
Reading message from channel...
Sender slept for 5 seconds
fatal error: all goroutines are asleep - deadlock!

goroutine 1 [chan receive]:
main.main()
        /chapter7/listing7.4/nosender.go:12 +0xbd
exit status 2
```

The key idea here is that by default, Go's channels are *synchronous*. A sender will block if there isn't a goroutine consuming its message, and a receiver will similarly block if there isn't a goroutine sending a message.

7.1.2 Buffering messages with channels

Although channels are synchronous, we can configure them so that they store a number of messages before they block (see figure 7.5). When we use a buffered channel, the sender goroutine will not block as long as there is space available in the buffer.

Figure 7.5   **Using a buffered channel between goroutines**

When we create a channel, we can specify its buffer capacity. Then, whenever a sender goroutine writes a message without any receiver consuming the message, the channel will store the message (shown in figure 7.6). This means that as long as there is space in the buffer, our sender does not block, and we don't have to wait for a receiver to read the message.

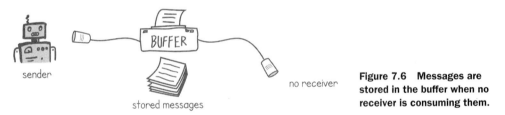

Figure 7.6   **Messages are stored in the buffer when no receiver is consuming them.**

The channel will keep on storing messages as long as capacity remains in the buffer. Once the buffer is filled up, the sender will block again, as shown in figure 7.7. This message buffer buildup can also happen if the receiving end is slow and does not consume the messages fast enough to keep up with the sender.

Once a receiver goroutine is available to consume the messages, the messages are fed to the receiver in the same order they were sent. This happens even if the sender

Figure 7.7   **A full buffer blocks the sender.**

goroutine is no longer sending any new messages (shown in figure 7.8). As long as there are messages in the buffer, a receiver goroutine will not block.

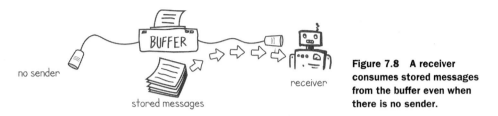

Figure 7.8 A receiver consumes stored messages from the buffer even when there is no sender.

Once the receiver goroutine consumes all the messages and the buffer is empty, the receiver goroutine will again block. When the buffer is empty, a receiver will block if we don't have a sender or if the sender is producing messages at a slower rate than the receiver can read them. This is shown in figure 7.9.

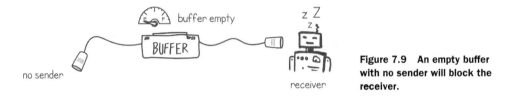

Figure 7.9 An empty buffer with no sender will block the receiver.

Let's now try this in practice. Listing 7.5 shows a slow message receiver that consumes messages from the integer channel at a rate of one per second. We use `time.Sleep()` to slow down the goroutine. Once the `receiver()` goroutine receives a -1 value, it stops receiving messages and calls `Done()` on a waitgroup.

Listing 7.5 Slow receiver reading a message every second

```go
package main

import (
    "fmt"
    "sync"
    "time"
)

func receiver(messages chan int, wGroup *sync.WaitGroup) {
    msg := 0
    for msg != -1 {
        time.Sleep(1 * time.Second)
        msg = <-messages
        fmt.Println("Received:", msg)
    }
    wGroup.Done()
}
```

Waits for 1 second

Keeps reading messages from the channel until it receives a -1

Reads the next message from the channel

Calls Done() on the waitgroup after reading all the messages

We can now write a `main()` function that creates a buffered channel and feeds messages into the channel at a faster rate than our reader can consume them. In listing 7.6, we create a buffered channel with a capacity of three messages. We then use this channel to send six messages quickly, each containing the next number in the sequence from 1 to 6. After this, we send a final message containing the value of -1. In the end, we wait for the `receiver()` goroutine to be done by waiting on the waitgroup.

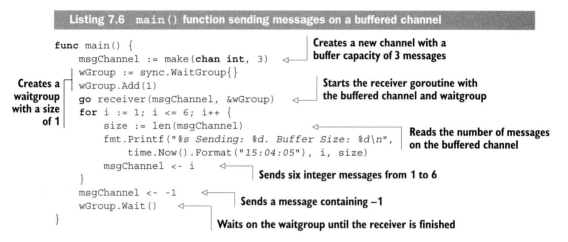

Listing 7.6   `main()` function sending messages on a buffered channel

```
func main() {
    msgChannel := make(chan int, 3)          ◁——  Creates a new channel with a
                                                   buffer capacity of 3 messages
    wGroup := sync.WaitGroup{}
    wGroup.Add(1)
    go receiver(msgChannel, &wGroup)         ◁——  Starts the receiver goroutine with
                                                   the buffered channel and waitgroup
    for i := 1; i <= 6; i++ {
        size := len(msgChannel)              ◁————— Reads the number of messages
        fmt.Printf("%s Sending: %d. Buffer Size: %d\n",   on the buffered channel
            time.Now().Format("15:04:05"), i, size)
        msgChannel <- i        ◁——  Sends six integer messages from 1 to 6
    }
    msgChannel <- -1           ◁——  Sends a message containing –1
    wGroup.Wait()             ◁——  Waits on the waitgroup until the receiver is finished
}
```

Creates a waitgroup with a size of 1

NOTE We can check how many messages are on the buffer by using the `len(buffer)` function.

Combining listings 7.5 and 7.6, we get a fast sender that is trying to send six messages. Since we have a much slower receiver, the `main()` goroutine will fill the channel buffer with three messages and then block. The receiver will consume a message every second, freeing a space in the buffer that the sender will quickly fill. Here is the output showing the timestamps of each send and receive operation:

```
11:09:15 Sending: 1. Buffer Size: 0
11:09:15 Sending: 2. Buffer Size: 1
11:09:15 Sending: 3. Buffer Size: 2
11:09:15 Sending: 4. Buffer Size: 3
11:09:16 Received: 1
11:09:16 Sending: 5. Buffer Size: 3
11:09:17 Received: 2
11:09:17 Sending: 6. Buffer Size: 3
11:09:18 Received: 3
11:09:19 Received: 4
11:09:20 Received: 5
11:09:21 Received: 6
11:09:22 Received: -1
```

7.1.3 *Assigning a direction to channels*

Go's channels are *bidirectional* by default. This means that a goroutine can act as both a receiver and a sender of messages. However, we can assign a direction to a channel so that the goroutine using the channel can only send or receive messages.

For example, when we declare a function's parameters, we can specify the direction of the channel. Listing 7.7 declares receiver and sender functions that allow messages to go in only one direction. In the receiver, when we declare the channel as being `messages <-chan int`, we are saying that the channel is a receive-only channel. The declaration of `messages chan<- int` in the sender function is saying the opposite—that the channel can only be used to send messages.

Listing 7.7 Declaring channels with a direction

```go
package main

import (
    "fmt"
    "time"
)

func receiver(messages <-chan int) {        // Declares a receive-only channel
    for {
        msg := <-messages                    // Receives messages from the channel
        fmt.Println(time.Now().Format("15:04:05"), "Received:", msg)
    }
}

func sender(messages chan<- int) {          // Declares a send-only channel
    for i := 1; ; i++ {
        fmt.Println(time.Now().Format("15:04:05"), "Sending:", i)
        messages <- i
        time.Sleep(1 * time.Second)         // Sends a message on the
    }                                        // channel every second
}

func main() {
    msgChannel := make(chan int)
    go receiver(msgChannel)
    go sender(msgChannel)
    time.Sleep(5 * time.Second)
}
```

In listing 7.7, if we try to use the receiver's channel to send messages, we would get a compilation error. For example, if in the `receiver()` function we do this

```go
messages <- 99
```

we would get an error message when we compile:

```
$ go build directional.go
# command-line-arguments
.\directional.go:11:9: invalid operation: cannot send to receive-only channel
  messages (variable of type <-chan int)
```

7.1.4   *Closing channels*

We've been using special value messages to signal that no more data is available on the channel. For example, in listing 7.6, the receiver is waiting for a -1 value to appear on the channel. This signals to the receiver that it can stop consuming messages. This message contains what is known as a *sentinel value.*

> **DEFINITION**   In software development, a *sentinel value* is a predefined value that signals to an execution, a process, or an algorithm that it should terminate. In the context of multithreading and a distributed system, this is sometimes referred to as a *poison pill* message.

Instead of using this sentinel value message, Go allows us to close a channel. We can do this in code by calling the close(channel) function. Once we close a channel, we shouldn't send any more messages to it because doing so raises errors. If we try to receive messages from a closed channel, we will get messages containing the default value for the channel's data type. For example, if our channel is of integer type, reading from a closed channel will result in the read operation returning a 0 value. This is illustrated in figure 7.10.

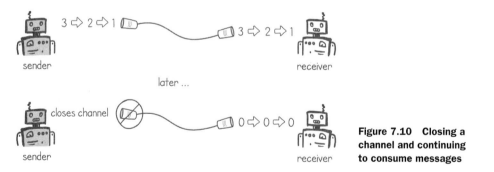

Figure 7.10   **Closing a channel and continuing to consume messages**

We can show this by implementing a receiver that continually consumes messages even after we close the channel. The following listing shows a receiver() function with a loop that reads messages from the channel and outputs them on the console every second.

Listing 7.8   Infinite channel receiver

```
package main

import (
```

```
    "fmt"
    "time"
)
```

**Declares a receive-
only channel**

```
func receiver(messages <-chan int) {
    for {
        msg := <-messages
        fmt.Println(time.Now().Format("15:04:05"), "Received:", msg)
        time.Sleep(1 * time.Second)
    }
}
```

**Reads one
message
from the
channel**

Waits for 1 second

Next, we can implement a `main()` function that sends a few messages on the channel, after which it closes the channel. In the following listing, we send three messages, one per second, and then close the channel. We have also added a sleep of 3 seconds to show what the `receiver()` goroutine reads from the closed channel.

Listing 7.9 `main()` function sending messages and closing channel

```
func main() {
    msgChannel := make(chan int)
    go receiver(msgChannel)
    for i := 1; i <= 3 ; i++ {
        fmt.Println(time.Now().Format("15:04:05"), "Sending:", i)
        msgChannel <- i
        time.Sleep(1 * time.Second)
    }
    close(msgChannel)
    time.Sleep(3 * time.Second)
}
```

Running listings 7.8 and 7.9 together, we get the receiver first outputting the messages from 1 to 3 and then reading 0s for 3 seconds:

```
$ go run closing.go
17:19:50 Sending: 1
17:19:50 Received: 1
17:19:51 Sending: 2
17:19:51 Received: 2
17:19:52 Sending: 3
17:19:52 Received: 3
17:19:53 Received: 0
17:19:54 Received: 0
17:19:55 Received: 0
```

Can we use this default value to let the receiver know that the channel has been closed? Using the default value is not ideal because the default value might be a valid value for our use case. Imagine, for example, a weather forecasting application sending temperatures over a channel. In this scenario, the receiver would think the channel has been closed whenever the temperature drops to 0.

Luckily, Go gives us a couple of ways to handle closed channels. Whenever we consume from a channel, an additional flag is returned, telling us the status of the channel. This flag is set to `false` only when the channel has been closed. The following listing shows how we can modify the receiver function in listing 7.8 to read this flag. By using this flag, we can decide to stop reading from the channel.

Listing 7.10   Receiver stopping when channel indicates that it's closed

```
func receiver(messages <-chan int) {
    for {
        msg, more := <-messages          ◁——   Reads message and an open channel flag,
        fmt.Println(time.Now().Format("15:04:05"), "Received:", msg, more)
        time.Sleep(1 * time.Second)            set to false when the channel is closed
        if !more {
            return        When there are no more messages, it
        }                 stops consuming from the channel.
    }
}
```

As expected, when we run listing 7.10 with the `main()` function from listing 7.9, we consume messages until the channel is closed. We can also see that when the channel is closed, the open channel flag is set to `false`:

```
$ go run closingFlag.go
08:07:41 Sending: 1
08:07:41 Received: 1 true
08:07:42 Sending: 2
08:07:42 Received: 2 true
08:07:43 Sending: 3
08:07:43 Received: 3 true
08:07:44 Received: 0 false
```

As we shall see in the next chapter, this syntax is useful in certain situations, such as when it's combined with the `select` statement. However, we can use a cleaner syntax to stop a receiver from reading on a closed channel. If we want to read all the messages until we close the channel, we can use the following `for` loop syntax:

```
for msg := range messages
```

Here, the `messages` variable is our channel. In this way, we can keep on iterating until the sender eventually closes the channel. The following listing shows how we can change the `receiver()` function from listing 7.9 to use this new syntax.

Listing 7.11   Receiver iterating on messages from the channel

```
                                          Consumes from the channel until it's closed,
func receiver(messages <-chan int) {      assigning messages to the msg variable
    for msg := range messages {    ◁——
        fmt.Println(time.Now().Format("15:04:05"), "Received:", msg)
        time.Sleep(1 * time.Second)
```

```
    }
    fmt.Println("Receiver finished.")
}
```

Running listing 7.11 with the same `main()` function from listing 7.9, we end up consuming all the messages sent from the `main()` goroutine until the `main()` goroutine closes the channel. The listing outputs the following:

```
$ go run forchannel.go
09:52:11 Sending: 1
09:52:11 Received: 1
09:52:12 Sending: 2
09:52:12 Received: 2
09:52:13 Sending: 3
09:52:13 Received: 3
Receiver finished.
```

7.1.5 *Receiving function results with channels*

We can execute functions concurrently in the background and then collect their results via channels once they finish. Typically, in normal sequential programming, we call a function and expect it to return a result. In concurrent programming, we can call functions in separate goroutines and later pick up their return values from an output channel.

Let's explore this with a simple example. The following listing shows a function that finds the factors of an input number. For example, if we call `findFactors(6)`, it will return the values `[1 2 3 6]`.

Listing 7.12 **Function to find all factors of a number**

```
package main

import (
    "fmt"
)
                                          Finds all the factors
func findFactors(number int) []int {  ◁──┘  for the input number
    result := make([]int, 0)
    for i := 1; i <= number; i++ {
        if number%i == 0 {
            result = append(result, i)
        }
    }
    return result
}
```

If we call the `findFactors()` function twice for two different numbers, in sequential programming, we would have two calls, one after the other. For example:

```
fmt.Println(findFactors(3419110721))
fmt.Println(findFactors(4033836233))
```

But what if we want to call the function with the first number, and while it's computing those factors, we call the function a second time with the second number? If we have multiple cores available, executing the first findFactors() call in parallel with the second will speed up our program. Finding factors of large numbers can be a lengthy operation, so it would be good to farm out the work on multiple processing cores.

We can, of course, start a goroutine for the first call and then make the second call:

```
go findFactors(3419110721)
fmt.Println(findFactors(4033836233))
```

However, how do we wait and collect the results from the first call easily? We could use something like a shared variable and a waitgroup, but there is an easier way: using channels. In the next listing, we use an anonymous function, running as a goroutine and making the first findFactors() call.

Listing 7.13   Collecting results using channels

```
func main() {
    resultCh := make(chan []int)         ⟵── Creates a new channel of type integer slice
    go func() {
        resultCh <- findFactors(3419110721)    ⟵┐ Calls the function in an anonymous
    }()                                         │ goroutine and places the results
    fmt.Println(findFactors(4033836233))        │ onto the channel
    fmt.Println(<- resultCh)          ⟵──┐
}                                        │ Collects the results from the channel
```

We use this anonymous goroutine to collect the results of the findFactors() function and write them on a channel. Later, after we finish the second call in our main() goroutine, we can read those results from the channel. If the first findFactors() call is not yet finished, reading from the channel will block the main() goroutine until we have the results. Here is the output showing all the factors:

```
$ go run collectresults.go
[1 7 131 917 4398949 30792643 576262319 4033836233]
[1 13 113 1469 2327509 30257617 263008517 3419110721]
```

7.2   *Implementing channels*

What does the inner logic of a channel look like? In its basic form, a buffered channel is similar to a fixed-size queue data structure. The difference is that it can safely be used from multiple concurrent goroutines. In addition, the channel needs to block the receiver goroutine if the buffer is empty or to block the sender if the buffer is full. In this section, we'll use concurrency primitives, built in previous chapters, to build the channel's send and receive functions so that we can better understand how it works internally.

7.2.1   *Creating a channel with semaphores*

We need a number of elements to build the functionality of our channel:

- A shared queue data structure that acts like a buffer to store the messages between sender and receiver
- Concurrent access protection for the shared data structure so that multiple senders and receivers do not interfere with each other
- Access control that blocks the execution of a receiver when the buffer is empty
- Access control that blocks the execution of a sender when the buffer is full

We have several options for implementing our shared data structure where we'll store our messages. We could, for example, build a queue structure on an array and use a Go slice or a linked list. Whatever tool we choose, it needs to give us the queue semantics—that is, first in, first out.

To protect our shared data structure from concurrent access, we can use a simple mutex. When we add or remove a message from the queue, we need to ensure that the concurrent modifications to the queue do not interfere.

To control access so that executions are blocked when the queue is full or empty, we can use semaphores. In this case, semaphores are a good base primitive since they allow concurrent access to a specific number of concurrent executions. From the receiver's side, we can think of using a semaphore as having as many free permits as there are messages in the shared queue. Once the queue is empty, the semaphore will block the next request to consume a message since the number of free permits on the semaphore will be 0. We can use the same trick on the sender's side—we can use another semaphore that goes down to 0 when the queue gets full. Once this happens, the semaphore will block the next send request.

These four elements make up our channel of buffer size 10 in figure 7.11. We use two semaphores, the capacity and buffer size semaphores, to block goroutines when the

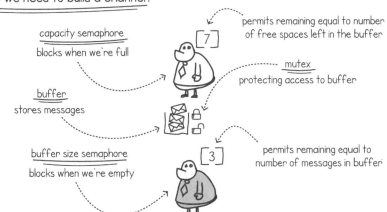

what do we need to build a channel?

capacity semaphore
blocks when we're full

permits remaining equal to number of free spaces left in the buffer

[7]

mutex
protecting access to buffer

buffer
stores messages

buffer size semaphore
blocks when we're empty

[3]

permits remaining equal to number of messages in buffer

Figure 7.11   The structures and tools needed to build a channel

capacity has been reached or when the buffer is empty, respectively. In the figure, we have three messages in the buffer, so the buffer size semaphore shows 3. This means we have seven spaces left until the buffer is full, and the capacity semaphore is set to this value.

We can translate this to code by creating a `channel` struct type with these four elements, as shown in listing 7.14. For our buffer, we'll use the linked list implementation from the `container` package. A linked list is an ideal structure for implementing a queue because we're always adding and removing messages from the head or tail of our linked list. In the `channel` struct type, we are also using Go's generics, which make our channel implementation easier to use with various data types.

Listing 7.14 Type struct for the custom channel implementation

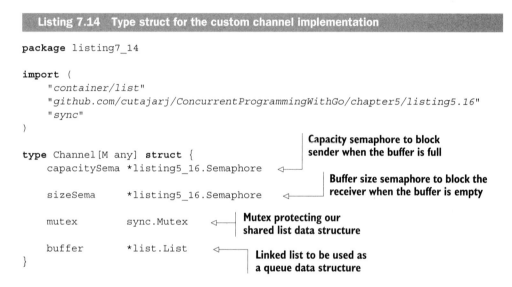

```
package listing7_14

import (
    "container/list"
    "github.com/cutajarj/ConcurrentProgrammingWithGo/chapter5/listing5.16"
    "sync"
)

type Channel[M any] struct {
    capacitySema  *listing5_16.Semaphore    ◁──  Capacity semaphore to block
                                                  sender when the buffer is full

    sizeSema      *listing5_16.Semaphore    ◁──  Buffer size semaphore to block the
                                                  receiver when the buffer is empty

    mutex         sync.Mutex    ◁──  Mutex protecting our
                                     shared list data structure

    buffer        *list.List    ◁──  Linked list to be used as
}                                    a queue data structure
```

Next, we need a function to initialize the elements in the `struct` type with default empty values. When we create a new channel, we need the buffer to be empty, the buffer size semaphore to have `0` permits, and the capacity semaphore to have a permit count equal to the input capacity. This will ensure we allow senders to add messages but block receivers because the buffer is currently empty. The `NewChannel()` function in the following listing does this initialization.

Listing 7.15 Function creating a new channel

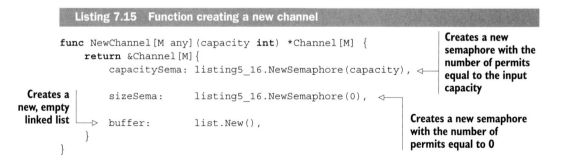

```
func NewChannel[M any](capacity int) *Channel[M] {          Creates a new
    return &Channel[M]{                                     semaphore with the
        capacitySema: listing5_16.NewSemaphore(capacity),   number of permits
                                                       ◁──  equal to the input
                                                            capacity
        sizeSema:     listing5_16.NewSemaphore(0),     ◁──
        buffer:       list.New(),                           Creates a new semaphore
    }                                                        with the number of
}                                                            permits equal to 0
}
```
Creates a new, empty linked list

7.2.2 *Implementing the Send() function in our channel*

Let's now explore how the semaphores, buffer, and mutex work together to give us the send functionality of the channel. The `Send(message)` function needs to fulfill these three requirements:

- Block the goroutine if the buffer is full.
- Otherwise, safely add the `message` to the buffer.
- If any receiver goroutines are blocked, waiting for messages, resume one of them.

We can meet all these requirements by performing the three steps outlined in figure 7.12:

1 The sender acquires a permit from the capacity semaphore, reducing the permit count by 1. This will meet the first requirement; if the buffer is full, the goroutine will block since no more permits will be available.

2 The sender pushes the message onto the buffer data structure. In our implementation, this data structure is the linked list queue. To protect the queue from concurrent updates, we can use a mutex to synchronize access.

3 The sender goroutine releases a permit on the buffer size semaphore by calling the `Release()` function on the semaphore. This meets the final requirement; if there is a blocked goroutine waiting for messages, it will be resumed.

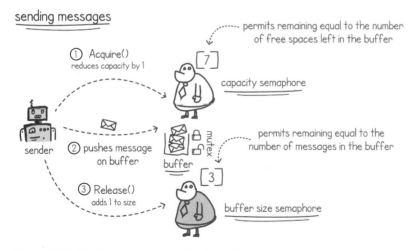

Figure 7.12 Sending messages on the channel

The next listing shows the implementation of the sender. The `Send(message)` function contains the three steps: reduce the permits on the capacity semaphore, push the message onto the queue, and increase the permits on the buffer size semaphore.

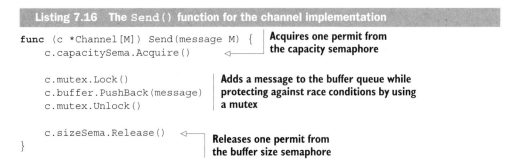

Listing 7.16   The `Send()` function for the channel implementation

```
func (c *Channel[M]) Send(message M) {
    c.capacitySema.Acquire()

    c.mutex.Lock()
    c.buffer.PushBack(message)
    c.mutex.Unlock()

    c.sizeSema.Release()
}
```

Acquires one permit from the capacity semaphore

Adds a message to the buffer queue while protecting against race conditions by using a mutex

Releases one permit from the buffer size semaphore

If the buffer is full, our capacity semaphore will not have any permits left, so the sender goroutine will be blocked on the first step (see figure 7.13). The sender will also block if we use a channel with an initial capacity of 0 and a receiver is not present, giving us the same synchronous functionality of the default channel in Go.

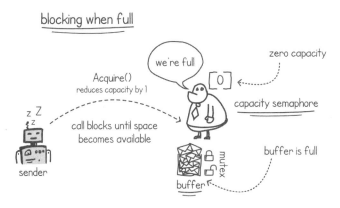

Figure 7.13   Blocking the sender when the buffer is full and we have 0 capacity

7.2.3   *Implementing the Receive() function in our channel*

Let's now look at the receiving side of our channel implementation. The `Receive()` function needs to satisfy the following requirements:

- Unblock a sender waiting for capacity space.
- If the buffer is empty, block the receiver.
- Otherwise, safely consume the next message from the buffer.

The steps needed to meet all these requirements are shown in figure 7.14:

1 The receiver releases a permit on the capacity semaphore. This will unblock a sender that is waiting for capacity to place its message.
2 The receiver tries to acquire a permit from the buffer size semaphore. This will have the effect of blocking the receiver goroutine if the buffer is empty of messages, meeting the second requirement.

3 Once the semaphore unblocks the receiver, the goroutine reads and removes
the next message from the buffer. Here we should use the same mutex used in
the sender function so that we protect the shared buffer from concurrent executions interfering with each other.

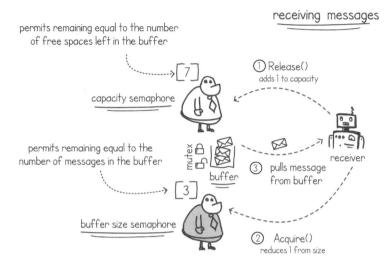

Figure 7.14   Receiving messages from the channel

NOTE The reason for releasing the permit on the capacity semaphore first is
that we want the implementation to also work when we have a zero-buffer
channel. This is when the sender and receiver wait until both are available
together.

Listing 7.17 shows the implementation of the `Receive()` function, performing the three
steps outlined in figure 7.14. It releases the capacity semaphore, acquires the buffer
semaphore, and pulls the first message from the linked list that implements the queue
buffer. The function uses the same mutex as the `Send()` function to protect the linked
list from concurrent interference.

Listing 7.17   The `Receive()` function for the channel implementation

```
func (c *Channel[M]) Receive() M {          Releases one permit from
    c.capacitySema.Release()         ◁────── the capacity semaphore

    c.sizeSema.Acquire()      ◁────── Acquires one permit from the buffer size semaphore

    c.mutex.Lock()                                  Removes one message from the
    v := c.buffer.Remove(c.buffer.Front()).(M)      buffer while protecting against
    c.mutex.Unlock()                                race conditions using the mutex

    return v    ◁────── Returns the message's value
}
```

If our buffer is empty, the buffer size semaphore will have 0 permits available. In this scenario, when a receiver goroutine tries to acquire the permit, the buffer size semaphore will block until a sender pushes a message and calls `Release()` on the same semaphore. Figure 7.15 shows the receiver goroutine blocking on a buffer size semaphore with 0 permits.

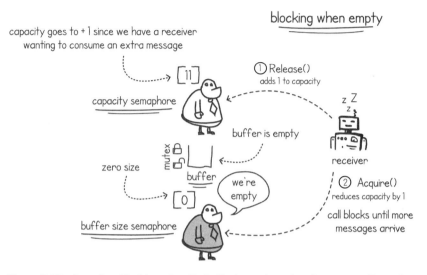

Figure 7.15   A receiver blocking when the buffer is empty and we have 0 permits on the buffer size semaphore

This blocking logic using semaphores will also work when the channel capacity is set to 0, as shown in figure 7.16. This is the default behavior of Go's channels. In such a case, the receiver would increase the permits on the capacity semaphore and block on acquiring the buffer size semaphore. Once a sender comes along, it will acquire the permit from the capacity semaphore, push a message onto the buffer, and release the buffer size semaphore. This will have the effect of unblocking the receiver goroutine. The receiver will then pull the message from the buffer.

If a sender arrives before a receiver in a zero-capacity channel, the sender will be blocked when it tries to acquire the capacity semaphore until a receiver comes along and releases a permit on the same semaphore.

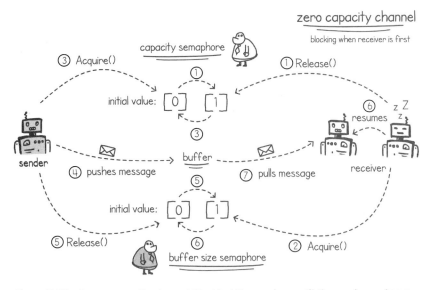

Figure 7.16 **A zero-capacity channel blocking the receiver until the sender pushes a message**

How are Go channels implemented?

The actual Go implementation of channels integrates with the runtime scheduler to improve performance. Unlike our implementation, it doesn't use a two-semaphore system to suspend goroutines. Instead, it uses two linked lists that store references to the suspended receiver and sender goroutines.

The implementation also has a buffer to store any pending messages. When this buffer is full or the channel is synchronous, any new sender goroutine is suspended and queued in the senders' list. Conversely, when the buffer is empty, any new receiver goroutine is suspended and queued in the receivers' list.

These lists are then used when a goroutine needs to be resumed. When a message becomes available, the first goroutine in the receivers' list is picked and resumed. When a new receiver becomes available, the first goroutine in the senders' list is resumed (if there is one). Unlike our implementation, this system ensures fairness amongst the suspended goroutines; the first goroutine that gets suspended will also be the first that gets resumed.

The channel's source code can be found in Go's GitHub project under the `runtime` package located at https://github.com/golang/go/blob/master/src/runtime/chan.go.

7.3 Exercises

NOTE Visit http://github.com/cutajarj/ConcurrentProgrammingWithGo to see all the code solutions.

1   In listings 7.1 and 7.2, the receiver doesn't output the last message STOP. This is because the `main()` goroutine terminates before the `receiver()` goroutine gets the chance to print out the last message. Can you change the logic, without using extra concurrency tools and without using the sleep function, so that the last message is printed?

2   In listing 7.8, the receiver reads a 0 when the channel is closed. Can you try it with different data types? What happens if the channel is of type string? What if it is of type slice?

3   In listing 7.13, we use a child goroutine to calculate the factors of one number and the `main()` goroutine to work out the factors of the other. Modify this listing so that, using multiple goroutines, we collect the factors of 10 random numbers.

4   Modify listings 7.14 through 7.17 to implement a channel using condition variables instead of semaphores. The implementation also needs to support channels with a zero-sized buffer.

Summary

- Message passing is another way for concurrent executions to communicate.
- Message passing is similar to our everyday way of communicating by passing a message and expecting an action or a reply.
- In Go, we can use channels to pass messages between our goroutines.
- Channels in Go are synchronous. By default, a sender will block if there is no receiver, and the receiver will also block if there is no sender.
- We can configure buffers on channels to store messages if we want to allow senders to send *N* messages before blocking on a receiver.
- With buffered channels, a sender can continue writing messages to the channel even without a receiver if the buffer has enough capacity. Once the buffer fills up, the sender will block.
- With buffered channels, a receiver can continue reading messages from the channel if the buffer is not empty. Once the buffer empties, the receiver will block.
- We can assign directions to channel declarations so that we can receive from or send to a channel, but not both.
- A channel can be closed by using the `close()` function.
- The read operation on a channel returns a flag telling us whether the channel is still open.
- We can continue to consume messages from a channel by using a `for range` loop until the channel is closed.
- We can use channels to collect the result of a concurrent goroutine execution.
- We can implement the channel functionality by using a queue, two semaphores, and a mutex.

Selecting channels

This chapter covers

- Selecting from multiple channels
- Disabling select cases
- Choosing between message passing and memory sharing

In the previous chapter, we used channels to implement message passing between two goroutines. In this chapter, we will see how to use Go's `select` statement to read and write messages on multiple channels and to implement timeouts and non-blocking channels. We will also examine a technique for excluding channels that have been closed and consuming only from the remaining open channels. Finally, we'll discuss memory sharing versus message passing and when we should choose one technique over the other.

8.1 Combining multiple channels

How can we have one goroutine respond to messages coming from different goroutines over multiple channels? Go's `select` statement lets us specify multiple channel operations as separate cases and then execute a case depending on which channel is ready.

8.1.1   *Reading from multiple channels*

Let's think of a simple scenario where a goroutine is expecting messages from separate channels, but we don't know on which channel the next message will be received. The `select` statement lets us group read operations on multiple channels together, blocking the goroutine until a message arrives on any one of the channels (see figure 8.1).

Figure 8.1   **Select blocks until a channel becomes available.**

Once a message arrives on any of the channels, the goroutine is unblocked, and a code handler for that channel is run, as shown in figure 8.2. We can then decide what else to do—either continue with our execution, or go back and wait for the next message by using the `select` statement again.

Figure 8.2   **Once a channel is available, select unblocks.**

Let's now look at how this translates to code. In listing 8.1, we have a function that creates an anonymous goroutine that periodically sends a message on a channel. The period is specified by the `seconds` input variable. As we shall see later in this chapter, using a pattern where the function returns an output-only channel enables us to reuse these functions as building blocks for more complex behaviors. We can do this because Go channels are first-class objects.

Listing 8.1   Function periodically outputting messages on a channel

```go
package main

import (
    "fmt"
    "time"
)

func writeEvery(msg string, seconds time.Duration) <-chan string {
```

```
              messages := make(chan string)  ◁──────
Creates    ┌─▷ go func() {                              Creates a new channel of type string
a new,     │      for {
anonymous  │          time.Sleep(seconds)   ◁───── Sleeps for the specified period
goroutine  │          messages <- msg        ◁──────
           │      }                                   Sends the specified message on the channel
           └─ }()
              return messages  ◁─────── Returns the newly created message channel
           }
```

> **DEFINITION** Channels are *first-class objects*, which means that we can store them as variables, pass or return them from functions, or even send them on a channel.

We can demonstrate the `select` statement by calling the `writeEvery()` function (shown in the previous listing) twice. If we specify a different message and sleep period, we'll end up with two channels and two goroutines sending messages at different times. The following listing reads from these two channels in a `select` statement, with each channel as a separate select case.

Listing 8.2 Reading from multiple channels using `select`

```
func main() {                                            Creates a goroutine
    messagesFromA := writeEvery("Tick", 1 * time.Second)  ◁──  sending messages every
    messagesFromB := writeEvery("Tock", 3 * time.Second)      second on channel A

    for {        ◁────── Loops forever
        select {
        case msg1 := <-messagesFromA:      Outputs message from channel
            fmt.Println(msg1)              A if one is available
        case msg2 := <-messagesFromB:      Outputs message from
            fmt.Println(msg2)             channel B if one is available
        }
    }
}
```

Creates a goroutine sending messages every 3 seconds on channel B

When we run listings 8.1 and 8.2 together, we get the `main()` goroutine looping and blocking each time until a message arrives from either channel. When we get a message, the `main()` goroutine executes the code underneath the `case` statement. In this example, the code just outputs the message to the console:

```
$ go run selectmanychannels.go
Tick
Tick
Tock
Tick
Tick
Tick
Tock
Tick
Tick
. . .
```

NOTE When using `select`, if multiple cases are ready, a case is chosen at random. Your code should not rely on the order in which the cases are specified.

Origins of the select statement

The UNIX operating system contains a system call named `select()` that accepts a set of file descriptors (such as files or network sockets) and blocks until one or more of the descriptors become ready for an I/O operation. The system call is useful when you want to monitor multiple files or sockets from a single kernel-level thread.

Go's `select` statement derives its name from the Newsqueak programming language's `select` command. Newsqueak (not to be confused with the fictional language Newspeak by George Orwell) is a language that, like Go, takes its concurrency model from C.A.R. Hoare's CSP formal language. Newsqueak's `select` statement might have gotten its name from the select system call that was built to provide multiplexed I/O for the Blit graphics terminal in 1983.

It is unclear whether the naming of Go's `select` statement was influenced by the UNIX system call; however, we can say that the UNIX `select()` system call is analogous to Go's `select` statement in that it multiplexes multiple blocking operations into a single execution.

8.1.2   *Using select for non-blocking channel operations*

Another use case for `select` is when we need to use channels in a non-blocking manner. Recall that when we were discussing mutexes, we saw that Go provides a non-blocking `tryLock()` operation. This function call tries to acquire the lock, but if the lock is being used, it will return immediately with a `false` return value. Can we adopt this pattern for channel operations? For example, can we try to read a message from a channel? Then, if no messages are available, instead of blocking, can we have the current execution work on a default set of instructions (see figure 8.3)?

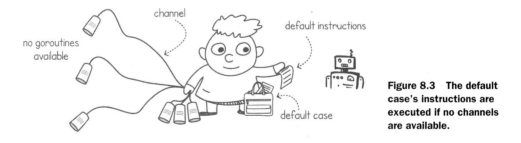

Figure 8.3   **The default case's instructions are executed if no channels are available.**

The `select` statement gives us the *default case* for exactly this scenario. The instructions under the default case will be executed if none of the other cases is available. This lets us try to access one or more channels, but if none is ready, we can do something else.

In the following listing, we have a `select` statement with a default case. In this listing, we are trying to read a message from a channel, but because the message arrives later, we get to execute the contents of the default case.

Listing 8.3   Non-blocking reads from a channel

```go
package main

import (
    "fmt"
    "time"
)

func sendMsgAfter(seconds time.Duration) <-chan string {
    messages := make(chan string)
    go func() {
        time.Sleep(seconds)
        messages <- "Hello"
    }()
    return messages
}

func main() {
    messages := sendMsgAfter(3 * time.Second)
    for {
        select {
        case msg := <-messages:
            fmt.Println("Message received:", msg)
            return
        default:
            fmt.Println("No messages waiting")
            time.Sleep(1 * time.Second)
        }
    }
}
```

Sends channel message after 3 seconds

Reads a message from the channel if there is one

When a message is available, terminates the execution

When no message is available, the default case is executed.

In the previous listing, since we have the select statement in a loop, the default case will be executed over and over again until we receive a message. When this happens, we print the message and return on the main() function, terminating the program. Here's the output:

```
$ go run nonblocking.go
No messages waiting
No messages waiting
No messages waiting
Message received: Hello
```

8.1.3   Performing concurrent computations on the default case

A useful scenario is to use the default select case for concurrent computations and then use a channel to signal when we need to stop. To illustrate this concept, suppose we have a sample application that will discover a forgotten password by brute force. To keep things simple, let's say we have a password-protected file that we remember has a password of six characters or less, using only the lowercase letters *a* to *z* and spaces.

The number of possible strings from "a" to "zzzzzz", including spaces, is $27^6 - 1$ (387,420,488). The function in the following listing gives us a way to convert the integers 1 to 387,420,488 into a string. For example, calling `toBase27(1)` gives us `"a"`, calling it with 2 gives us `"b"`, 28 gives us `"aa"`, and so on.

Listing 8.4 Enumerating all possible combinations of a string

```go
package main

import (
    "fmt"
    "time"
)

const (
    passwordToGuess = "go far"
    alphabet = " abcdefghijklmnopqrstuvwxyz"
)

func toBase27(n int) string {
    result := ""
    for n > 0 {
        result = string(alphabet[n%27]) + result
        n /= 27
    }
    return result
}
```

Sets the password that we need to guess

Defines all possible characters that the password is made of

Algorithm converts a decimal integer into a string of base 27 using the alphabet constant

---

If we had to use a brute force approach in a sequential program, we would just create a loop enumerating all strings from `"a"` to `"zzzzzz"`, and every time, we would check to see whether it matched with the variable `passwordToGuess`. In a real-life scenario, we wouldn't have the value of the password; instead, we would try to gain access to our resource (such as a file) using each string enumeration as the password.

To find our password faster, we can divide the range of our guesses among several goroutines. For example, goroutine A would try guesses from string enumerations 1 to 10 million, goroutine B would try guesses from 10 million to 20 million, and so on (see figure 8.4). In this way, we can have many goroutines, each working on a separate part of our problem space.

To avoid unnecessary computations, we want to stop the execution of each goroutine when any goroutine makes a correct guess. To achieve this, we can use a channel to notify all other goroutines when one execution discovers the password, as shown in figure 8.4. Once a goroutine finds the matching password, it closes a common channel. This has the effect of interrupting all participating goroutines and stopping the processing.

> **NOTE** We can use the `close()` operation on a channel to act like a signal being broadcast to all consumers.

How can we implement the logic to stop processing in all goroutines after a common channel is closed? One solution is to perform the necessary computation in the `select`

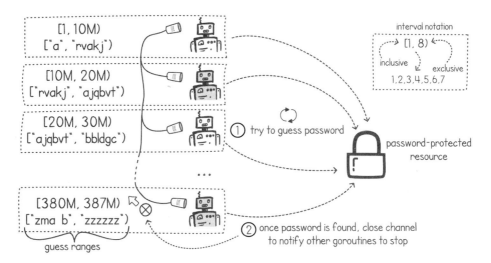

Figure 8.4 Dividing the work among executions and closing the channel to stop them

statement's default case and then have another case waiting on the common channel. In our example, we can call our `toBase27()` function and try to guess passwords in the default case, each time guessing just one password. We can have the logic to stop generating and trying passwords in a separate select case, which will be triggered when the common channel is closed.

Listing 8.5 shows a function that accepts this common channel, called `stop`. In the function, we generate all password guesses from the given range, represented by the `from` and `upto` integer variables. Each time we generate the next password guess, we try to match it against the `passwordToGuess` constant. This simulates the program trying to access a resource that is password protected. Once a password matches, the function closes the channel, resulting in all the goroutines receiving a close message on their own select case and stopping their processing because of the `return` statement.

Listing 8.5 Brute force password discovery goroutine

> Loops over all password combinations using from and upto as starting and end points

```
func guessPassword(from int, upto int, stop chan int, result chan string) {
    for guessN := from; guessN < upto; guessN += 1 {        ⟵

        select {

        case <-stop:        ⟵   Upon receiving a message on the stop channel,
            fmt.Printf("Stopped at %d [%d,%d]\n", guessN, from, upto)   outputs a message and stops processing
            return

        default:
            if toBase27(guessN) == passwordToGuess {        ⟵
                result <- toBase27(guessN)
```

Sends matching password on the result channel

Checks whether the password matches (in a real-life system, we would try to access the protected resource)

```
                    close(stop)   ◁────┐  Closes the channel so that other goroutines
                    return             │  stop checking the password
                }
            }
        }
        fmt.Printf("Not found between [%d,%d]\n", from, upto)
    }
```

We can now create several goroutines executing the previous listing. Each goroutine will try to find the correct password within a certain range. In the following listing, the `main()` function creates the necessary channels and starts all the goroutines with their input ranges in steps of 10 million.

Listing 8.6   `main()` function creating several goroutines with various password ranges

```
                                       ┌─ Creates a common channel used in the goroutines
                                       │  that signals when a password has been found
func main() {
    finished := make(chan int)   ◁─────┘
                                          ┌─ Creates a channel that will contain the
    passwordFound := make(chan string)  ◁─┘  discovered password after it's found

    for i :- 1; i <= 387_420_488; i += 10_000_000 {
        go guessPassword(i, i+ 10_000_000, finished, passwordFound)
    }
    fmt.Println("password found:", <-passwordFound)
    close(passwordFound)
    time.Sleep(5 * time.Second)
}
```

Waits for the password to be found ─→ `fmt.Println("password found:", <-passwordFound)`

Creates a goroutine with input ranges [1, 10M), [10M, 20M), . . . [380M, 390M)

Simulates the program using the password to access the resource

After starting up all the goroutines, the `main()` function waits for an output message on the `passwordFound` channel. Once a goroutine discovers the correct password, it will send the password on its `result` channel to the `main()` function. When we run all the listings together, we get the following output:

```
Not found between [1,10000001)
Stopped at 277339743 [270000001,280000001)
Stopped at 267741962 [260000001,270000001)
Stopped at 147629035 [140000001,150000001)
. . .
password found: go far
Stopped at 378056611 [370000001,380000001)
Stopped at 217938567 [210000001,220000001)
Stopped at 357806660 [350000001,360000001)
Stopped at 287976025 [280000001,290000001)
. . .
```

8.1.4   *Timing out on channels*

Another useful scenario is blocking for only a specified amount of time, waiting for an operation on a channel. Just like in the previous two examples, we want to check to see whether a message has arrived on a channel, but we want to wait for a few seconds to see if a message arrives, instead of unblocking immediately and doing something else. This is useful in many situations when channel operations are time sensitive. Consider, for example, a financial trading application, where if we don't receive a stock price update within a time window, we need to raise alerts.

We can implement this behavior by using a separate goroutine that sends a message on an extra channel after a specified timeout. We can then use this extra channel in our `select` statement, together with the other channels. This will give us the effect of blocking on the `select` statement until any of the channels becomes available or the timeout occurs (see figure 8.5).

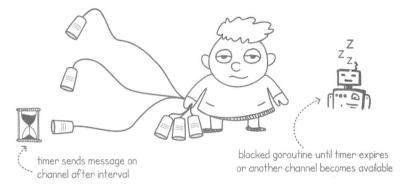

timer sends message on
channel after interval

blocked goroutine until timer expires
or another channel becomes available

Figure 8.5 Using a timer to send a message on a channel to implement blocking with a timeout

Thankfully, the `time.Timer` type in Go provides us with this functionality, and we don't have to implement our own timer goroutine. We can create one of these timers by calling `time.After(duration)`. This will return a channel on which a message is sent after the duration time elapses. The following listing shows an example of how we can use this with a `select` statement to implement channel blocking with a timeout.

Listing 8.7 Blocking with a timeout

```go
package main

import (
    "fmt"
    "os"
    "strconv"
    "time"
)

func sendMsgAfter(seconds time.Duration) <-chan string {
    messages := make(chan string)
    go func() {
        time.Sleep(seconds)
```

Sends the message "Hello" on the returned channel after the specified number of seconds

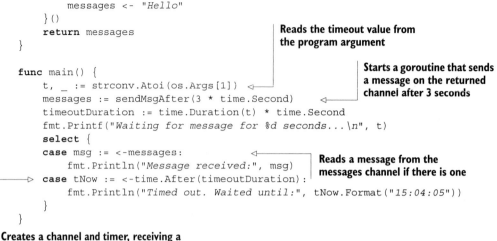

```
                messages <- "Hello"
        } ()
        return messages
    }

    func main() {
        t, _ := strconv.Atoi(os.Args[1])
        messages := sendMsgAfter(3 * time.Second)
        timeoutDuration := time.Duration(t) * time.Second
        fmt.Printf("Waiting for message for %d seconds...\n", t)
        select {
        case msg := <-messages:
            fmt.Println("Message received:", msg)
        case tNow := <-time.After(timeoutDuration):
            fmt.Println("Timed out. Waited until:", tNow.Format("15:04:05"))
        }
    }
```

Reads the timeout value from the program argument

Starts a goroutine that sends a message on the returned channel after 3 seconds

Reads a message from the messages channel if there is one

Creates a channel and timer, receiving a message after the specified duration

Listing 8.7 accepts a timeout value as a program argument. We use this timeout to wait for a message to arrive on the messages channel, which arrives after 3 seconds. Here's the output of this program when we specify a timeout of less than 3 seconds:

```
$ go run selecttimer.go 2
Waiting for message for 2 seconds...
Timed out. Waited until: 16:31:50
```

When we specify a timeout greater than 3 seconds, the message arrives, as expected:

```
$ go run selecttimer.go 4
Waiting for message for 4 seconds...
Message received: Hello
```

When we use the time.After(duration) call, the returned channel will receive a message containing the time when the message was sent. In listing 8.7, we are simply outputting it.

8.1.5   *Writing to channels with select*

We can also use the select statement when we need to write messages to channels, not just when we are reading messages from channels. Select statements can combine read or write blocking channel operations together, selecting the case that unblocks first. As in the previous scenarios, we can use select to implement non-blocking channel sending or sending on a channel with a timeout. Let's demonstrate a scenario that combines writing and reading from channels in a single select statement.

Imagine we have to come up with 100 random prime numbers. In real life, we could pick a random number from a bag with a large set of numbers and then keep that number only if it is prime (see figure 8.6).

Figure 8.6 Filtering primes from random numbers

In programming, we can have a primes filter that, given a stream of random numbers, picks out any prime number it finds and outputs it on another stream. In listing 8.8, the `primesOnly()` function does exactly this: it accepts a channel with input numbers and filters for prime numbers. The primes are output on the returned channel.

To prove that a number, *C*, is non-prime, we just need to find a prime number in the range from 2 to the square root of *C* that is a factor of *C*. A *factor* is a number that divides another number, leaving no remainder. If no such factor exists, then *C* is prime. To keep our `primesOnly()` function implementation simple, we'll check every integer in this range instead of checking every prime.

Listing 8.8 Goroutine filtering for prime numbers

```go
package main

import (
    "fmt"
    "math"
    "math/rand"
)

func primesOnly(inputs <-chan int) <-chan int {          // Accepts numbers in the inputs channel and returns a channel containing only prime numbers
    results := make(chan int)
    go func() {                                            // Creates an anonymous goroutine that will filter for prime numbers only
        for c := range inputs {
            isPrime := c != 1                              // Checks to ensure c is not 1, since 1 is not a prime
            for i := 2; i <= int(math.Sqrt(float64(c))); i++ {   // Checks to see if c has a factor in the range from 2 to the square root of c
                if c%i == 0 {
                    isPrime = false
                    break
                }
            }
            if isPrime {
                results <- c                               // If c is prime, outputs c on the results channel
            }
        }
    }()
    return results
}
```

Notice that in listing 8.8, our goroutine outputs a subset of the numbers it receives on the input channel. Often, the goroutine receives a non-prime number that is thrown away, meaning no number is output. How can we feed in a stream of random numbers while reading the primes returned on another channel in one goroutine? The answer is to use a `select` statement to both feed in the random numbers and read the primes. This is shown in the following listing, where the `main()` goroutine uses two select cases: one feeds the random numbers and another reads the primes.

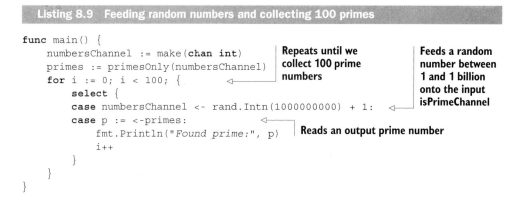

Listing 8.9   Feeding random numbers and collecting 100 primes

```
func main() {
    numbersChannel := make(chan int)          Repeats until we       Feeds a random
    primes := primesOnly(numbersChannel)      collect 100 prime      number between
    for i := 0; i < 100; {                    numbers                1 and 1 billion
        select {                                                     onto the input
        case numbersChannel <- rand.Intn(1000000000) + 1:           isPrimeChannel
        case p := <-primes:
            fmt.Println("Found prime:", p)     Reads an output prime number
            i++
        }
    }
}
```

In listing 8.9, we continue executing until we collect 100 prime numbers. After running this, we get the following output:

```
$ go run selectsender.go
Found prime: 646203301
Found prime: 288845803
Found prime: 265690541
Found prime: 263958077
Found prime: 280061603
Found prime: 214167823
. . .
```

8.1.6   *Disabling select cases with nil channels*

In Go, we can assign `nil` values to channels. This has the effect of blocking the channel from sending or receiving anything, as demonstrated in the following listing. The `main()` goroutine tries to send a string on a nil channel, and the operation blocks, stopping any further statements from executing.

Listing 8.10   Blocking on a nil channel

```
package main

import "fmt"

func main() {
    var ch chan string = nil      Creates a nil channel
```

```
   ch <- "message"
   fmt.Println("This is never printed")
}
```

**Blocks execution as it tries to send
message on the nil channel**

When we run listing 8.10, the `Println()` command never gets executed because the execution blocks on the message sending. Go has deadlock detection, so when Go notices that the program is stuck with no hope of recovering, it gives us the following message:

```
$ go run blockingnils.go
fatal error: all goroutines are asleep - deadlock!

goroutine 1 [chan send (nil chan)]:
main.main()
   /ConcurrentProgrammingWithGo/chapter8/listing8.10/blockingnils.go:7 +0x28
exit status 2
```

The same logic applies to `select` statements. Trying to send to or receive from a nil channel on a `select` statement has the same effect of blocking the case using that channel (see figure 8.7).

Figure 8.7   Blocking on nil channels

Using `select` with just one nil channel is not that useful, but we can use the pattern of assigning `nil` to a channel to disable a case in a `select` statement. Consider a scenario where we are consuming messages from two separate goroutines on two separate channels, and the goroutines close their channels at different times.

For example, we might be developing accounting software that receives sales and expense amounts from various sources. At the close of business, we want to output the total profit or loss for that day. We can model this by having a goroutine outputting sales details on one channel and another goroutine doing the same on another channel for expenses. We can then collate the two sources in another goroutine, and once both channels are closed, output the end-of-day balance to the user (see figure 8.8).

Listing 8.11 simulates our expense and sales application. The `generateAmounts()` function will create n random transaction amounts and send them on an output channel. We can then call this function twice, once for sales and again for expenses, and our main goroutine can combine both channels.

Figure 8.8   An accounting application reading sales and expenses from two sources

There is a small sleep inside the loop so that we can interleave both the sales and expense goroutines.

Listing 8.11   A `generateAmounts()` function generating sales and expenses

```
package main

import (
    "fmt"
    "math/rand"
    "time"
)

func generateAmounts(n int) <-chan int {
    amounts := make(chan int)          ⟵── Creates an output channel
    go func() {
        defer close(amounts)
        for i := 0; i < n; i++ {
            amounts <- rand.Intn(100) + 1
            time.Sleep(100 * time.Millisecond)
        }
    }()
    return amounts      ⟵── Returns the output channel
}
```

Closes the output channel when we're done (annotation pointing to `defer close(amounts)`)

Writes n random amounts in the range of [1, 100] to the output channel every 100 ms (annotation)

If we were to use a normal `select` statement to consume from both the sales and expense goroutines, with one of the goroutines closing its channel earlier than the other, we would end up always executing on the closed channel case. Every time we consume from a closed channel, it will return the default data type without blocking. This also applies to select cases. In our simple accounting application, if we used a `select` statement to consume from both sources, we would end up needlessly looping on the closed channel select case, receiving 0 every time (see figure 8.9).

> **WARNING**   When we use a select case on a closed channel, that case will always execute.

One solution to this problem is to have both the sales and expense goroutines output onto the same channel and then close the channel only when both goroutines are done. However, this might not always be an option, since it requires us to change the

Figure 8.9 Using a select case with a closed channel will result in that select case always executing.

goroutine function's signature so we can pass the same output channel to both sources. Sometimes, such as when using third-party libraries, changing the function's signature is not possible.

Another solution would be to change the channel into a nil channel whenever it is closed. Reading from a channel always returns two values: the message and a flag telling us if the channel is still open. We can read the flag, and if the flag indicates that the channel has been closed, we can set the channel reference to `nil` (see figure 8.10).

Figure 8.10 Assigning a nil channel when the channel is closed to disable the select case

Assigning a `nil` value to the channel variable after the receiver detects that the channel has been closed has the effect of disabling that `case` statement. This allows the receiving goroutine to read from the remaining open channels.

Listing 8.12 shows how we can use this nil channel pattern for our accounting application. In the `main()` goroutine, we initialize the sales and expense sources, and then we use a `select` statement to consume from both. If either of the channels returns a flag indicating that the channel has been closed, we set the channel to `nil` to disable the select case. We continue selecting from the channels for as long as there is one non-nil channel.

Listing 8.12 A `main()` goroutine using the nil select pattern

```
func main() {
    sales := generateAmounts(50)        Generates 50 amounts on the sales channel
    expenses := generateAmounts(40)     Generates 40 amounts on the expenses channel
```

```
        endOfDayAmount := 0
        for sales != nil || expenses != nil {
            select {
            case sale, moreData := <-sales:
                if moreData {
                    fmt.Println("Sale of:", sale)
                    endOfDayAmount += sale
                } else {
                    sales = nil
                }
            case expense, moreData := <-expenses:
                if moreData {
                    fmt.Println("Expense of:", expense)
                    endOfDayAmount -= expense
                } else {
                    expenses = nil
                }
            }
        }
        fmt.Println("End of day profit and loss:", endOfDayAmount)
    }
```

Continues to loop while there is a non-nil channel

Consumes the next amount and channel open flag from the sales channel

Adds the sales amount to the total end-of-day balance

If the channel has been closed, marks the channel as nil, disabling this select case

Consumes the next amount and channel open flag from the expenses channel

Subtracts the expense amount from the total end-of-day balance

If the channel has been closed, marks the channel as nil, disabling this select case

In listing 8.12, once both channels are closed and set to nil, we exit the select loop and output the end-of-day balance. Running listings 8.11 and 8.12 together, we get the sales and expense amounts interleaved until we have consumed all the expenses and the channel has been closed. At this point, the select statement drains the sales channel and then exits the loop, printing the total balance:

```
$ go run selectwithnil.go
Expense of: 82
Sale of: 88
Sale of: 48
Expense of: 60
Sale of: 82
. . .
Sale of: 34
Sale of: 44
Sale of: 92
Sale of: 3
End of day profit and loss: 387
```

> **NOTE** This pattern of merging channel data into one stream is referred to as a *fan-in* pattern. Using the select statement to merge different sources only works when we have a fixed number of sources. In the next chapter, we will see a fan-in pattern that merges a dynamic number of sources.

8.2 *Choosing between message passing and memory sharing*

We can decide whether to use memory sharing or message passing for our concurrent applications depending on the type of solution we are trying to implement. In this section, we will examine the factors and implications that we should keep in mind when deciding which of the two approaches to use.

8.2.1   Balancing code simplicity

Producing simple, readable, and easy-to-maintain software code is ever more important with today's complex business requirements and large development teams. Concurrent programming using message passing tends to produce code containing well-defined modules, each module running its own concurrent execution that passes messages to other executions. This makes code simpler and easier to understand. In addition, having clear input and output channels to the concurrent executions means that our program data flow is easier to grasp and, if needed, modify.

In contrast, memory sharing means that we need to use a more primitive way of managing concurrency. Just like reading a low-level language, code that uses concurrency primitives (such as mutexes and semaphores) tends to be harder to follow. The code is usually more verbose and is littered with protected critical sections. Unlike message passing, it's harder to determine how data flows through the application (see figure 8.11).

Figure 8.11   Achieving the right balance between code simplicity and performance

8.2.2   Designing tightly versus loosely coupled systems

The terms *tightly* and *loosely* coupled software refer to how dependent different modules are on each other. Tightly coupled software means that when we change one component, it will have a ripple effect on many other parts of the software, which usually require changes as well. In loosely coupled software, components tend to have clear boundaries and few dependencies on other modules. In loosely coupled software, introducing a change in one component requires few or no changes in others (see figure 8.12). Loosely coupling is usually a software design goal and a desirable code property. It means that our software is easier to test and more maintainable, requiring less work whenever we introduce a new feature.

Concurrent programming using memory sharing typically produces more tightly coupled software. The inter-thread communication uses a common block of memory, and the boundaries of each execution are not clearly defined. Any execution can read and write to the same location. Writing loosely coupled software while using memory sharing is more difficult than when using message passing because changing the way

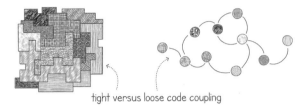

tight versus loose code coupling

Figure 8.12   The difference between tight and loose code coupling

we update the shared memory from one execution will have a significant effect on the rest of the application.

In contrast, with message passing, executions can have clearly defined input and output contracts, which means we know exactly how a change in one execution will affect another. For example, we can easily change the inside logic of a goroutine if the input and output contracts through our channels are maintained. This allows us to build loosely coupled systems more easily, and refactoring the logic in one module does not have a large ripple effect on the rest of the application.

> **NOTE**   This is not to say that all code that uses message passing is loosely coupled. Nor is all software that uses memory sharing tightly coupled. It is just easier to come up with a loosely coupled design using message passing because we can define simple boundaries for each concurrent execution with clear input and output channels.

8.2.3   *Optimizing memory consumption*

With message passing, each goroutine has its own isolated state stored in memory. When we pass messages from one goroutine to another, each organizes the data in its memory to compute its task. Often, there is some replication of the same data across multiple goroutines.

For example, consider the letter-frequency application we implemented in chapter 3. In our implementation, we used a Go slice shared among our goroutines. The program downloaded web pages using concurrent goroutines and used this shared slice to store the number of times that each letter in the English alphabet appeared in the downloaded document (see the left side of figure 8.13). We could change the program to use message passing by having each goroutine build a local instance of a slice with the frequencies encountered while downloading its web page. After counting the letter frequencies, each goroutine would send a message on an output channel with the slice containing the results. In our `main()` function, we could then collect the results and merge them (see the right side of figure 8.13).

Listing 8.13 shows how we could implement a goroutine that downloads a web document and counts the occurrences of each letter in the alphabet. It has its own local slice data structure instead of a shared one.

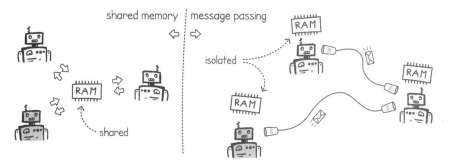

Figure 8.13   Message passing can result in more memory consumption.

Once it's done, it sends the results to its output channel.

Listing 8.13   Letter-frequency function using message passing (imports omitted)

```go
package main

import (...)

const allLetters = "abcdefghijklmnopqrstuvwxyz"

func countLetters(url string) <-chan []int {
    result := make(chan []int)          // Creates output channel of type int slice
    go func() {
        defer close(result)
        frequency := make([]int, 26)    // Creates a local frequency slice
        resp, _ := http.Get(url)
        defer resp.Body.Close()
        if resp.StatusCode != 200 {
            panic("Server returning error code: " + resp.Status)
        }
        body, _ := io.ReadAll(resp.Body)
        for _, b := range body {
            c := strings.ToLower(string(b))
            cIndex := strings.Index(allLetters, c)
            if cIndex >= 0 {
                frequency[cIndex] += 1    // Updates each character count
            }                            // in the local frequency slice
        }
        fmt.Println("Completed:", url)
        result <- frequency              // Once it's finished, the frequency
    }()                                  // slice is sent over the channel.
    return result
}
```

We can now add a `main()` function that starts a goroutine for each web page and waits for messages from each output channel. Once we start receiving messages containing the slices, we can merge them into a final slice. The following listing shows how we can do this, summing each slice into the `totalFrequencies` slice.

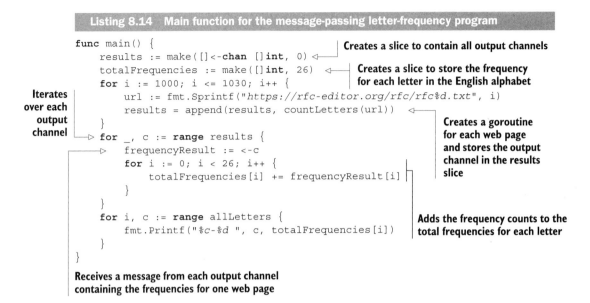

Listing 8.14   Main function for the message-passing letter-frequency program

```
func main() {
    results := make([]<-chan []int, 0)          ◁——  Creates a slice to contain all output channels
    totalFrequencies := make([]int, 26)   ◁——  Creates a slice to store the frequency
    for i := 1000; i <= 1030; i++ {             for each letter in the English alphabet
        url := fmt.Sprintf("https://rfc-editor.org/rfc/rfc%d.txt", i)
        results = append(results, countLetters(url))  ◁——
    }                                                     Creates a goroutine
    for _, c := range results {                          for each web page
        frequencyResult := <-c                           and stores the output
        for i := 0; i < 26; i++ {                         channel in the results
            totalFrequencies[i] += frequencyResult[i]     slice
        }
    }
    for i, c := range allLetters {              Adds the frequency counts to the
        fmt.Printf("%c-%d ", c, totalFrequencies[i])  total frequencies for each letter
    }
}
```

Iterates over each output channel → `for _, c := range results {`

Receives a message from each output channel containing the frequencies for one web page

In converting our program to use message passing, we have avoided using mutexes to control access to shared memory since each goroutine is now only working on its own data. However, in doing so, we have increased the memory use since we have allocated a slice for each web page. For this simple application, the memory increase is minimal because we're only using a small slice of size 26. For applications that pass structures containing larger amounts of data, we might be better off using memory sharing to reduce memory consumption.

8.2.4   Communicating efficiently

Message passing will degrade the performance of our application if we are spending too much time passing messages around. Since we pass copies of messages from one goroutine to another, we suffer the performance penalty of spending time copying the data in the message. This extra performance cost is noticeable if the messages are large or numerous.

One scenario is when the message size is too large. Consider, for example, an image or video processing application applying various filters on the images concurrently. Copying huge blocks of memory containing images or videos just to pass them on channels might greatly reduce our performance. If the amount of data shared is large and we have performance constraints, we might be better off using memory sharing.

The other scenario is when our executions are very chatty—when concurrent executions need to send many messages to each other. For example, we can imagine a weather forecasting application that uses concurrent programming to speed up its weather calculations. Figure 8.14 shows how we could split the weather forecasting area into a grid and distribute the computational work of forecasting the weather for each grid square to a separate goroutine.

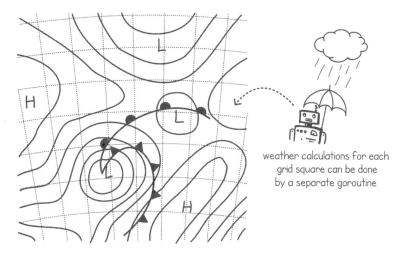

weather calculations for each
grid square can be done
by a separate goroutine

Figure 8.14 Using concurrent executions to speed up weather forecasting

To calculate the weather forecast in each grid square, a goroutine might need information from calculations in all the other grids. Each goroutine might need to send and receive partial calculation results from all the other goroutines, and this process might have to be repeated multiple times until the forecasting calculations converge. Our made-up algorithm, running in each goroutine, might look like this:

1 Calculate partial results for the goroutine's grid square.
2 Send partial results to all other goroutines, each working on its own grid square.
3 Receive partial results from every other goroutine, and include them in the next calculation.
4 Repeat from 1 until the calculation is fully complete.

Using message passing for such a scenario would mean that we would be sending a huge number of messages on every iteration. Every goroutine would have to send its partial results to all other goroutines and then receive the other grid results from every goroutine. In this scenario, our application would end up spending a lot of time and memory to copy and pass the values around.

In such scenarios, we are likely better off using memory sharing. For example, we could allocate a shared two-dimensional array space and let the goroutines read each other's grid results, using the appropriate synchronization tools, such as readers–writer locks.

8.3 Exercises

NOTE Visit http://github.com/cutajarj/ConcurrentProgrammingWithGo to see all the code solutions.

1   In listing 8.15, we have two goroutines. The `generateTemp()` function simulates reading and sending the temperature on a channel every 200 ms. The `output-Temp()` function simply outputs a message found on a channel every 2 seconds. Can you write a `main()` function, using a `select` statement, that reads messages coming from the `generateTemp()` goroutine and sends only the latest temperature to the `outputTemp()` channel? Since the `generateTemp()` function outputs values faster than the `outputTemp()` function, you'll need to discard some values so that only the most up-to-date temperature is displayed.

Listing 8.15   Latest temperature exercise

```go
package main

import (
    "fmt"
    "math/rand"
    "time"
)

func generateTemp() chan int {
    output := make(chan int)
    go func() {
        temp := 50 //fahrenheit
        for {
            output <- temp
            temp += rand.Intn(3) - 1
            time.Sleep(200 * time.Millisecond)
        }
    }()
    return output
}

func outputTemp(input chan int) {
    go func() {
        for {
            fmt.Println("Current temp:", <-input)
            time.Sleep(2 * time.Second)
        }
    }()
}
```

2   In listing 8.16, we have a goroutine in the `generateNumbers()` function that outputs random numbers. Can you write a `main()` function using a `select` statement that continuously consumes from the output channel, printing the output on the console until 5 seconds have elapsed from the start of the program? After 5 seconds, the function should stop consuming from the output channel, and the program should terminate.

Listing 8.16   Stop-reading-after-5-seconds exercise

```
package main

import (
    "math/rand"
    "time"
)

func generateNumbers() chan int {
    output := make(chan int)
    go func() {
        for {
            output <- rand.Intn(10)
            time.Sleep(200 * time.Millisecond)
        }
    }()
    return output
}
```

3 Consider listing 8.17 containing the `player()` function. This function creates a goroutine simulating a player in a game moving along a two-dimensional plane. The goroutine returns the movements at random times by writing UP, DOWN, LEFT, or RIGHT on an output channel. Create a `main()` function that creates four player goroutines and outputs on the console all movements from the four players. The `main()` function should terminate only when there is one player left in the game. Here is an example of what the output should look like:

```
Player 1: DOWN
Player 0: LEFT
Player 3: DOWN
Player 2 left the game. Remaining players: 3
Player 1: UP
. . .
Player 0: LEFT
Player 3 left the game. Remaining players: 2
Player 1: RIGHT
. . .
Player 1: RIGHT
Player 0 left the game. Remaining players: 1
Game finished
```

Listing 8.17   Simulating game players

```
package main

import (
    "fmt"
    "math/rand"
    "time"
)
```

```go
func player() chan string {
    output := make(chan string)
    count := rand.Intn(100)
    move := []string{"UP", "DOWN", "LEFT", "RIGHT"}
    go func() {
        defer close(output)
        for i := 0; i < count; i++ {
            output <- move[rand.Intn(4)]
            d := time.Duration(rand.Intn(200))
            time.Sleep(d * time.Millisecond)
        }
    }()
    return output
}
```

Summary

- When multiple channel operations are combined using the `select` statement, the operation that is unblocked first gets executed.
- We can have non-blocking behavior on a blocking channel by using the default case on the `select` statement.
- Combining a send or receive channel operation with a `Timer` channel on a `select` statement results in blocking on a channel up to the specified timeout.
- The `select` statement can be used not just for receiving messages but also for sending.
- Trying to send to or receive from a nil channel results in blocking the execution.
- Select cases can be disabled when we use nil channels.
- Message passing produces simpler code that is easier to understand.
- Tightly coupled code results in applications in which it is difficult to add new features.
- Code written in a loosely coupled way is easier to maintain.
- Loosely coupled software with message passing tends to be simpler and more readable than using memory sharing.
- Concurrent applications using message passing might consume more memory because each execution has its own isolated state instead of a shared one.
- Concurrent applications requiring the exchange of large chunks of data might be better off using memory sharing because copying this data for message passing may greatly degrade performance.
- Memory sharing is more suited for applications that would exchange a huge number of messages if they were to use message passing.

Programming
with channels

This chapter covers

- Introducing communicating sequential processes
- Reusing common channel patterns
- Taking advantage of channels being first-class objects

Working with channels requires a different way of programming than when using memory sharing. The idea is to have a set of goroutines, each with its own internal state, exchanging information with other goroutines by passing messages on Go's channels. In this way, each goroutine's state is isolated from direct interference by other executions, reducing the risk of race conditions.

Go's own mantra is not to communicate by shared memory but to instead share memory by communicating. Since memory sharing is more prone to race conditions and requires complex synchronization techniques, we should avoid it when possible and instead use message passing.

In this chapter, we will start by discussing communicating sequential processes (CSP) and then move on to look at the common patterns used when using message passing with channels. We'll finish this chapter by demonstrating the value of treating

187

channels as first-class objects, meaning that we can pass channels as function arguments and receive them as function return types.

9.1   *Communicating sequential processes*

In previous chapters, we discussed a model of concurrency using goroutines, shared memory, and primitives, such as mutexes, condition variables, and semaphores. This is the classic way to model concurrency. The main criticism of this model is that for many applications, it is too low-level.

> ### The SRC model
>
> Using shared memory with concurrent primitives, such as mutexes, is sometimes referred to as the *SRC model*. The name comes from a paper by Andrew D. Birrell titled "An Introduction to Programming with Threads" (Systems Research Center, 1989). The paper is a popular introduction to concurrent programming, using threads with shared memory, and synchronizing with concurrency primitives.

Programming with a low-level model of concurrency means that as programmers, we need to work harder to manage the complexity and reduce bugs in our software. We don't know when a thread of execution will be scheduled by the operating system, and this creates a non-deterministic environment—instructions are interleaved without us knowing beforehand the order of execution. This non-determinism, combined with memory sharing, creates the potential for race conditions. To avoid these, we must keep track of which execution is accessing the memory at the same time as other executions, and we need to restrict this access using synchronization primitives such as mutexes or semaphores.

Programming with such low-level tools for concurrency, when combined with modern software development teams and ever-increasing business complexity, leads to buggy, complex, and high-maintenance code. Software containing race conditions is difficult to debug because race conditions are tricky to reproduce and test. In some industries and applications, such as health and infrastructure software, code reliability is of critical importance (see figure 9.1). For these applications, it is hard to prove that concurrent code written in this manner is correct due to its non-deterministic nature.

Figure 9.1   Proving that software is correct is important for critical applications.

9.1.1 Avoiding interference with immutability

One way to greatly reduce the risk of race conditions is to not allow our programming to modify the same memory from multiple concurrent executions. We can restrict this by making use of immutable concepts when we are sharing memory.

> **DEFINITION** *Immutable* literally means *unchangeable*. In computer programming, we use immutability when we initialize structures without providing any way to modify them. When the programming requires changes to these structures, we create a new copy of the structure containing the required changes, leaving the old copy as it is.

If our threads of execution only share memory containing data that is never updated, we can rest assured that there are no data race conditions. After all, most race conditions happen because multiple executions write to the same memory locations at the same time. If an execution needs to modify shared data, such as a variable, it can instead create a separate, local copy with the updates needed.

Creating a copy when we need to update shared data leaves us with a problem: How do we share the new, updated data that is now in a separate location in memory? We need a model for managing and sharing this new, modified data. This is where message passing and CSP come in handy.

9.1.2 Concurrent programming with CSP

A different, higher-level model of concurrency was proposed by C.A.R Hoare in his 1978 article "Communicating Sequential Processes" (https://www.cs.cmu.edu/~crary/819-f09/Hoare78.pdf). CSP, short for *communicating sequential processes*, is a formal language used to describe concurrent systems. Instead of using memory sharing, it is based on message passing via channels. Ideas and concepts from CSP have been adopted for concurrency models in programming languages and frameworks such as Erlang, Occam, Go, Scala's Akka framework, Clojure's core.async, and many others.

In CSP, processes communicate with each other by exchanging copies of values. Communication is done through named unbuffered channels. A CSP process is not to be confused with an OS process (the ones we discussed in chapter 2); rather, a CSP process is a sequential execution, which has its own isolated state, as shown in figure 9.2.

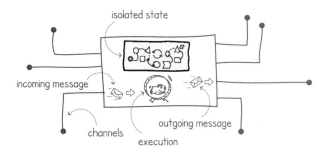

Figure 9.2 A sequential process communicating with others

The key difference when using the CSP model is that executions are not sharing memory. Instead, they pass copies of data to each other. Like when using immutability, if each execution is not modifying shared data, there is no risk of interference, and thus we avoid most race conditions. If each execution has its own isolated state, we can eliminate data race conditions without needing to use complex synchronization logic involving mutexes, semaphores, or condition variables.

Go implements this model with the use of goroutines and channels. Just like in the CSP model, Go's channels are synchronized and unbuffered by default. One key difference between the CSP model and Go's implementation is that in Go, channels are first-class objects, meaning we can pass them around in functions or even in other channels. This gives us more programming flexibility. Instead of creating a static topology of connected sequential processes, we can instead create and remove channels at runtime, depending on our logic needs.

> **CSP in other languages**
>
> Many other languages implement some aspects of the CSP model. For example, in Erlang, processes communicate with each other by sending messages. However, in Erlang, there is no notion of a channel, and the messages sent are not synchronous.
>
> In Java and Scala, the Akka framework uses an Actor model. This is a message-passing framework in which units of execution are called *actors*. Actors have their own isolated memory space and pass messages to each other. Unlike in CSP, there is no notion of channels, and message passing is not synchronous.

9.2   *Reusing common patterns with channels*

When we use message passing with channels in Go, there are two main guidelines to follow:

- *Try to only pass copies of data on channels*. This implies that you shouldn't pass direct pointers on channels in most cases. Passing pointers can result in multiple goroutines sharing memory, which can create race conditions. If you have to pass pointer references, use data structures in an immutable fashion—create them once, and don't update them. Alternatively, pass a reference via a channel, and then never use it again from the sender.
- *As much as possible, try not to mix message passing patterns with memory sharing*. Using memory sharing together with message passing might create confusion as to the approach adopted in the solution.

Let's now look at some examples of common concurrency patterns, best practices, and reusable components to understand how we can apply some of the CSP ideas to our applications.

9.2.1 Quitting channels

The first pattern we will examine is having a common channel that instructs goroutines to stop processing messages. In the previous chapter, we saw how we can use Go's close(channel) call to notify a goroutine that no more messages are coming. The goroutine can then terminate its execution. But what should we do if our goroutine is consuming from more than one channel? Should we terminate execution when we receive the first close() call or when all the channels are closed?

One solution is to use a quit channel together with the select statement. Figure 9.3 shows an example of a goroutine that generates numbers until it is instructed to stop on another quit channel. The goroutine on the right receives 10 of these numbers and then calls close(channel) on the quit channel, instructing the number generation to stop.

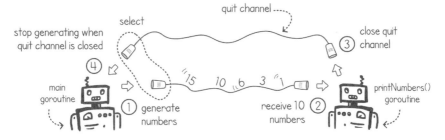

Figure 9.3 Using the quit channel to stop a goroutine's execution

Let's start by implementing the goroutine that receives and prints the numbers. Listing 9.1 shows a function accepting both an input numbers channel and a quit channel. The function simply takes 10 items from the numbers channel and then closes the quit channel. The data type we use for the quit channel does not really matter, since no data is ever sent on it except the close signal.

Listing 9.1 Prints 10 numbers and then closes the `quit` channel

```go
package main

import "fmt"

func printNumbers(numbers <-chan int, quit chan int) {
    go func() {
        for i := 0; i < 10; i++ {            Consumes 10 items from
            fmt.Println(<-numbers)           the numbers channel
        }
        close(quit)    <——— Closes the quit channel
    }()
}
```

Next, let's look at generating a stream of numbers on a channel to be consumed by our previous function. In our number stream, we can write the triangular number sequence shown in figure 9.4.

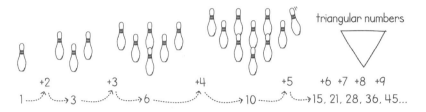

Figure 9.4   Generating a triangular number sequence

In listing 9.2, we have the `main()` goroutine creating the `numbers` and `quit` channels and calling the `printNumbers()` function. We can then continue generating the numbers and sending them on the `numbers` channel until the `select` statement tells us that the `quit` channel has unblocked. Once the `quit` channel has unblocked, we can terminate the `main()` goroutine.

Listing 9.2   Generating numbers until the `quit` channel is closed

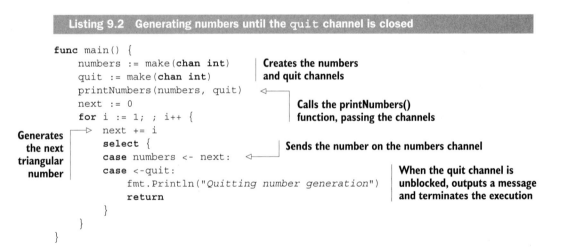

NOTE We are passing copies of the numbers on the channel. We are not sharing any memory because the goroutine has its own isolated memory space.

None of the variables used in the goroutines are being shared. For example, in listing 9.2, the `next` variable stays local on the `main()` function's stack. Running listings 9.1 and 9.2 together, we get the following result:

```
$ go run closingchannel.go
1
3
6
```

```
10
15
21
28
36
45
55
Quitting number generation
```

9.2.2 *Pipelining with channels and goroutines*

Let's now look at a pattern of connecting goroutines to form an execution pipeline. We can demonstrate this with an application that processes the text contents of web pages. In chapters 3 and 4, we used a concurrent memory-sharing application that downloaded text documents from the internet and counted the frequencies of characters. In the following section, we will develop a similar application that uses message passing via channels instead of memory sharing.

The first step in our application is to generate URLs of web pages that we can download later. We can have a goroutine generate several URLs and send them on a channel to be consumed (see figure 9.5). For starters, we can simply print out the URLs on the console from our `main()` goroutine. Once we're done, the goroutine generating the URLs will close the output channel to notify the `main()` goroutine that there aren't any more web pages to process.

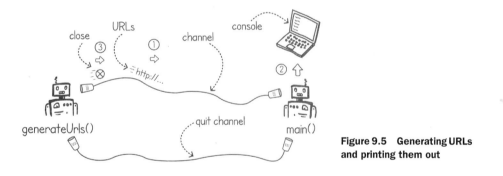

Figure 9.5   Generating URLs and printing them out

Listing 9.3 shows an implementation of the `generateUrls()` function, which creates a goroutine that generates URL strings on an output channel. The output channel is returned by the function. The function also accepts a quit channel, which it listens to in case it needs to stop generating URLs earlier. We'll adopt a common pattern where we pass the input channel as a function argument and return the output channel (the `generateUrls()` function doesn't have any input channels). This allows us to easily plug these goroutines together in the form of a pipeline. In our implementation, just as in chapter 3, we're using documents obtained from https://rfc-editor.org. This provides us with static online text documents that have predictable web addresses.

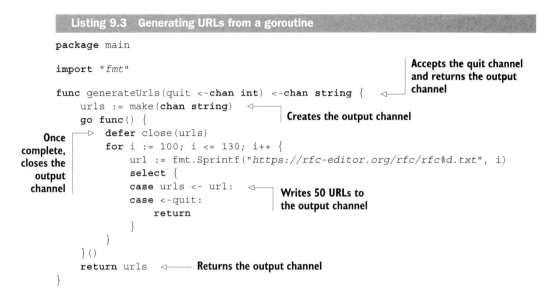

Listing 9.3   Generating URLs from a goroutine

```go
package main

import "fmt"

func generateUrls(quit <-chan int) <-chan string {
    urls := make(chan string)
    go func() {
        defer close(urls)
        for i := 100; i <= 130; i++ {
            url := fmt.Sprintf("https://rfc-editor.org/rfc/rfc%d.txt", i)
            select {
            case urls <- url:
            case <-quit:
                return
            }
        }
    }()
    return urls
}
```

Accepts the quit channel and returns the output channel

Creates the output channel

Once complete, closes the output channel

Writes 50 URLs to the output channel

Returns the output channel

Next, let's complete our simple application by writing the `main()` function, shown in listing 9.4. In the `main()` function, we create the `quit` channel and then call `generateUrls()`, which returns the goroutine's output channel (called `results` in this example). We then listen to both the output and the `quit` channel. We continue writing messages from the output channel to the console until the `quit` channel is closed, at which point we terminate the application by returning on the `main()` function.

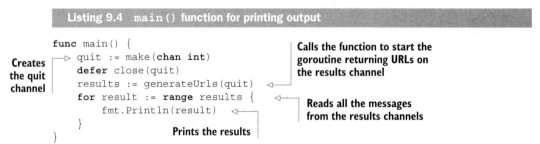

Listing 9.4   `main()` function for printing output

```go
func main() {
    quit := make(chan int)
    defer close(quit)
    results := generateUrls(quit)
    for result := range results {
        fmt.Println(result)
    }
}
```

Creates the quit channel

Calls the function to start the goroutine returning URLs on the results channel

Reads all the messages from the results channels

Prints the results

Running listings 8.7 and 8.8 together, we get the following output:

```
$ go run generateurls.go
https://rfc-editor.org/rfc/rfc100.txt
https://rfc-editor.org/rfc/rfc101.txt
https://rfc-editor.org/rfc/rfc102.txt
https://rfc-editor.org/rfc/rfc103.txt
https://rfc-editor.org/rfc/rfc104.txt
. . .
```

Next, let's write the logic to download the contents of these pages. For this task, we just need a goroutine that accepts a stream of URLs and outputs the text contents into another output stream. This goroutine can be plugged into the output of the generateUrls() goroutine and the input of the main() goroutine, as shown in figure 9.6.

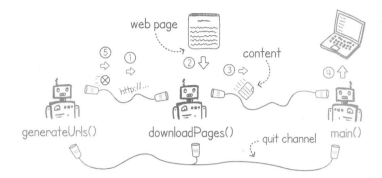

Figure 9.6 Adding a goroutine that downloads web pages to our pipeline

Listing 9.5 shows an implementation of the downloadPages() function. It accepts both the quit and urls channels and returns an output channel containing the downloaded pages. The function creates a goroutine that uses the select statement to download each page until the urls channel or the quit channel is closed. The goroutine checks to see whether the input channel is still open by reading the moreData Boolean flag that is returned when it reads the next message. When this returns false, meaning the channel has been closed, we stop iterating on the select statement.

Listing 9.5 Goroutine to download pages (imports omitted for brevity)

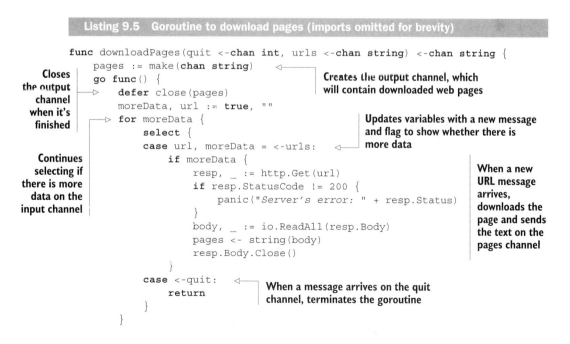

```go
func downloadPages(quit <-chan int, urls <-chan string) <-chan string {
    pages := make(chan string)          // Creates the output channel, which
    go func() {                         // will contain downloaded web pages
        defer close(pages)
        moreData, url := true, ""
        for moreData {                  // Updates variables with a new message
            select {                    // and flag to show whether there is
            case url, moreData = <-urls:  // more data
                if moreData {
                    resp, _ := http.Get(url)
                    if resp.StatusCode != 200 {
                        panic("Server's error: " + resp.Status)
                    }
                    body, _ := io.ReadAll(resp.Body)
                    pages <- string(body)
                    resp.Body.Close()
                }
            case <-quit:
                return
            }
        }
    }()
}
```

Closes the output channel when it's finished

Continues selecting if there is more data on the input channel

When a new URL message arrives, downloads the page and sends the text on the pages channel

When a message arrives on the quit channel, terminates the goroutine

```
    }()
    return pages     ◁——— Returns the output channel
}
```

> **WARNING** In listing 9.5, we're passing a copy of the web document on the channel. We can do this since the web pages are only a few KB in size. Using message passing for large objects, such as images or video, in this fashion might have a detrimental effect on performance. Using a memory-sharing architecture might be more suitable for applications sharing large amounts of data and requiring high performance.

We can now connect this new goroutine to our pipeline easily since it accepts the same channel datatype as the output of the `generateUrls()` function. It also returns the same output channel datatype as the one that our `main()` goroutine can use. In the following listing, we change the `main()` function to also call the `downloadPages()` function.

Listing 9.6 Modified `main()` function to call `downloadPages()`

```
func main() {
    quit := make(chan int)
    defer close(quit)
    results := downloadPages(quit, generateUrls(quit))     ◁——┐  Adds the new goroutine
    for result := range results {                              │  that downloads pages to
        fmt.Println(result)                                    │  our existing pipeline
    }
}
```

When we run the preceding `main()` function, we get the text from the web pages, and they are printed on the console. Printing out our text pages is not very useful, so instead we can add another goroutine on our pipeline to extract words from the downloaded text.

Following this pattern of accepting the input channel as a function input parameter and returning the output channel makes building pipelines easy. We just need to create a new goroutine that extracts the words and then connect it to our pipeline, as shown in figure 9.7.

Listing 9.7 shows the implementation of the `extractWords()` function. The same pattern as for `downloadPages()` is used. The function accepts an input channel containing texts, and it returns an output channel containing all the words found in the received texts. It extracts the words from the document by using regular expressions (regex).

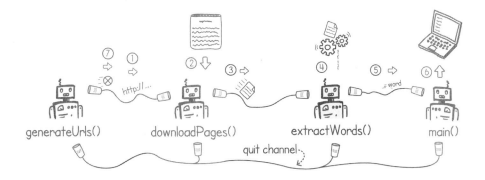

Figure 9.7 Adding a goroutine to extract words from pages

Just like in listing 9.6, we continue reading from the input channel until we get a close on the input or on the `quit` channel. We do this by using the `select` statement and reading the `moreData` flag on the input channel.

Listing 9.7 Extracting words from text pages (imports omitted for brevity)

```
func extractWords(quit <-chan int, pages <-chan string) <-chan string {
    words := make(chan string)                      ⊲──── Creates the output channel, which
    go func() {                                            will contain extracted words
        defer close(words)
        wordRegex := regexp.MustCompile(`[a-zA-Z]+`)
        moreData, pg := true, ""
        for moreData {                                    Updates variables with a new
            select {                                      message and flag to show
            case pg, moreData = <-pages:       ⊲───       whether there is more data
                if moreData {
                    for _, word := range wordRegex.FindAllString(pg, -1) {
                        words <- strings.ToLower(word)  ⊲──┐
                    }                                      │
                }                                          │ When a new text page
            }                        When a message arrives on the  │ is received, extracts all
            case <-quit:        ⊲──  quit channel, terminates goroutine │ words with the regex
                return                                     │ and sends them on the
            }                                              │ output channel
        }
    }()
    return words    ⊲──── Returns the output channel
}
```

Creates a regular expression to extract the words (label pointing to `wordRegex := regexp.MustCompile(`[a-zA-Z]+`)`)

Again, we can modify our `main()` function to include this new goroutine in our pipeline, as shown in listing 9.8. Each function in the pipeline is a goroutine that takes the `quit` channel and an input channel and returns an output channel that results are sent to. Using the `quit` channel will later allow us to control the flow of different parts of the pipeline.

Listing 9.8 Adding `extractWords()` to the pipeline

```
func main() {
    quit := make(chan int)
    defer close(quit)
    results := extractWords(quit, downloadPages(quit, generateUrls(quit)))
    for result := range results {
        fmt.Println(result)
    }
}
```

Running the previous listings with the new `extractWords()` in our pipeline, we get a list of words contained in the texts:

```
$ go run extractwords.go
network
working
group
p
karp
request
for
comments
. . .
```

> **NOTE** This pipeline pattern gives us the ability to easily plug executions together. Each execution is represented by a function that starts a goroutine accepting input channels as arguments and returning the output channels as return values.

When running listing 9.8, the web pages are downloaded sequentially, one after the other, making execution quite slow. Ideally, we'll want to speed this up and do the downloads concurrently. This is where the next pattern (fan-in and fan-out) comes in handy.

9.2.3 Fanning in and out

In our example application, if we want to speed things up, we can perform the downloads concurrently by load-balancing the URLs to multiple goroutines. We can create a fixed number of goroutines, each reading from the same URL input channel. Each one of the goroutines will receive a separate URL from the `generateUrls()` goroutine, and they can perform the downloads concurrently. The downloaded text pages can then be written on each goroutine's own output channel.

> **DEFINITION** In Go, a *fan-out* concurrency pattern is when multiple goroutines read from the same channel. In this way, we can distribute the work among a set of goroutines.

Figure 9.8 shows how we can fan out the URLs to multiple `downloadPage()` goroutines, each doing a different download. In this example, the concurrent goroutines are

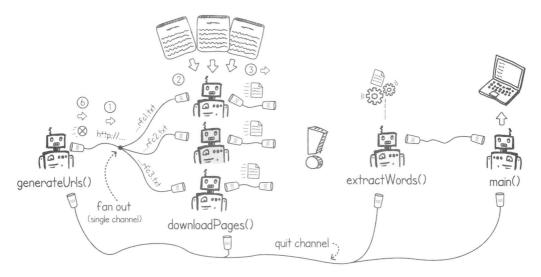

Figure 9.8 Load-balancing requests by using a fan-out pattern with the connection to `extractWords()` missing

load-balancing the URLs sent from the `generateUrls()` goroutine; when a `download-Page()` goroutine is free, it will read the next URL from the shared input channel. This is similar to having multiple baristas serving customers from a single queue at your local coffee shop.

NOTE Since concurrent processing is non-deterministic, some messages will be processed quicker than others, resulting in messages being processed in an unpredictable order. The fan-out pattern makes sense only if we don't care about the order of the incoming messages.

In our code, we can implement this simple fan-out pattern by creating a set of `download-loadPages()` goroutines and setting the same channel as an input channel parameter. This is shown in the following listing.

Listing 9.9 Fanning out to multiple `downloadPages()` goroutines

```
const downloaders = 20

func main() {
    quit := make(chan int)
    defer close(quit)
    urls := generateUrls(quit)
    pages := make([]<-chan string, downloaders)
    for i := 0; i < downloaders; i++ {
        pages[i] = downloadPages(quit, urls)
    }
    . . .
```

Creates a slice to store output channels from the download goroutines

Creates 20 goroutines to download web pages and stores the output channels

The fan-out pattern in our application has created a problem: the outputs of our download goroutines are in separate channels. How can we connect them to the single input channel of our next stage: the `extractWords()` goroutine?

One solution is to change the `downloadPages()` goroutines and make them all output on the same channel. For this, we would have to pass the same output channel to each downloader. This would break our pattern of having easily pluggable units where each one accepts input channels as arguments and returns the output channels as return values.

To keep to this pattern, we need a mechanism that merges the output messages from the different channels into a single output channel. We can then plug the single output channel into the `extractWords()` goroutine. This is what is called the *fan-in* pattern.

> **DEFINITION** In Go, a *fan-in* concurrency pattern occurs when we merge the content from multiple channels into one.

Since goroutines are very lightweight, we can implement this fan-in pattern as a single unit by creating a set of goroutines, one per output channel, and having each goroutine feed a common channel, as shown in figure 9.9. Each goroutine listens to messages from the output channel, and when a message arrives, it simply forwards it to the common channel.

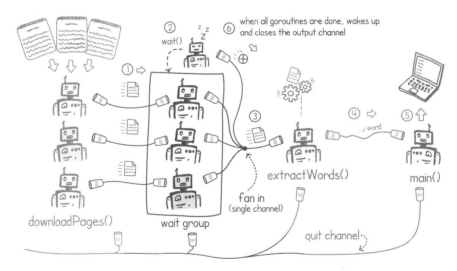

Figure 9.9 Merging channels by using a fan-in

Having multiple goroutines all feeding into a single common channel creates a problem. When we have a one-to-one input-to-output channel goroutine, the channel-closing strategy is simple: close the output after the input channel has been closed. When we have a many-to-one fan-in scenario, we must make a decision about when to close the common channel. If we continue with the same approach of closing the channel when a goroutine notices that the channel it's consuming from has been closed, we might end up closing the channel too soon. Another goroutine might still be outputting messages.

The solution is to only close the common channel when *all* the goroutines have noticed that the channels from which they are consuming have been closed. As shown in figure 9.9, we can use a waitgroup for this. Each goroutine in the fan-in group marks the waitgroup as done after it has sent its last message. We have a separate goroutine that calls `wait()` on this waitgroup, which will have the effect of suspending its execution until all the fan-in goroutines are done. Once this goroutine resumes, it will close the output channel. This technique is shown in the following listing.

Listing 9.10 Implementing a fan-in function

```
package listing9_10

import (
    "sync"
)

func FanIn[K any](quit <-chan int, allChannels ...<-chan K) chan K {
    wg := sync.WaitGroup{}
    wg.Add(len(allChannels))         // Creates a waitgroup, setting the size to be equal to the number of input channels
    output := make(chan K)           // Creates the output channel
    for _, c := range allChannels {
        go func(channel <-chan K) {  // Starts a goroutine for every input channel
            defer wg.Done()          // Once the goroutine terminates, marks the waitgroup as done
            for i := range channel {
                select {
                case output <- i:    // Forwards each received message to the shared output channel
                case <-quit:
                    return           // If quit channel is closed, terminates the goroutine
                }
            }
        }(c)                         // Passes one input channel to the goroutine
    }
    go func() {
        wg.Wait()                    // Waits for all the goroutines to finish and then closes the output channel
        close(output)
    }()
    return output                    // Returns the output channel
}
```

We can now connect our fan-in pattern to our application and include it in the pipeline. Listing 9.11 modifies our `main()` function to include the `fanIn()` function from listing 9.10. The `fanIn()` function accepts the list of channels containing the web pages and returns a common aggregated channel, which we then feed into our `extractWords()` function.

Listing 9.11   Adding the `fanIn()` function to the pipeline

```
const downloaders = 20

func main() {
    quit := make(chan int)
    defer close(quit)
    urls := generateUrls(quit)
    pages := make([]<-chan string, downloaders)
    for i := 0; i < downloaders; i++ {
        pages[i] = downloadPages(quit, urls)
    }
    results := extractWords(quit, listing9_10.FanIn(quit, pages...))
    for result := range results {
        fmt.Println(result)
    }
}
```

> Joins all the pages
> channels into one channel
> using the fan-in pattern

When we run our new implementation, it runs a lot faster because the downloads are being performed concurrently. As a side effect of doing the downloads together, the order of the extracted words is different every time we run the program.

9.2.4 *Flushing results on close*

We haven't really done anything interesting with our URL download application, apart from extracting the words. What if we use the downloaded web pages for something useful? How about trying to find the 10 longest words in these text documents?

This task is easy if we continue to follow our pipeline-building pattern. We just need to add a new goroutine that accepts an input channel and returns an output one. In figure 9.10, this new goroutine, called `longestWords()`, is inserted just after our `extractWords()` goroutine.

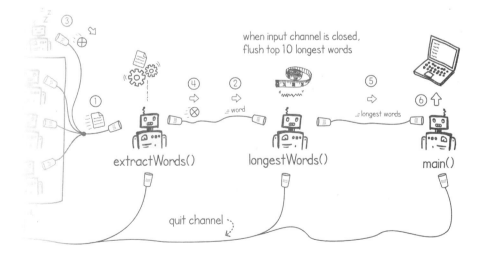

Figure 9.10   Adding the `longestWords()` goroutine to find the 10 longest words in our texts

This new `longestWords()` goroutine is slightly different from the other goroutines we have developed in our pipeline. It accumulates a set of unique words in its memory. Once it has read all the words from the web pages and receives the close message, it will review this set and output the 10 longest ones. Our `main()` goroutine will then print it on the console.

The implementation of `longestWords()` is shown in listing 9.12. In this function, we use a map to store the set of unique words. Since this map is isolated from our concurrent execution and only our `longestWords()` goroutine is accessing it, we do not need to worry about data race conditions. We also store the words in a separate slice to make sorting easier.

Listing 9.12 Goroutine to output longest words (imports omitted for brevity)

```go
func longestWords(quit <-chan int, words <-chan string) <-chan string {
    longWords := make(chan string)
    go func() {
        defer close(longWords)
        uniqueWordsMap := make(map[string]bool)      // Creates a map to
                                                      // store unique words
        uniqueWords := make([]string, 0)             // Creates slices to store the list of
        moreData, word := true, ""                   // unique words for easy sorting later
        for moreData {
            select {
            case word, moreData = <-words:
                if moreData && !uniqueWordsMap[word] {
                    uniqueWordsMap[word] = true
                    uniqueWords = append(uniqueWords, word)
                }
            case <-quit:
                return
            }
        }
        sort.Slice(uniqueWords, func(a, b int) bool {
            return len(uniqueWords[a]) > len(uniqueWords[b])
        })
        longWords <- strings.Join(uniqueWords[:10], ", ")
    }()
    return longWords
}
```

If the channel is not closed and the word is a new one, adds the new word to the map and list

Once the input channel is closed, sorts the unique words list by word length

Once the input channel is closed, sends a string with the 10 longest words on the output channel

In listing 9.12, the goroutine stores all the unique words on a map and a list. Once the input channel closes, meaning there are no more messages, the goroutine sorts the list of unique words by length. Then, on the output channel, it sends the first 10 items on the list, which are the 10 longest words. In this way, we flush the results after we have collected all the data.

We can now connect this new component to our pipeline in the `main()` function. In the following listing, the `longestWords()` goroutine consumes from the output channel of `extractWords()`.

Listing 9.13 Adding `longestWords()` to our pipeline

```
func main() {
    quit := make(chan int)
    defer close(quit)
    urls := generateUrls(quit)
    pages := make([]<-chan string, downloaders)
    for i := 0; i < downloaders; i++ {
        pages[i] = downloadPages(quit, urls)
    }
    results := longestWords(quit,
        extractWords(quit, listing8_14.FanIn(quit, pages...)))
    fmt.Println("Longest Words:", <-results)
}
```

Connects the longestWords() goroutine to the pipeline just after extractWords()

Prints the single message containing the longest words

When we run the listings together, the pipeline will find the longest words on the downloaded documents and output them on the console. Here's the output:

```
$ go run longestwords.go
Longest Words: interrelationships, misunderstandings, telecommunication,
    administratively, implementability, characteristics, insufficiencies,
    implementations, synchronization, representatives
```

9.2.5 *Broadcasting to multiple goroutines*

What if we want to find out more stats from our download pages? For this scenario, let's say that in addition to finding the longest words, we want to find which words occur most frequently.

For this scenario, we'll feed the output of `extractWords()` to two goroutines: the existing `longestWords()` and an additional one called `frequentWords()`. The pattern of the new function will be the same as that of `longestWords()`. It will store the frequency of each unique word, and when the input channel closes, it will output the top 10 most often-occurring words.

In the previous section, we used the fan-out pattern when we needed to feed the output of one computation to multiple concurrent goroutines. We load-balanced the messages, with each goroutine receiving a distinct subset of the output data. That pattern will not work here, since we want to send a copy of each output message to both the `longestWords()` and `frequentWords()` goroutines.

Instead of fan-out, we can use a broadcast pattern—one that replicates messages to a set of output channels. Figure 9.11 shows how we can use a separate goroutine that broadcasts to multiple channels. In our pipeline, we can connect the outputs of the broadcast to the inputs of both the `frequentWords()` and `longestWords()` goroutines.

To implement this broadcast utility, we just need to create a list of output channels and then use a goroutine that writes every received message to each channel. In listing 9.14, the broadcast function accepts the input channel and an integer, n, specifying the number of outputs that are needed. The function then returns these n output

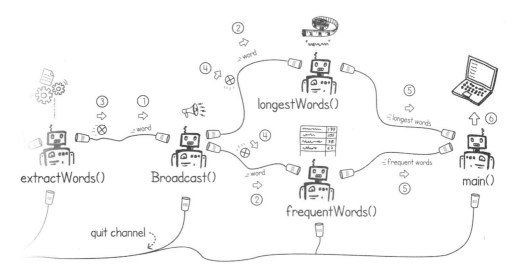

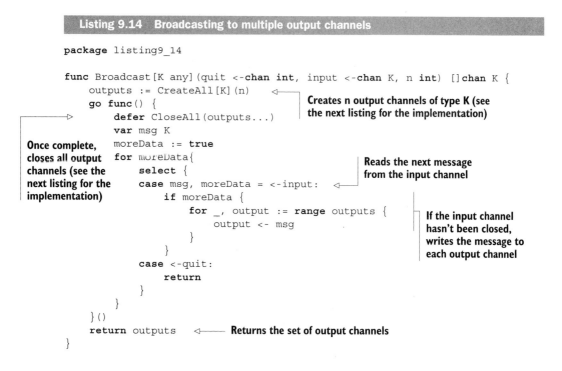

Figure 9.11 Connecting a concurrent `frequentWords()` goroutine to our pipeline

channels in a slice. In this implementation, we're using generics so that the broadcast can be used with any channel data type.

Listing 9.14 Broadcasting to multiple output channels

```
package listing9_14

func Broadcast[K any](quit <-chan int, input <-chan K, n int) []chan K {
    outputs := CreateAll[K](n)
    go func() {
        defer CloseAll(outputs...)
        var msg K
        moreData := true
        for moreData{
            select {
            case msg, moreData = <-input:
                if moreData {
                    for _, output := range outputs {
                        output <- msg
                    }
                }
            case <-quit:
                return
            }
        }
    }()
    return outputs
}
```

Creates n output channels of type K (see the next listing for the implementation)

Once complete, closes all output channels (see the next listing for the implementation)

Reads the next message from the input channel

If the input channel hasn't been closed, writes the message to each output channel

Returns the set of output channels

NOTE In the broadcast implementation in listing 9.14, we read the next message only after the current message has been sent to all the channels. A slow consumer from this broadcast implementation would slow all consumers to the same rate.

The previous listing makes use of two functions, `CreateAll()` and `CloseAll()`, that create and close a set of channels, respectively. The following listing shows their implementation.

Listing 9.15   The `CreateAll()` and `CloseAll()` functions

```go
func CreateAll[K any](n int) []chan K {        // Creates n channels of type K
    channels := make([]chan K, n)
    for i, _ := range channels {
        channels[i] = make(chan K)
    }
    return channels
}

func CloseAll[K any](channels ...chan K) {      // Closes all the channels
    for _, output := range channels {
        close(output)
    }
}
```

We can now write our `frequentWords()` function, which will identify the top 10 most frequently occurring words in our downloaded pages. The implementation in the following listing is similar to the `longestWords()` function. This time, we're using a map, called `mostFrequentWords`, to count each word's occurrence. After the input channel is closed, we sort the word list by the occurrence count in the map.

Listing 9.16   Finding the most frequent words (imports omitted for brevity)

```go
func frequentWords(quit <-chan int, words <-chan string) <-chan string {
    mostFrequentWords := make(chan string)
    go func() {
        defer close(mostFrequentWords)          // Creates a map to store the frequency
        freqMap := make(map[string]int)         // occurrence of each unique word
        freqList := make([]string, 0)           // Creates a slice to store a list of unique words
        moreData, word := true, ""
        for moreData {
            select {
            case word, moreData = <-words:      // If the message contains
                if moreData {                   // a new word, adds it to
                    if freqMap[word] == 0 {     // the slice of unique words
                        freqList = append(freqList, word)
                    }
                    freqMap[word] += 1          // Increments the
                }                               // count of the word
            case <-quit:
                return
```

Consumes the next message on the input channel

Writes the 10 most frequent words onto the output channel
```
            }
        }
        sort.Slice(freqList, func(a, b int) bool {
            return freqMap[freqList[a]] > freqMap[freqList[b]]
        })
        mostFrequentWords <- strings.Join(freqList[:10], ", ")
    }()
    return mostFrequentWords
}
```

Once all input messages are consumed, sorts the list of words by the occurrence count

Now we can wire in the `frequentWords()` unit with the broadcast utility we developed previously. In the following listing, we call the `Broadcast()` function to create two output channels and make it consume from `extractWords()`. Then we use the two output channels from the broadcast as inputs for the `longestWords()` and `frequentWords()` goroutines.

Listing 9.17 Wiring in the broadcast pattern to find the most frequent and longest words

```
const downloaders = 20

func main() {
    quit := make(chan int)
    defer close(quit)
    urls := generateUrls(quit)
    pages := make([]<-chan string, downloaders)
    for i := 0; i < downloaders; i++ {
        pages[i] = downloadPages(quit, urls)
    }
    words := extractWords(quit, listing9_10.FanIn(quit, pages...))
    wordsMulti := listing9_14.Broadcast(quit, words, 2)
    longestResults := longestWords(quit, wordsMulti[0])
    frequentResults := frequentWords(quit, wordsMulti[1])
    fmt.Println("Longest Words:", <-longestResults)
    fmt.Println("Most frequent Words:", <-frequentResults)
}
```

Creates the goroutine to find the most frequently used words from the input channel

Creates a goroutine that will broadcast the contents of the words channel to two output channels

Creates the goroutine to find the longest words from the input channel

Reads the result from the longestWords() goroutine and prints it

Reads the result from the mostFrequentWords() goroutine and prints it

Since both the `longestWords()` and `frequentWords()` goroutines output only one message containing the results, our `main()` function can just consume one message from each and print it on the console. The following snippet contains the output when we run the full pipeline. Not surprisingly, *the* is the most frequent word:

```
$ go run wordstats.go
Longest Words: interrelationships, telecommunication, misunderstandings,
    implementability, administratively, transformations, reconfiguration,
    representatives, experimentation, interpretations
Most frequent Words: the, to, a, of, is, and, in, be, for, rfc
```

9.2.6   *Closing channels after a condition*

So far, we haven't really used the quit channels that we have wired into every goroutine in our application. These quit channels can be used to stop parts of the pipeline on certain conditions.

In our application, we are reading a fixed number of web pages and then processing them, but what if we wanted to process only the first 10,000 words that we download? The solution is to add another execution that stops a section of our pipeline after it has consumed a specified number of messages. If we insert this new goroutine, called `Take(n)`, just after the `extractWords()` goroutine, we can instruct it to close the `quit` channel after receiving a specified number of messages (see figure 9.12). The `Take(n)` goroutine will only terminate parts of the pipeline by calling `close()` on the `quit` channel. We can do this by wiring the left part of the pipeline, before the `take(n)` goroutine, with a separate `quit` channel.

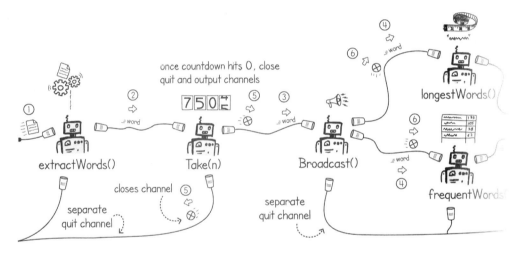

Figure 9.12   Adding the `Take(n)` goroutine to our pipeline

To implement `Take(n)`, we need a goroutine that simply forwards the messages received from the input to the output channel while keeping a countdown, with every message forwarded reducing the countdown by 1. Once the countdown is 0, the goroutine closes the `quit` and output channels. Listing 9.18 shows an implementation of `Take(n)`, where the countdown is represented by the variable n. The goroutine continues forwarding messages as long as there is more data, the countdown is greater than 0, and the `quit` channel hasn't been closed. It will close the `quit` channel only if the countdown hits 0.

Listing 9.18   Implementing the Take(n) function

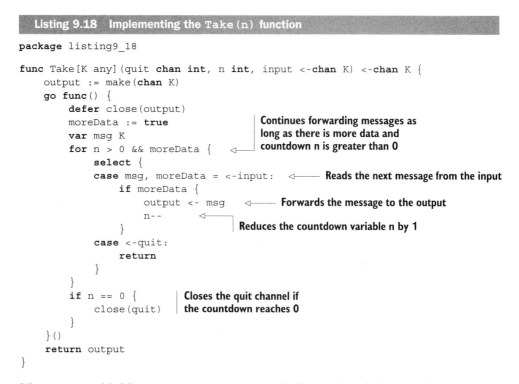

```
package listing9_18

func Take[K any](quit chan int, n int, input <-chan K) <-chan K {
    output := make(chan K)
    go func() {
        defer close(output)
        moreData := true                        Continues forwarding messages as
        var msg K                               long as there is more data and
        for n > 0 && moreData {          ◁──── countdown n is greater than 0
            select {
            case msg, moreData = <-input:   ◁──── Reads the next message from the input
                if moreData {
                    output <- msg       ◁──── Forwards the message to the output
                    n--                 ◁─┐
                }                         └ Reduces the countdown variable n by 1
            case <-quit:
                return
            }
        }
        if n == 0 {           Closes the quit channel if
            close(quit)       the countdown reaches 0
        }
    }()
    return output
}
```

We can now add this new component to our pipeline and make it stop the processing when it reaches a specific word count. The following listing shows how we can modify our `main()` function to include the `Take(n)` goroutine, configured to stop processing when it reaches the count of 10,000 words.

Listing 9.19   Wiring Take(n) into our pipeline

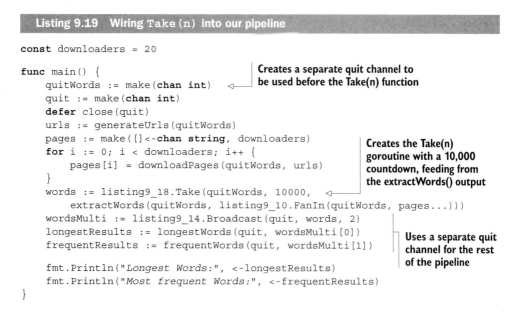

```
const downloaders = 20

func main() {                               Creates a separate quit channel to
    quitWords := make(chan int)     ◁────── be used before the Take(n) function
    quit := make(chan int)
    defer close(quit)
    urls := generateUrls(quitWords)
    pages := make([]<-chan string, downloaders)    Creates the Take(n)
    for i := 0; i < downloaders; i++ {             goroutine with a 10,000
        pages[i] = downloadPages(quitWords, urls)  countdown, feeding from
    }                                              the extractWords() output
    words := listing9_18.Take(quitWords, 10000,  ◁─┐
        extractWords(quitWords, listing9_10.FanIn(quitWords, pages...)))
    wordsMulti := listing9_14.Broadcast(quit, words, 2)
    longestResults := longestWords(quit, wordsMulti[0])
    frequentResults := frequentWords(quit, wordsMulti[1])   Uses a separate quit
                                                            channel for the rest
    fmt.Println("Longest Words:", <-longestResults)         of the pipeline
    fmt.Println("Most frequent Words:", <-frequentResults)
}
```

Running listing 9.19 results in the word stats being processed only on the first 10,000 words downloaded. Since the downloads are done in parallel, the order of the downloaded pages cannot be predicted and might be different every time the application is run. Thus, the first 10,000 words encountered will vary, depending on which pages get downloaded first. Here's the output of one such run:

```
$ go run wordstatsearlyquit.go
Longest Words: implementations, characteristics, recommendations,
    considerations, implementation, effectiveness, simultaneously,
    specifications, irrecoverable, informational
Most frequent Words: the, to, of, is, a, and, be, for, in, not
```

9.2.7   *Adopting channels as first-class objects*

In his CSP language paper, C.A.R. Hoare uses an example of generating prime numbers up to 10,000 with a list of communicating sequential processes. The algorithm is based on the sieve of Eratosthenes, which is a simple method for checking whether a number is prime. The approach in the CSP paper uses a static linear pipeline where each process in the pipeline filters the multiple of a prime number and then passes it on to the next process. Because the pipeline is static (it doesn't grow with the problem size), it will generate prime numbers only up to a fixed number.

The improvement available in Go over the CSP language that was defined in the original paper is that channels are first-class objects. This means that a channel can be stored as a variable and passed around to other functions. In Go, a channel can also be passed on another channel. This allows us to improve on the original solution by using a dynamic linear pipeline, one that grows with the problem's size and that allows us to generate up to n prime numbers, instead of up to a fixed number.

> **Origins of the prime numbers pipeline algorithm**
>
> Although the solution of using a pipeline to generate prime numbers was mentioned in the CSP paper, the original idea has been attributed to the mathematician and programmer Douglas McIlroy.

Figure 9.13 shows how we can generate prime numbers using a concurrent pipeline. A number, c, is prime if c is not a multiple of all the prime numbers less than c. For example, to check whether 7 is a prime number, we need to ensure that 7 is not divisible by 2, 3, or 5. Since 7 is not divisible by any of these, 7 is a prime number. However, the number 9 is divisible by 3, so 9 is not a prime number.

> **Checking to see whether a number is prime**
>
> To check whether the number c is prime, we only need to check that c is not divisible by all primes less than the square root of c. However, for this section, we're simplifying the requirements to keep the listings simpler and shorter.

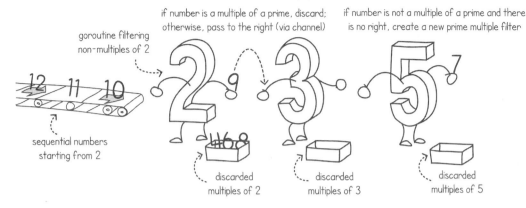

Figure 9.13 Checking to see whether a number is a prime by using a pipeline

For our prime-checking pipeline, we can have a goroutine generate candidate sequential numbers starting from 2. The output of this goroutine will feed into a pipeline that consists of a chain of goroutines, each filtering out the multiples of a prime number. A goroutine in this chain is assigned a prime number, p, and it will discard numbers that are multiples of p. If a number is not discarded, it is passed on to the right side of the chain. If it survives all the way to the end, that means we have a new prime number, and a new goroutine is created with its p equal to the new prime. This process is shown in figure 9.14.

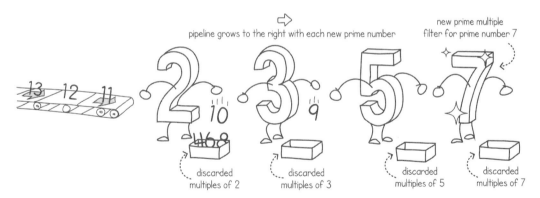

Figure 9.14 When a new prime is found, we start a new goroutine that filters multiples of that new prime.

In our pipeline, when a number passes through all the existing goroutines and is not discarded, that means we have found a new prime number. The last goroutine in the pipeline will then initialize a new goroutine at the tail of the pipeline and connect to it. This new goroutine will become the new tail of the pipeline, and it will filter out the multiples of the newly found prime. In this way, the pipeline grows dynamically with the number of primes.

Having this pipeline grow dynamically with the number of primes shows the advantage of treating channels as first-class objects, compared to the original channel in the CSP paper by C.A.R. Hoare. Go gives us the ability to treat channels like normal variables.

Listing 9.20 implements this prime-filtering goroutine. Upon creation, the goroutine receives its first message on the channel containing the prime number, p, that will be used for the multiple filtering. Then it listens for new numbers on its input channel, and it checks to see whether any number received is a multiple of p. If it is, the goroutine simply discards it; otherwise, it passes the number on to its right channel. If the goroutine happens to be at the tail of the pipeline, it creates a new right channel and passes the channel to a newly created goroutine.

Listing 9.20 The `primeMultipleFilter()` goroutine

```go
package main

import "fmt"

func primeMultipleFilter(numbers <-chan int, quit chan<- int) {
    var right chan int
    p := <-numbers
    fmt.Println(p)
    for n := range numbers {
        if n%p != 0 {
            if right == nil {
                right = make(chan int)
                go primeMultipleFilter(right, quit)
            }
            right <- n
        }
    }
    if right == nil {
        close(quit)
    } else {
        close(right)
    }
}
```

Reads the next number from the input channel

Discards any received number that is a multiple of p

Receives the first message containing the prime number p on the input channel and prints it

If the current goroutine has no right, it starts a new goroutine and connects to it with a channel.

Passes the filtered number to the right channel

Closes the quit channel if there are no more numbers to filter and the goroutine has no right channel

Otherwise, closes right channel

All we need now is to connect our prime multiple filters to a sequential number generator. We can use the main() goroutine for this task. In listing 9.21, our main() function starts our first prime multiple filter goroutine with an input channel and then feeds it sequential numbers from 2 to 100,000. After that, it closes the input channel and waits for the quit channel to close. In this way, we ensure that the last prime number is printed before we terminate the main() goroutine.

Listing 9.21 The `main()` function feeding sequential numbers to the prime filters

```go
func main() {
    numbers := make(chan int)
```

Creates an input channel that will feed the prime multiple filters

Starts
the first
goroutine in
the pipeline,
passing the
numbers and
quit channels

```
quit := make(chan int)                    ←——— Creates a common quit channel
go primeMultipleFilter(numbers, quit)
for i := 2; i < 100000; i++ {             Feeds sequential numbers, starting from
    numbers <- i                          2 up to 100,000, onto the input channel
}
close(numbers)    ←——┤  Closes the input channel, signaling
<-quit    ←————┐         that there will be no more numbers
}
          Waits for the quit channel to close
```

Running listings 9.20 and 9.21 together gives us all the prime numbers less than 100,000:

```
$ go run primesieve.go
2
3
5
7
11
13
. . .
99989
99991
```

9.3 Exercises

NOTE Visit http://github.com/cutajarj/ConcurrentProgrammingWithGo to see all the code solutions.

1 Write a generator goroutine similar to listing 9.2 that, instead of generating URL strings, generates an infinite stream of square numbers $(1, 4, 9, 16, 25 \ldots)$ on an output channel. Here is the signature:

```
func GenerateSquares(quit <-chan int) <-chan int
```

2 In listing 9.18, we developed a take(n) goroutine. Extend the functionality of this goroutine to implement TakeUntil(f), where f is a function returning a Boolean. The goroutine needs to continue consuming and forwarding the messages on its input channel while the return value of f is true. Using generics ensures that we can reuse the TakeUntil(f) function and plug it into many other pipelines. Here's the function signature:

```
func TakeUntil[K any](f func(K) bool,quit chan int,input <-chan K) <-chan K
```

3 Write a goroutine that prints to the console the contents of any message it receives on a channel and then forwards the message to the output channel. Again, use generics so that the function can be reused in many situations:

```
func Print[T any](quit <-chan int, input <-chan T) <-chan T
```

4 Write a goroutine that drains the contents of its input channel without doing anything with them. The goroutine simply reads a message and throws it away:

```
func Drain[T any](quit <-chan int, input <-chan T)
```

5 Connect the components developed in exercises 1 to 4 together in a `main()` function using the following pseudocode:

```
Create quit channel
Drain(quitChannel,
    Print(quitChannel,
        TakeUntil({ s <= 1000000 }, quitChannel,
            GenerateSquares(quitChannel)))))
Wait on quit channel
```

Summary

- Communicating sequential processes (CSP) is a formal language concurrency model that uses message passing through synchronized channels.
- Executions in CSP have their own isolated state and do not share memory with other executions.
- Go borrows core ideas from CSP, with the addition that it treats channels as first-class objects, which means we can pass channels around in function calls and even on other channels.
- A quit channel pattern can be used to notify goroutines to stop their execution.
- Having a common pattern where a goroutine accepts input channels and returns outputs allows us to easily connect various stages of a pipeline.
- A fan-in pattern merges multiple input channels into one. This merged channel is closed only after all input channels are closed.
- A fan-out pattern is where multiple goroutines read from the same channel. In this case, messages on the channel are load-balanced among the goroutines.
- The fan-out pattern makes sense only when the order of the messages is not important.
- With the broadcast pattern, the contents of an input channel are replicated to multiple channels.
- In Go, having channels behave as first-class objects means that we can modify the structure of our message-passing concurrent program dynamically while the program is executing.

Part 3

More concurrency

In this part of the book, we'll look at more advanced concurrency topics: concurrency patterns, deadlocking, atomic variables, and futexes.

We'll start by reviewing some common patterns used to break down problems into multiple parts that can be executed in parallel, and we'll see how some patterns are better suited for different types of problems. We'll also explore patterns such as loop-level parallelism, fork/join, worker pools, and pipelining, and we'll discuss the properties of each.

Deadlocks can be a bad side effect of a concurrent system. Deadlocks happen when we have two or more threads of execution blocking each other in a circular fashion. We'll examine some examples of deadlocks, with both memory sharing and message passing, and discuss various options for avoiding and preventing deadlocks in our programs.

In this book, we've looked at the implementations of various concurrency tools. Here we'll look at the most primitive of our concurrent tools: the mutex. We'll explore how the mutex uses an atomic operation internally, together with an operating system call, to achieve the best results in terms of performance.

Concurrency patterns

When we have a job to do and many helping hands, we need to decide how to divide the work so that it's completed efficiently. A significant task in developing a concurrent solution is identifying mostly independent computations—tasks that do not affect each other if they are executed at the same time. This process of breaking down our programming into separate concurrent tasks is known as *decomposition*.

In this chapter, we shall see techniques and ideas for performing this decomposition. Later, we'll discuss common implementation patterns used in various concurrent scenarios.

10.1 Decomposing programs

How can we convert a program or an algorithm so that it can run more efficiently using concurrent programming? *Decomposition* is the process of subdividing a program into many tasks and recognizing which of these tasks can be executed concurrently. Let's pick a real-life example to see how decomposition works.

Imagine we are in a car, driving along with a group of friends. Suddenly, we hear weird noises coming from the front of the car. We stop to check and find that we have a flat tire. Not wanting to be late, we decide to replace the wheel with the spare instead of waiting for a tow truck. Here are the steps we need to perform:

1 Apply the handbrake.
2 Unload the spare wheel.
3 Loosen the wheel nuts.
4 Jack the car off the ground.
5 Remove the flat tire.
6 Place the spare tire.
7 Tighten the nuts.
8 Lower the car.
9 Stow the bad tire.

Since we are not alone, we can assign some steps to other people so that we can complete the job more quickly. For example, we can have someone unload the spare tire while someone else is loosening the wheel nuts. To decide which steps can be done in parallel with others, we can perform a dependency analysis on the job by drawing a task dependency graph as shown in figure 10.1.

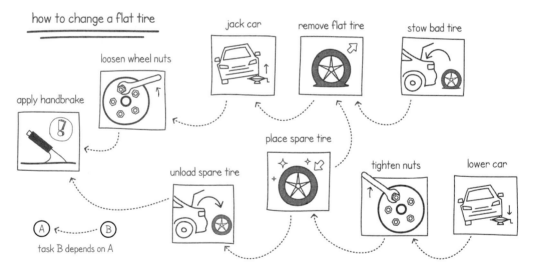

Figure 10.1   Task dependency graph for changing a flat tire

By looking at the task dependency graph, we can make informed decisions about how best to allocate the tasks so we complete the job more efficiently. In this example, we could assign one person to unload the spare tire from the trunk while someone else is loosening the wheel nuts. We could also have another person stowing the bad tire after we remove it while another is placing the spare tire.

Building a task dependency graph is a good start. However, how do we come up with the list of steps that are needed? What if we can come up with a different list of steps that could be performed more efficiently when executed in parallel? To help us break down our programming task and think about the various concurrent tasks, we can consider our programs from two different sides: task and data decomposition. We'll use these two decomposition techniques together and try to apply common concurrency patterns to our problem.

10.1.1 *Task decomposition*

Task decomposition occurs when we think about the various actions in our program that can be performed in parallel. In task decomposition, we ask the question, "What are the different parallel actions we can perform to accomplish the job more quickly?" As an analogy, think about two pilots dividing up the work of landing an airplane and performing various tasks in parallel (see figure 10.2). In our analogy, the pilots have access to the same input data through the aircraft's instruments, but each is performing different tasks to get the aircraft on the ground safely and efficiently.

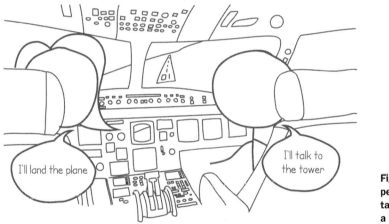

Figure 10.2 Pilots performing separate tasks while landing a plane

In the previous chapter, we saw various ways we could distribute different tasks to different executions, such as when we built a program to find the longest words in a group of web documents. In task decomposition, we need to break down the problem into several tasks, such as

- Downloading the web pages
- Extracting the words
- Finding the longest words

After obtaining this breakdown of tasks, we can start by outlining the dependencies of each. In our program to find the longest words, each task has a dependency on the previous one. For example, we cannot extract the words before we download the web pages.

10.1.2 Data decomposition

We can also break down our program by thinking about how data flows through it. We can, for example, divide the input data and feed it to multiple parallel executions (see figure 10.3). This is known as *data decomposition*, where we ask the question, "How can we organize the data in our program so that we can execute more work in parallel?"

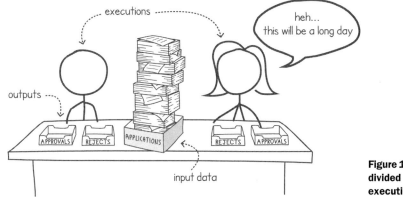

Figure 10.3   Data can be divided between multiple executions.

DEFINITION Data decomposition can be done at various points in our process. *Input data decomposition* occurs when we divide the program's input data and process it through multiple concurrent executions.

In input data decomposition, we divide the program input and feed it to our various executions. For example, in chapter 3, we wrote a concurrent program that downloaded various web documents and counted the letter frequencies. We opted for an input data decomposition design where each input URL was given to a separate goroutine. The goroutine downloaded the document from the input URL and counted the letters on a shared data structure.

DEFINITION In *output data decomposition*, we use the program's output data to distribute the work amongst our executions.

In contrast, our matrix multiplication in chapter 6 was based on output data decomposition. In that example, we had separate goroutines, each responsible for working out the results for one output matrix row (see figure 10.4). For a 3 × 3 matrix, we had goroutine 0 work out the result for row 0, goroutine 1 work out the result for row 1, and so on, for the entire matrix.

NOTE Task and data decomposition are principles that should be applied together when designing a concurrent program. Most concurrent applications apply a mixture of task and data decomposition to achieve an efficient solution.

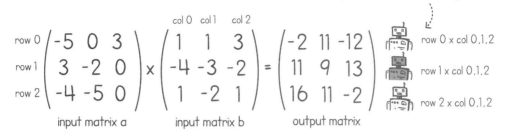

Figure 10.4   Output data decomposition using one output row for each execution

10.1.3 *Thinking about granularity*

How big should our subtasks or data chunks be when we distribute parts of a problem to various concurrent executions? This is what we call *task granularity*. At one end of the granularity spectrum, we have *fine-grained* tasks, in which the problem is broken down into a large number of small tasks. At the other end, when a problem is split into a few large tasks, we say we have *coarse-grained* tasks.

To understand task granularity, we can think of a team of developers working together to deliver an online web shop. We can break down the project delivery into smaller tasks and distribute them amongst the developers. If we make our tasks too coarse, the tasks are few and large. With so few tasks, we might not have enough tasks for everyone. Even if we do have tasks for every developer, if they are too coarse, we might have some developers busy working on their large tasks, with others idling after finishing their smaller tasks quickly. This happens because the amount of work in each task will vary.

If, on the other hand, we break down our project into tasks that are too fine-grained, we will be able to distribute the work to more developers (if they're available). In addition, it's less likely that we'll have an imbalance where some developers will be idle without work while others are busy working on a large task. However, in breaking down the tasks too finely, we create a situation where developers waste a lot of time in meetings talking about who's doing what and when. A lot of effort will be spent coordinating and synchronizing the various tasks, and the overall efficiency will drop.

Somewhere between these two extremes lies an optimal point that will give us the maximum speedup—a task granularity that will enable us to deliver the project in the shortest time. The location of this sweet spot (see figure 10.5) will depend on many factors, such as how many developers we have and how many meetings they will have to attend (time spent on communication). The biggest factor will be the nature of our project, which will dictate how much we can parallelize the tasks since parts of the project will have dependencies on other tasks.

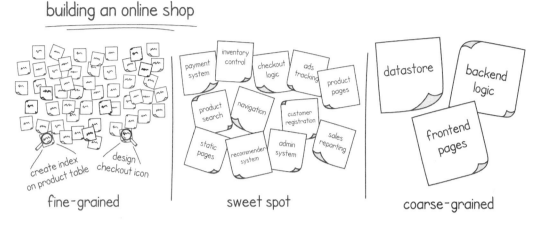

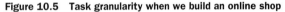

Figure 10.5   Task granularity when we build an online shop

The same principles apply to choosing the right type of task granularity for our algorithms and programs. Task granularity has big effects on the parallel execution performance of our software. Determining the best granularity depends on many factors but is dictated mainly by the problem you're trying to solve. Splitting a problem into many small tasks (fine grained) means that when our program is executing, it will have more parallelism (if extra processors are present) and a bigger speedup. However, increased synchronization and communication due to our tasks being too fine grained will constrain scalability. As we increase the parallelism, we will have a negligible or even a negative effect on speedup.

If we choose coarse granularity, we'll reduce the need for a lot of communication and synchronization between executions. However, having a few large tasks may result in a smaller speedup, and can lead to load imbalances between our executions. Just as in our online shop example, we need to find the right balance that works for our scenario. This can be done by modeling, experimentation, and testing.

> **TIP**   Concurrent solutions that require very little communication and synchronization (due to the nature of the problem being solved) generally allow us to have finer-grained solutions and achieve bigger speedups.

10.2   Concurrency implementation patterns

Once we have decomposed our problem using a mixture of task and data decomposition, we can apply common concurrent patterns for our implementation. Each of these patterns is suitable for specific scenarios, although we can sometimes combine more than one pattern in a single solution.

10.2.1   Loop-level parallelism

When we have a collection of data that we need to perform a task on, we can use concurrency to perform multiple tasks on different parts of the collection at the same time. A serial program might have a loop to perform the task on each item of the collection, one after the other. The loop-level parallelism pattern transforms each iteration task into a concurrent task so it can be performed in parallel.

Suppose we have to come up with a program to compute the hash code for a list of files in a specific directory. In sequential programming, we would come up with a file hashing function (shown in the following listing). Then we'd have our program collect a list of files from the directory and iterate over them. On each iteration, we would call our hash function and print the results.

Listing 10.1 SHA256 file hashing function (error handling omitted for brevity)

```go
package listing10_1

import (
    "crypto/sha256"
    "io"
    "os"
)

func FHash(filepath string) []byte {
    file, _ := os.Open(filepath)      ⟵——— Opens file
    defer file.Close()

    sha := sha256.New()               │ Calculates the hash code using
    io.Copy(sha, file)                │ the crypto sha256 library

    return sha.Sum(nil)    ⟵——— Returns the hash result
}
```

Instead of processing each file in the directory one after the other sequentially, we could use loop-level parallelism and feed each file to a separate goroutine. Listing 10.2 reads all the files from a specified directory and then iterates over every file in a loop. For each iteration, it starts a new goroutine to compute the hash code for the file in that iteration. This listing uses a waitgroup to pause the `main()` goroutine until all the tasks are complete.

Listing 10.2 Using loop-level parallelism to compute file hash codes

```go
package main

import (
    "fmt"
    "github.com/cutajarj/ConcurrentProgrammingWithGo/chapter10/listing10.1"
    "os"
    "path/filepath"
    "sync"
)

func main() {
    dir := os.Args[1]
```

```
files, _ := os.ReadDir(dir)
wg := sync.WaitGroup{}
for _, file := range files {
    if !file.IsDir() {
        wg.Add(1)
        go func(filename string) {
            fPath := filepath.Join(dir, filename)
            hash := listing10_1.FHash(fPath)
            fmt.Printf("%s - %x\n", filename, hash)
            wg.Done()
        }(file.Name())
    }
}
wg.Wait()
}
```

Gets a list of files from the specified directory

Starts a goroutine to compute the hash code for the file in the iteration

Computes and outputs the hash code for the file using the previously developed function

Waits for all the tasks, which are computing the hashes, to be complete

Running the previous listing on a specific directory results in a list of hash codes for the files in the directory:

```
$ go run dirfilehash.go ~/Pictures/
surf.jpg - e3b0c44298fc1c149afbf4c8996fb92427ae41e4649b934ca495991b7852b855
wave.jpg - 89e723f1dbd4c1e1cedb74e9603a4f84df617ba124ffa90b99a8d7d3f90bd535
sand.jpg - dd1b143226f5847dbfbcdc257fe3acd4252e45484732f17bdd110d99a1e451dc
. . .
```

In this example, we can easily use the loop-level parallelism pattern because there is no dependence between the tasks. The result of computing the hash code for one file does not affect the hash code computation for the next file. If we had enough processors, we could execute each iteration on a separate processor. But what if the computation of an iteration depends on a step being computed in a previous iteration?

> **DEFINITION**   *Loop-carried dependence* is when a step in one iteration depends on another step in a different iteration in the same loop.

Let's extend our program to compute a single hash code for an entire directory to illustrate an example of loop-carried dependence. Computing a hash code for the contents of the entire directory will tell us if any file is added, removed, or modified. To keep things simple, we're only going to consider the files in one directory and assume that there are no subdirectories. To achieve this, we can iterate over every file and compute its hash code. In the same iteration, we can combine each hash result into a single hash value. At the end, we'll have a single hash value representing the entire directory.

In listing 10.3, we do this with a sequential main() function. The sequential program shows that each iteration has a dependency on the previous iteration. Step i in the loop requires step i-1 to be complete. The order in which we add the hash codes to our sha256 function matters. If we change this order, we'll produce different results.

Listing 10.3   Computing the hash code of an entire directory (imports omitted)

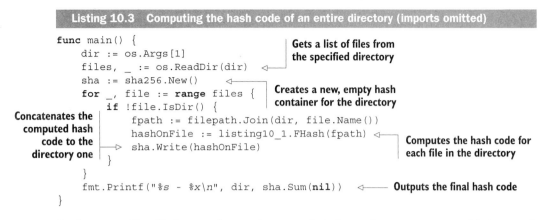

```
func main() {
    dir := os.Args[1]
    files, _ := os.ReadDir(dir)
    sha := sha256.New()
    for _, file := range files {
        if !file.IsDir() {
            fpath := filepath.Join(dir, file.Name())
            hashOnFile := listing10_1.FHash(fpath)
            sha.Write(hashOnFile)
        }
    }
    fmt.Printf("%s - %x\n", dir, sha.Sum(nil))
}
```

Gets a list of files from the specified directory

Creates a new, empty hash container for the directory

Concatenates the computed hash code to the directory one

Computes the hash code for each file in the directory

Outputs the final hash code

In the preceding listing, we have a loop-carried dependence; we must add the previous iteration hash code to the global directory hash before we add the current one. This creates a problem for our concurrent program. We cannot just use the same trick as we did before because now we have to wait for the previous iteration to finish before starting the next one. Instead, we can take advantage of the fact that parts of the instructions inside each iteration are independent and execute those concurrently. We can then use synchronization techniques to compute the carried dependence steps in the correct order.

In our directory hashing application, we can compute the file hash code in parallel because it is independent. In each iteration, we need to wait for the previous iteration to finish and only then add the file hash code to the global directory hash. Figure 10.6

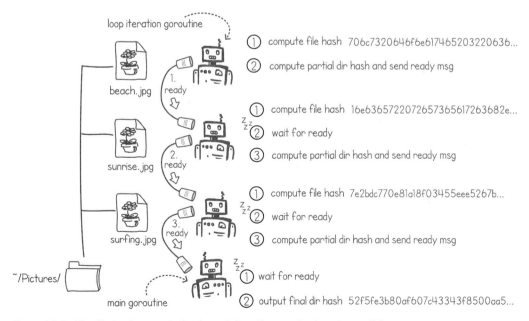

Figure 10.6   The file hash computation in each iteration can be done in parallel.

shows how this can be done. The lengthy part of each iteration—reading the file and computing the file hash code—is completely independent of any other iteration in the same loop. This means that we can execute this part in a goroutine without waiting.

Once the goroutine finishes computing the file hash, it must wait for the previous iteration to finish. In our implementation, we use channels to implement this wait. Each goroutine waits to receive a signal from the previous iteration. Once it has computed the partial directory hash code, it then signals that it is complete by sending a channel message to the next iteration. This is shown in the following listing.

Listing 10.4   Loop-carried dependency in directory hashing (imports omitted)

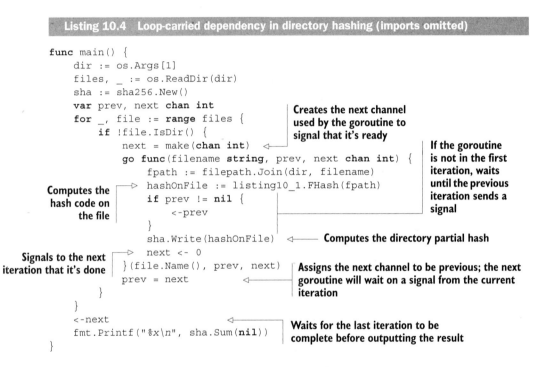

```
func main() {
    dir := os.Args[1]
    files, _ := os.ReadDir(dir)
    sha := sha256.New()
    var prev, next chan int
    for _, file := range files {
        if !file.IsDir() {
            next = make(chan int)         ◁──┐   Creates the next channel
            go func(filename string, prev, next chan int) {      used by the goroutine to
                fpath := filepath.Join(dir, filename)            signal that it's ready
                hashOnFile := listing10_1.FHash(fpath)
                if prev != nil {
                    <-prev
                }
                sha.Write(hashOnFile)     ◁──────  Computes the directory partial hash
                next <- 0
            }(file.Name(), prev, next)
            prev = next
        }
    }
    <-next
    fmt.Printf("%x\n", sha.Sum(nil))
}
```

Creates the next channel used by the goroutine to signal that it's ready

If the goroutine is not in the first iteration, waits until the previous iteration sends a signal

Computes the hash code on the file

Computes the directory partial hash

Signals to the next iteration that it's done

Assigns the next channel to be previous; the next goroutine will wait on a signal from the current iteration

Waits for the last iteration to be complete before outputting the result

> **NOTE** Go's os.ReadDir() function returns entries in the directory order. This is a key requirement for our listing to work properly. If the order was undefined, the hash result might be different each time we ran the program without the directory changing.

The main() goroutine waits for the final iteration to be complete by expecting a ready message on the next channel. It then prints out the result of the directory hash code. In the previous listing, the ready message is just a 0 sent on the channel. Here is the output from listing 10.4:

```
$ go run dirhashsequential.go ~/Pictures/
7200bdf2b90fc5e65da4b2402640986d37c9a40c38fd532dc0f5a21e2a160f6d
```

10.2.2   The fork/join pattern

The fork/join pattern is useful in situations where we need to create a number of executions to perform tasks in parallel, and then we collect and merge the results from these executions. In this pattern, the program spawns one execution per task and then waits until all of these tasks are complete before proceeding. Let's use the fork/join pattern in a program to search for source files that have deeply nested code blocks.

Deeply nested code is hard to read. The following code has a nested depth level of 3 because it opens three nested blocks of code before closing them:

```
if x > 0 {
    if y > 0 {
        if z > 0 {
            //do something
        }
    } else {
        //do something else
    }
}
```

We want to write a program that recursively scans through a directory and finds the source file that has the deepest nested block. Listing 10.5 shows a function that, when given a filename, reads the file and returns the nested code depth for that source file. It does this by increasing a counter every time it finds an open curly bracket and reducing it when it finds a closed one. The function keeps track of the highest value found and returns it with the filename.

Listing 10.5   Finding the deepest nested code block (imports and error handling omitted)

```
package main

import (...)

type CodeDepth struct {file  string; level int}

func deepestNestedBlock(filename string) CodeDepth {          Reads the full file into
    code, _ := os.ReadFile(filename)              ←————————   a memory buffer
    max := 0
    level := 0
    for _, c := range code {          When the character is an          Records
        if c == '{' {                 opening curly bracket,            the maximum
            level += 1      ←————      increments level by 1            value of level
            max = int(math.Max(float64(max), float64(level)))  ←————    variable
        } else if c == '}' {
            level -= 1      ←————
        }                         When the curly brackets are
    }                             closed, decrements level by 1
    return CodeDepth{filename, max}   ←————
}                                          Returns the result with the filename
```

Iterates over every single character in the file

We now need logic to run this function on all the source files found recursively in a directory. In a sequential program, we would simply call this function on all the files, one after the other, and keep track of the code depth with the maximum value. Figure 10.7 shows how we can employ the fork/join pattern to solve this problem concurrently. In the fork part, the `main()` goroutine spawns a number of goroutines that execute the `deepestNestedBlock()` function, and it then outputs the result on a common channel.

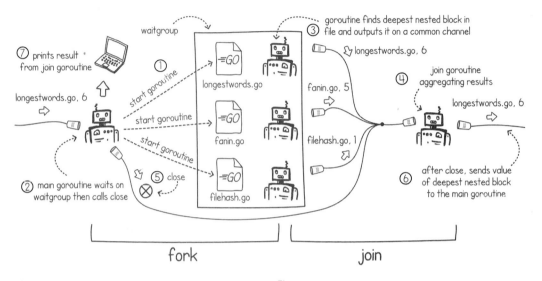

Figure 10.7   Using the fork/join pattern to scan source files

The join part of the pattern is when we consume the common output channel and wait for all the goroutines to be complete. In this example, we implement this part with a separate join goroutine that collects the results and keeps track of the deepest nested block. When it's complete, this goroutine sends the result to the `main()` goroutine to output on the console.

In our implementation, the `main()` goroutine waits on a waitgroup until all the forked goroutines are complete. When the waitgroup is done (meaning the forked goroutines are finished), it closes the common output channel. When the join goroutine notices that the common channel has been closed, it sends the result, containing the filename with the deepest nested block, on another channel to `main()`. The `main()` goroutine simply waits for this result and prints it on the console.

Listing 10.6 implements the fork section of this pattern. It verifies that the given path is not a directory, adds one to the waitgroup, and starts a goroutine executing the `deepestNestedBlock()` function on the filename. In this listing, we don't handle directories, as we call this function from `filepath.Walk()` later in our `main()` function. The return value of `deepestNestedBlock()` is sent on the common result channel. Once the function completes, it calls `Done()` on the waitgroup.

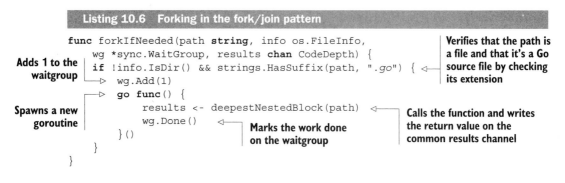

Listing 10.6 Forking in the fork/join pattern

```go
func forkIfNeeded(path string, info os.FileInfo,
        wg *sync.WaitGroup, results chan CodeDepth) {
    if !info.IsDir() && strings.HasSuffix(path, ".go") {
        wg.Add(1)
        go func() {
            results <- deepestNestedBlock(path)
            wg.Done()
        }()
    }
}
```

- **Adds 1 to the waitgroup** → `wg.Add(1)`
- **Spawns a new goroutine** → `go func() {`
- **Marks the work done on the waitgroup** → `wg.Done()`
- **Verifies that the path is a file and that it's a Go source file by checking its extension** → `if !info.IsDir() && strings.HasSuffix(path, ".go") {`
- **Calls the function and writes the return value on the common results channel** → `results <- deepestNestedBlock(path)`

For the joining part of the fork/join pattern, we need a goroutine that collects the results from the common output channel, shown in listing 10.7. The `joinResults()` goroutine consumes from this common channel and records the maximum value of the deepest nested block from the received results. Once the common channel closes, it writes the result to the main channel, `finalResult`.

Listing 10.7 Joining results onto a final result channel

```go
func joinResults(partialResults chan CodeDepth) chan CodeDepth {
    finalResult := make(chan CodeDepth)
    max := CodeDepth{"", 0}
    go func() {
        for pr := range partialResults {
            if pr.level > max.level {
                max = pr
            }
        }
        finalResult <- max
    }()
    return finalResult
}
```

- **Creates a channel that will contain the final result** → `finalResult := make(chan CodeDepth)`
- **Receives results from the channel until it's closed** → `for pr := range partialResults {`
- **Records the value of the deepest nested block** → `max = pr`
- **After the channel is closed, writes result on the the output channel** → `finalResult <- max`

In listing 10.8, our `main()` function wires everything together. We start by creating the common channel and the waitgroup. Then we walk recursively through all the files in the directory specified in the arguments, and we fork a goroutine for each source file encountered. In the end, we join everything by starting the goroutine to collect the results, and we wait on the waitgroup for the forked goroutines to be complete, closing the common channel and then finally reading the result from the `finalResult` channel.

Listing 10.8 `main()` function forking and then outputting the result

```go
func main() {
    dir := os.Args[1]
    partialResults := make(chan CodeDepth)
    wg := sync.WaitGroup{}
```

- **Reads root directory from arguments** → `dir := os.Args[1]`
- **Creates common channel used by all forked goroutines** → `partialResults := make(chan CodeDepth)`

```
        filepath.Walk(dir,
              func(path string, info os.FileInfo, err error) error {
                  forkIfNeeded(path, info, &wg, partialResults)
                  return nil
              })

        finalResult := joinResults(partialResults)

        wg.Wait()

        close(partialResults)

        result := <-finalResult
        fmt.Printf("%s has the deepest nested code block of %d\n",
            result.file, result.level)
}
```

Waits for all the forked goroutines to complete their work

Walks the root directory, and for every file, calls the fork function, creating goroutines

Calls the join function and gets the channel that will contain the final result

Closes the common channel, signaling the join goroutine that the work is complete

Receives the final result and outputs it on the console

NOTE Unlike the previous directory hashing scenario, this example does not rely on the order of the partial results to compute the complete result. Not having this requirement allows us to easily adopt the fork/join pattern, where we can aggregate the results in the join part.

When we put all the listings together, we can use it to scan our top source directory to find out which file has the deepest code block. Here's the output:

```
$ go run deepestnestedfile.go ~/projects/ConcurrentProgrammingWithGo/
~/projects/ConcurrentProgrammingWithGo/chapter9/listing9.12_13/longestwords.g
    o has the deepest nested code block of 6
```

10.2.3 *Using worker pools*

In some cases, we don't know how much work we are going to get. It can be difficult to decompose our algorithms and make them work concurrently if the workload will vary depending on the demand. For example, we might have an HTTP server that handles a varying number of requests per second depending on how many users are accessing a website.

In real life, the solution is to have a number of workers and a queue of work. Imagine a bank branch with several tellers serving a single queue of customers. In concurrent programming, the worker pool pattern copies this real-life queue and workers model in programming.

> **Different names for the same pattern**
> The worker pool pattern and slight variations of it are known under many different names, such as the thread pool pattern, replicated workers, master/worker, or worker-crew model.

In the worker pool pattern, we have a fixed number of goroutines created and ready to accept work. In this pattern, the goroutines are either idle, waiting for a task, or they're busy executing one. The work gets passed to the worker pool through a common work queue. When all the workers are busy, the work queue increases in size. If the work queue fills to its full capacity, we can stop accepting more work. In some worker pool implementations, the worker pool can also be increased in size by increasing the number of goroutines, up to a limit, to handle the extra load.

To see this concurrency pattern in action, let's implement a very simple HTTP web server that serves static files as web resources. The worker pool pattern in our HTTP server can be seen in figure 10.8. In our design, several goroutines take part in the worker pool, waiting for work to arrive in the work queue. We implement the work queue with a Go channel. When all the worker goroutines are reading from the same channel, this has the effect of load-balancing the items on the channel to all the workers.

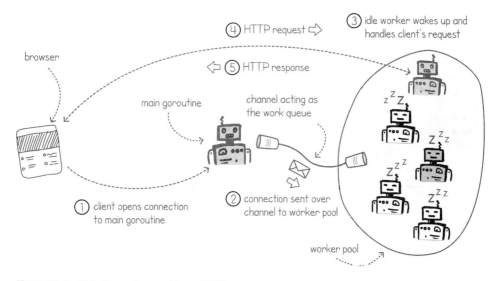

Figure 10.8   Using a worker pool in an HTTP server

In our HTTP web server, we have our `main()` goroutine accepting socket connections from clients. Once a connection is open, the `main()` goroutine passes it to any idle worker by putting the connection on the channel. The idle worker handles the HTTP requests and replies with the appropriate response. Once the response is sent, the worker goroutine goes back to wait for the next connection by waiting on the channel.

Listing 10.9 shows the minimal HTTP protocol handling. In the listing, we read the request from the connection (using regex), load the requested file from the resources directory, and return the contents of the file as a response with the appropriate headers. If the file does not exist or the request is invalid, the function responds with a suitable HTTP error. This is the logic that every goroutine in the worker pool will execute upon receiving a connection from the `main()` goroutine on the channel.

Listing 10.9 A simple HTTP response handler

```
package listing10_9

import (
    "fmt"
    "net"
    "os"
    "regexp"
)

var r, _ = regexp.Compile("GET (.+) HTTP/1.1\r\n")

func handleHttpRequest(conn net.Conn) {          Creates buffer to store HTTP request
    buff := make([]byte, 1024)          ◄───────
    size, _ := conn.Read(buff)
    if r.Match(buff[:size]) {                If the request is a valid one, reads the
        file, err := os.ReadFile(            request file from the resources directory
            fmt.Sprintf("../resources/%s", r.FindSubmatch(buff[:size])[1]))
        if err == nil {
            conn.Write([]byte(fmt.Sprintf(
                "HTTP/1.1 200 OK\r\nContent-Length: %d\r\n\r\n",len(file))))
            conn.Write(file)
        } else {
            conn.Write([]byte(                If the file does not exist, responds with an error
                "HTTP/1.1 404 Not Found\r\n\r\n<html>Not Found</html>"))
        }
    } else {          ◄────────   If the HTTP request is not valid, responds with an error
        conn.Write([]byte("HTTP/1.1 500 Internal Server Error\r\n\r\n"))
    }
    conn.Close()   ◄───── Closes the connection after handling the request
}
```

Annotations: **Reads from the connection into the buffer** points to `size, _ := conn.Read(buff)`. **If the file exists, responds to the client with the HTTP header and file contents** points to `if err == nil {`.

The following listing initializes all the goroutines in the worker pool. The function simply starts n goroutines, each reading from the input channel containing the client connections. When a new connection is received on the channel, the `handleHttpRequest()` function is called to handle the client's request.

Listing 10.10 Starting up the worker pool

```
func StartHttpWorkers(n int, incomingConnections <-chan net.Conn) {
    for i := 0; i < n; i++ {          Starts n goroutines          Consumes connections from
        go func() {                                                the work queue channel until
            for c := range incomingConnections {  ◄────────────   the channel is closed
                handleHttpRequest(c)   ◄─────
            }
        }()
    }                                     Handles the HTTP request
}                                         from the received connection
```

Next, we need the `main()` goroutine to listen for new connections on a port and pass on any newly established connection on the work queue channel. In listing 10.11, the `main()` function creates the work queue channel, starts up the worker pool, and then binds a TCP listen connection on port 8080. In an infinite loop, when a new connection is established, the `Accept()` function unblocks and returns the connection. This connection is then passed on the channel to be used by one of the goroutines in the worker pool.

> **Listing 10.11** `main()` function passing work to the worker pool (error handling omitted)

```
package main

import (
    "github.com/cutajarj/ConcurrentProgrammingWithGo/chapter10/listing10.9"
    "net"
)

func main() {
    incomingConnections := make(chan net.Conn)        ← Creates a work
                                                          queue channel
    listing10_9.StartHttpWorkers(3, incomingConnections)  ← Starts the worker
                                                             pool with three
    server, _ := net.Listen("tcp", "localhost:8080")  ←  goroutines
    defer server.Close()
    for {                                                  Binds the TCP listening
        conn, _ := server.Accept()  ←                     connection to port 8080
        incomingConnections <- conn
    }                               Blocks until there is a new
}                                   connection from a client
}
```

Passes the connection on the work queue channel

We can test the previous listings either by pointing a browser to http://localhost:8080/index.html or by using the following `curl` command:

```
$ go run httpserver.go &
. . .
$ curl localhost:8080/index.html
<!DOCTYPE html>
<html>
<head>
    <title>Learn Concurrent Programming with Go</title>
</head>
<body><h1>Learn Concurrent Programming with Go</h1><img src="cover.png"></body>
```

NOTE The worker pool pattern is especially useful when creating new threads of execution is expensive. Instead of creating threads on the fly when we have new work, this pattern creates the worker pool before processing begins, and the workers are reused. This way, less time is wasted when we need new work to be done. In Go, creating goroutines is a very fast process, so this pattern doesn't bring much benefit in terms of performance.

Even though worker pools do not offer much performance benefit in Go, they can still be used to limit the amount of concurrency so that programs and servers don't run out of resources. In our HTTP server, we can opt to stop handling client connections when the entire worker pool is busy, as shown in figure 10.9. We can use the channel in a non-blocking manner so that the `main()` goroutine returns a "server busy" error to the client.

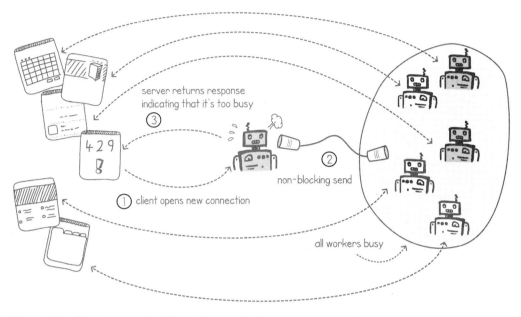

Figure 10.9   Server detects that it's too busy and returns an error message

Listing 10.12 implements this non-blocking behavior on the work queue channel. In this listing, we use a `select` statement that triggers the default case when there are no free worker pool goroutines. The logic in the default case returns a "busy" error message to the client.

Listing 10.12   Using `select`'s default case to limit the load on the server

```go
package main

import (
    "fmt"
    "github.com/cutajarj/ConcurrentProgrammingWithGo/chapter10/listing10.9"
    "net"
)

func main() {
    incomingConnections := make(chan net.Conn)
    listing10_9.StartHttpWorkers(3, incomingConnections)
    server, _ := net.Listen("tcp", "localhost:8080")
    defer server.Close()
    for {
        conn, _ := server.Accept()
```

```
select {
case incomingConnections <- conn:
default:
    fmt.Println("Server is busy")
    conn.Write([]byte("HTTP/1.1 429 Too Many Requests\r\n\r\n" +
        "<html>Busy</html>\n")
    conn.Close()
}
    }
}
```

When no goroutines are consuming from the work queue, the default case triggers.

Returns "busy" message to client

Closes client connection

We can trigger this "busy" error message when we open many simultaneous connections. Our worker pool is very small, with only three goroutines, so it's quite easy to get the entire pool busy. Using the following command, we can see that the server returns this error message. In this command, the `xargs` with `-P100` option executes `curl` requests in parallel, with 100 processes:

```
$ seq 1 2000 | xargs -Iname  -P100  curl -s
    "http://localhost:8080/index.html" | grep Busy
</html><html>Busy</html>
</html><html>Busy</html>
</html><html>Busy</html>
. . .
```

10.2.4 Pipelining

What if the only way to decompose our problem is to have a set of tasks where each task completely depends on the previous one being complete? For example, consider a scenario in which we are running a cupcake factory. Baking cupcakes in our factory involves the following steps:

1 Prepare the baking tray.
2 Pour the cupcake mixture.
3 Bake the mixture in the oven.
4 Add toppings.
5 Pack the cupcakes in a box for delivery.

If we wanted to speed things up, simply hiring staff and asking them to pick up any task that needs doing would not be a very effective strategy in terms of efficiency, because each step, apart from the first one, depends on the previous one. When we have this heavy task dependency, applying a pipeline pattern will allow us to do more work in the same amount of time.

The pipeline pattern is used in many manufacturing industries. One common example is a modern car assembly line. The frame of a car moves along the line, and at each stage, a different robot performs a different action (such as attaching a part) on the car being built.

We can use the same principle in our example. We can have people working in parallel on different cupcakes batches. Each person is working on a different one of the previously outlined steps, and the output of one step feeds into the input of the next (see figure 10.10). In this way, we can utilize the full workforce and increase the number of cupcakes we can produce in a given time.

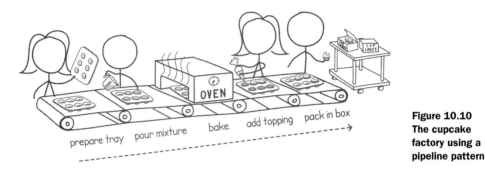

Figure 10.10
The cupcake factory using a pipeline pattern

There are technical problems where we can only decompose tasks in this manner. For example, consider a sound processing application in which multiple filters, such as noise reduction, high cut, bandpass, etc., need to be applied to a sound stream on top of each other. There are similar examples that apply to video and image processing. In the previous chapter, we built an application using a pipeline pattern that downloaded documents from web pages, extracted words, and then counted word frequencies.

Let's stay with our cupcake example and try to implement a program that simulates this. We can then use this program to examine the various properties of a typical pipeline. In the following listing, the steps that we outlined in figure 10.10 are in separate functions. In each function, we are simulating work by sleeping for 2 seconds, except for the `Bake()` function, where we sleep for 5 seconds.

Listing 10.13 Steps for making cupcakes

```
package listing10_13

import (
    "fmt"
    "time"
)

const (
    ovenTime          = 5
    everyThingElseTime = 2
)


func PrepareTray(trayNumber int) string {
    fmt.Println("Preparing empty tray", trayNumber)
    time.Sleep(everyThingElseTime * time.Second)     ◁
    return fmt.Sprintf("tray number %d", trayNumber)  ◁
}
```

Every step, except the bake step, sleeps for 2 seconds to simulate work.

Each function returns a description of what was done.

```go
func Mixture(tray string) string {
    fmt.Println("Pouring cupcake Mixture in", tray)
    time.Sleep(everyThingElseTime * time.Second)
    return fmt.Sprintf("cupcake in %s", tray)
}

func Bake(mixture string) string {
    fmt.Println("Baking", mixture)
    time.Sleep(ovenTime * time.Second)
    return fmt.Sprintf("baked %s", mixture)
}

func AddToppings(bakedCupCake string) string {
    fmt.Println("Adding topping to", bakedCupCake)
    time.Sleep(everyThingElseTime * time.Second)
    return fmt.Sprintf("topping on %s", bakedCupCake)
}

func Box(finishedCupCake string) string {
    fmt.Println("Boxing", finishedCupCake)
    time.Sleep(everyThingElseTime * time.Second)
    return fmt.Sprintf("%s boxed", finishedCupCake)
}
```

The oven step sleeps for 5 seconds instead of 2.

To compare the speedup of parallel vs. sequential execution, let's first execute all the steps, one after the other, by using the sequential program outlined in the following listing. Here we are simulating one person producing 10 boxes of cupcakes by performing one step after the other.

> **Listing 10.14   `main()` function producing 10 boxes of cupcakes sequentially**

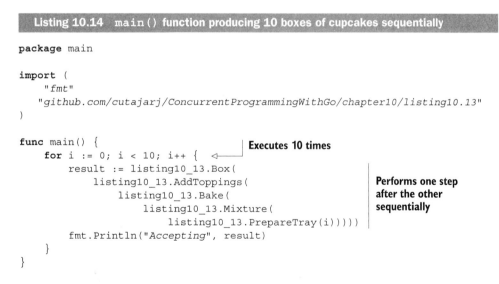

```go
package main

import (
    "fmt"
    "github.com/cutajarj/ConcurrentProgrammingWithGo/chapter10/listing10.13"
)

func main() {
    for i := 0; i < 10; i++ {
        result := listing10_13.Box(
            listing10_13.AddToppings(
                listing10_13.Bake(
                    listing10_13.Mixture(
                        listing10_13.PrepareTray(i)))))
        fmt.Println("Accepting", result)
    }
}
```

Executes 10 times

Performs one step after the other sequentially

When performing one step after the other, sequentially, finishing a box of cupcakes takes us about 13 seconds. In our program, finishing 10 boxes takes around 130 seconds, as shown in the output when we execute the previous two listings together:

```
$ time go run cupcakeoneman.go
Preparing empty tray 0
Pouring cupcake Mixture in tray number 0
Baking cupcake in tray number 0
Adding topping to baked cupcake in tray number 0
Boxing topping on baked cupcake in tray number 0
Accepting topping on baked cupcake in tray number 0 boxed
Preparing empty tray 1
. . .
Boxing topping on baked cupcake in tray number 9
Accepting topping on baked cupcake in tray number 9 boxed

real    2m10.979s
user    0m0.127s
sys     0m0.152s
```

Let's now convert our program to run with multiple executions in a pipeline fashion. The steps in a simple pipeline all follow the same pattern: accept input from an input channel of type X, process X, and produce the result Y on an output channel of type Y. Figure 10.11 shows how we can build a reusable component that creates a goroutine reading from an input channel consuming type X, calls a function that maps X to Y, and outputs Y on an output channel.

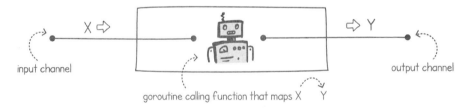

Figure 10.11   Pipeline step accepts X, calls a function to map to Y, and outputs Y

In listing 10.15, we implement this. In the signature, we accept both input and output channels and a mapping function f. The AddOnPipe() function creates an output channel and starts up a goroutine that calls the mapping function in an infinite loop. In the implementation, we use the usual quit channel pattern where we stop if the quit channel (the parameter named q in the listing) is closed. We make use of Go's generics so that the types from the channels and the mapping function match.

Listing 10.15   A reusable pipeline node

```
package main

import (
    "fmt"
    "github.com/cutajarj/ConcurrentProgrammingWithGo/chapter10/listing10.13"
)
```

```
func AddOnPipe[X, Y any](q <-chan int, f func(X) Y, in <-chan X) chan Y {
    output := make(chan Y)
    go func() {
        defer close(output)
        for {
            select {
            case <-q:
                return
            case input := <-in:
                output <- f(input)
            }
        }
    }()
    return output
}
```

Creates an output channel of type Y

Starts the goroutine

Calls select in an infinite loop

When the quit channel is closed, exits the loop and terminates the goroutine

Receives a message on the input channel if one is available

Calls the function f and outputs the function's return value on the output channel

We can now add all the steps of our cupcake factory on a common pipeline, using the function in listing 10.15. In the following listing, we have a `main()` function that wraps each step using the `AddOnPipe()` function. It then starts a goroutine that feeds 10 messages into the `PrepareTray()` step. This has the effect of running our pipeline 10 times.

Listing 10.16 Wiring and starting our cupcake pipeline

```
func main() {
    input := make(chan int)
    quit := make(chan int)
    output := AddOnPipe(listing10_1.Box, quit,
        AddOnPipe(quit, listing10_1.AddToppings,
            AddOnPipe(quit, listing10_1.Bake,
                AddOnPipe(quit, listing10_1.Mixture,
                    AddOnPipe(quit, listing10_1.PrepareTray, input)))))
    go func() {
        for i := 0; i < 10; i++ {
            input <- 1
        }
    }()
    for i := 0; i < 10; i++ {
        fmt.Println(<-output, "received")
    }
}
```

Creates the first input channel to be used to connect to the first step

Creates the quit channel

Wires each step on the pipeline, feeding the output of each step to the input of the next one

Creates a goroutine that sends 10 integers onto the pipeline to produce 10 cupcake boxes

Reads 10 cupcake boxes as output from the last pipeline step

At the end of our `main()` function, we wait for 10 messages to arrive and print out the message on the console. Here's the output when we run the previous listing:

```
$ time go run cupcakefactory.go
Preparing empty tray 0
Preparing empty tray 1
Pouring cupcake Mixture in tray number 0
Pouring cupcake Mixture in tray number 1
Preparing empty tray 2
Baking cupcake in tray number 0
Baking cupcake in tray number 1
```

```
Pouring cupcake Mixture in tray number 2
Preparing empty tray 3
Adding topping to baked cupcake in tray number 0
. . .
Boxing topping on baked cupcake in tray number 8
topping on baked cupcake in tray number 8 boxed received
Adding topping to baked cupcake in tray number 9
Boxing topping on baked cupcake in tray number 9
topping on baked cupcake in tray number 9 boxed received

real    0m58.780s
user    0m0.106s
sys     0m0.289s
```

Using the pipelining version of our algorithm resulted in a faster execution of around 58 seconds instead of 130. Can we improve it even further by speeding up the time it takes to complete some of the steps? Let's experiment with the timings, and along the way, we'll discover some properties of the pipeline pattern.

10.2.5 *Pipelining properties*

What would happen if we sped up all our manual steps (excluding the baking time)? In our program, we can reduce the constant everyThingElseTime (from listing 10.1) to a smaller value. In this way, all the steps, excluding the baking time, will run faster. Here's the output when we set everyThingElseTime = 1:

```
$ time go run cupcakefactory.go
Preparing empty tray 0
. . .
topping on baked cupcake in tray number 9 boxed received

real    0m55.579s
user    0m0.117s
sys     0m0.242s
```

What is going on here? We have doubled the speed of almost every step, but the total time to produce 10 boxes has stayed almost the same. To understand what is going on, have a look at figure 10.12.

> **NOTE** In a pipeline, the *throughput rate* is dictated by the slowest step. The *latency* of the system is the sum of the time it takes to perform every step along the way.

If our pipeline were real, four people would be working twice as fast but making hardly any difference in terms of throughput. This is because the bottleneck in our pipeline is the baking time. Our slowest step is limited by the fact that we have a slow oven, and it is slowing everything down. To increase the number of cupcakes created per unit of time, we should focus on speeding up our slowest step.

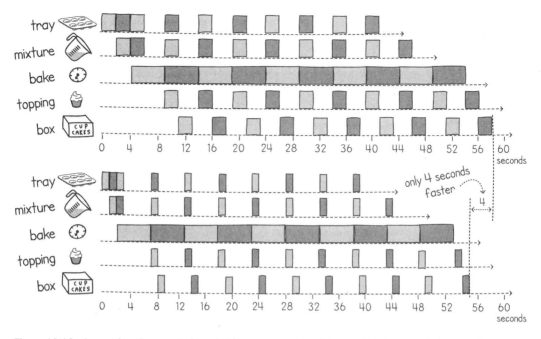

Figure 10.12 **Increasing the speed of non-baking parts does not increase the throughput significantly.**

TIP To increase the throughput of a system, it's always best to focus on the bottleneck of that system. This is the part that is having the greatest effect on slowing down our performance.

Speeding up most of the steps has made a difference in how much time it takes to produce a single box of cupcakes from start to finish. In the first run, it took us 13 seconds to produce one box. When we set everyThingElseTime = 1, this went down to 9 seconds. We can think of this as the system latency. For some applications (such as backend batch processing), it's more important to have high throughput, while for other applications (such as real-time systems), it's better to improve latency.

TIP To reduce the latency of a pipeline system, we need to improve the speed of most steps in the pipeline.

Let's experiment further with our pipeline by improving the baking step and making it faster. In real life, we could get a more powerful oven or perhaps have multiple ovens that can work in parallel. In our program, we can simply set the variable ovenTime = 2 instead of 5 and set everyThingElseTime back to 2. When we run the program again, we get the following output:

```
$ time go run cupcakefactory.go
Preparing empty tray 0
. . .
topping on baked cupcake in tray number 9 boxed received
```

```
real    0m30.197s
user    0m0.094s
sys     0m0.135s
```

We have greatly improved the time it takes to produce 10 boxes of cupcakes. The reason for this speedup is clear in figure 10.13. We can see that we're now more efficient with time. Every goroutine is constantly busy without any idle time. This means we have improved throughput—the number of cupcakes produced per unit of time.

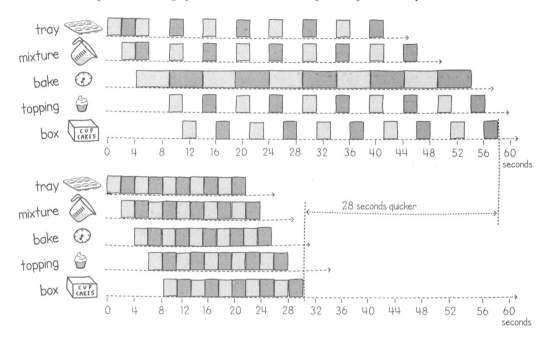

Figure 10.13 Speeding up our slowest step has bigger effects on throughput.

It's worth noting that although we have increased throughput, the time it takes to produce a box of cupcakes (the system latency) has not been greatly affected. It now takes 10 seconds to produce a box from start to finish instead of 13 seconds.

10.3 *Exercises*

NOTE Visit http://github.com/cutajarj/ConcurrentProgrammingWithGo to see all the code solutions.

1 Implement the same directory hashing that we did in listing 10.4, but instead of using channels to synchronize between iterations, try using waitgroups.

2 Change listing 10.2 so that the work queue channel between the `main()` goroutine and the worker pool has a buffer of 10 messages. Doing so will give you a

capacity buffer so that when all the goroutines are busy, some of the requests are queued before they can be picked up.

3 The following listing downloads 30 web pages and counts the total number of lines on all the documents sequentially. Convert this program to use concurrent programming, using a concurrency pattern explained in this chapter.

Listing 10.17 Line count for web pages

```go
package main

import (
    "fmt"
    "io"
    "net/http"
    "strings"
)

func main() {
    const pagesToDownload = 30
    totalLines := 0
    for i := 1000; i < 1000 + pagesToDownload; i++ {
        url := fmt.Sprintf("https://rfc-editor.org/rfc/rfc%d.txt", i)
        fmt.Println("Downloading", url)
        resp, _ := http.Get(url)
        if resp.StatusCode != 200 {
            panic("Server's error: " + resp.Status)
        }
        bodyBytes, _ := io.ReadAll(resp.Body)
        totalLines += strings.Count(string(bodyBytes), "\n")
        resp.Body.Close()
    }
    fmt.Println("Total lines:", totalLines)
}
```

Summary

- Decomposition is the process of breaking a program into different parts and figuring out which parts can be executed concurrently.
- Building dependency graphs helps us understand which tasks can be performed in parallel with others.
- Task decomposition is about breaking down a problem into the different actions needed to complete the entire job.
- Data decomposition is partitioning data in a way so that tasks on the data can be performed concurrently.
- Choosing fine granularity when breaking down programs means more parallelism at the cost of limiting scalability due to time spent on synchronization and communication.
- Choosing coarse granularity means less parallelism, but it reduces the amount of synchronization and communication required.

- Loop-level parallelism can be used to perform a list of tasks concurrently if there is no dependency on the tasks.
- In loop-level parallelism, splitting the problem into parallel and synchronized parts allows for a dependency on a previous task iteration.
- Fork/join is a concurrency pattern that can be used when we have a problem with an initial parallel part and a final step that merges the various results.
- A worker pool is useful when the concurrency needs to scale on demand.
- Pre-creating executions in a worker pool is faster than creating them on the fly for most languages.
- In Go, the performance of pre-creating a worker pool versus creating goroutines on the fly is minimal due to the lightweight nature of goroutines.
- Worker pools can be used to limit concurrency so as not to overload servers when there is an unexpected increase in demand.
- Pipelines are useful to increase throughput when each task depends on the previous one to be complete.
- Increasing the speed of the slowest node in a pipeline results in an increase in the throughput performance of the entire pipeline.
- Increasing the speed of any node in a pipeline results in a reduction in the pipeline's latency.

Avoiding deadlocks

This chapter covers
- Identifying deadlocks
- Avoiding deadlocks
- Deadlocking with channels

A *deadlock*, in a concurrent program, occurs when executions block indefinitely, waiting for each other to release resources. Deadlocks are an undesirable side effect of certain concurrent programs where concurrent executions are trying to acquire exclusive access to multiple resources at the same time. In this chapter, we will analyze the conditions under which deadlocks might occur and offer strategies to prevent them. We'll also discuss certain deadlocking conditions that can occur when using Go channels.

Deadlocks can be quite tricky to identify and debug. As with race conditions, we can have a program that runs without hitches for a long time, and then suddenly the execution halts, for no obvious reason. Understanding the reasons why deadlocks happen allows us to make programming decisions to avoid them.

11.1 Identifying deadlocks

What is the simplest concurrent program we can write that creates all the conditions for a deadlock to occur? We can create a simple program with just two goroutines competing for two exclusive resources, as shown in figure 11.1. The two

245

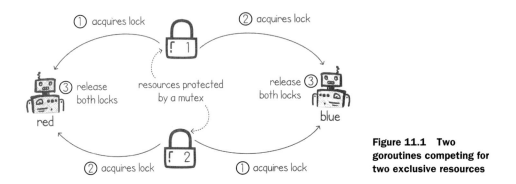

Figure 11.1 Two goroutines competing for two exclusive resources

goroutines, called `red()` and `blue()`, each try to hold two mutex locks at the same time. Since the locks are exclusive, the only time one goroutine can acquire both locks is when the other goroutine is not holding any of them.

Listing 11.1 shows a simple implementation of the `red()` and `blue()` goroutines. The two functions accept our two mutexes, and when we run the functions as separate goroutines, they will try to acquire both locks at the same time before releasing them. This process repeats in an infinite loop. In the listing, there are multiple messages to indicate when we are acquiring, holding, and releasing the locks.

Listing 11.1 `red()` and `blue()` goroutines (imports omitted for brevity)

```go
func red(lock1, lock2 *sync.Mutex) {
    for {
        fmt.Println("Red: Acquiring lock1")
        lock1.Lock()                              // Acquires and
        fmt.Println("Red: Acquiring lock2")       // holds both locks
        lock2.Lock()
        fmt.Println("Red: Both locks Acquired")
        lock1.Unlock(); lock2.Unlock()     // ◁── Releases both locks
        fmt.Println("Red: Locks Released")
    }
}

func blue(lock1, lock2 *sync.Mutex) {
    for {
        fmt.Println("Blue: Acquiring lock2")
        lock2.Lock()                              // Acquires and
        fmt.Println("Blue: Acquiring lock1")      // holds both locks
        lock1.Lock()
        fmt.Println("Blue: Both locks Acquired")
        lock1.Unlock(); lock2.Unlock()     // ◁── Releases both locks
        fmt.Println("Blue: Locks Released")
    }
}
```

We can now create our two mutexes and start up the `red()` and `blue()` goroutines in the `main()` function, as shown in listing 11.2. After starting up the goroutines, the main() function sleeps for 20 seconds, during which we expect the red() and blue() goroutines to continuously output the console messages. After 20 seconds, the main() goroutine terminates, and the program exits.

Listing 11.2 main() **function starting up** red() **and** blue() **goroutines**

```
func main() {
    lockA := sync.Mutex{}
    lockB := sync.Mutex{}
    go red(&lockA, &lockB)      ◁──────  Starts red() goroutine
    go blue(&lockA, &lockB)     ◁──────  Starts blue() goroutine
    time.Sleep(20 * time.Second) ◁──┐
    fmt.Println("Done")             │  Allows the red() and blue()
}                                      goroutines to run for 20 seconds
```

The following is an example of output from running listings 11.1 and 11.2:

```
$ go run simpledeadlock.go
. . .
Blue: Locks Released
Blue: Acquiring lock2
Red: Acquiring lock1
Red: Acquiring lock2
Blue: Acquiring lock1
```

After a while, the program stops outputting messages, and it appears to be stuck prior to the end of the 20-second sleep period. At this point, our red() and blue() goroutines are stuck in a deadlock, unable to proceed. After about 20 seconds have elapsed, the main() goroutine finishes and the program quits. To understand what is going on and how the deadlock has occurred, we'll look at a resource allocation graph in the following section.

> **NOTE** Due to the non-deterministic nature of concurrent executions, running listings 11.1 and 11.2 will not always result in a deadlock. We can further increase the chances of a deadlock by adding Sleep() calls in our red() and blue() goroutines between the first and second mutex.Lock() calls.

11.1.1 Picturing deadlocks with resource allocation graphs

A *resource allocation graph* (RAG) shows the resources utilized by various executions. They are used in operating systems for various functions, including deadlock detection.

Drawing these graphs can help us picture deadlocks in our concurrent programs. Figure 11.2 shows the simple deadlock situation that occurs in listings 11.1 and 11.2.

In a resource allocation graph, the nodes represent the executions or resources. For example, in figure 11.2, the nodes are our two goroutines, interacting with the two exclusive locks. In the figure, we use rectangular nodes for resources and circular ones for goroutines. The edges show us which resources are being requested or held by the executions. An edge pointing from an execution to a resource (the dashed

deadlock between two goroutines

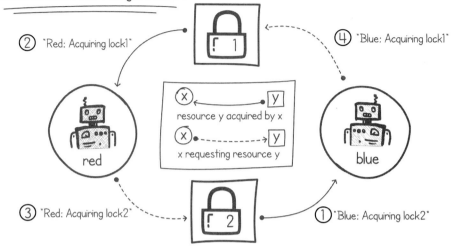

Figure 11.2   Resource allocation graph of the `red()` and `blue()` goroutines

lines in figure 11.2) means that the execution is requesting the use of that resource. An edge pointing from a resource to an execution (the solid lines) tells us that the resource is being used by that execution.

Figure 11.2 shows how the deadlock happens in our simple program. After the `blue()` goroutine acquires lock 2, it needs to request lock 1. The `red()` goroutine is holding lock 1, and it needs to request lock 2. Each goroutine is holding one lock, and then it goes ahead to request the other. Since the other lock is held by another goroutine, the second lock is never acquired. This creates the deadlock situation where the two goroutines will each be forever waiting for the other goroutine to release its lock.

> **NOTE** Figure 11.2 contains a graph cycle: starting from any node, we can trace a path along the edges that leads us back to our starting node. Whenever a resource allocation graph contains such a cycle, it means that a deadlock has occurred.

Deadlocks don't just happen in software. Sometimes, real-life scenarios create the conditions for a deadlock to occur. Consider, for example, a rail-crossing layout, as shown in figure 11.3. In this simple layout, a long train might need to use more than one rail-crossing at a time.

Rail crossings, by their nature, are exclusive resources—only one train can use them at any point in time. Thus, a train approaching a crossing needs to request and reserve access to it so that no other train can use it. If another train is already using a crossing, any other train needing the same crossing must wait until the crossing is free again.

A train that is long enough to span multiple crossings might need to use more than one crossing at the same time. This is akin to our executions holding more than one exclusive resource (such as a mutex) at the same time. Figure 11.3 shows that

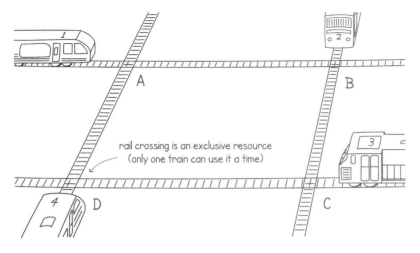

Figure 11.3   A rail-crossing layout that might cause a deadlock

each train approaching from a different direction will require the use of two crossings at the same time. For example, train 1 moving from left to right requires crossings A and B, train 2 moving from top to bottom requires crossings B and C, and so on.

Acquiring the use of multiple crossings is not an atomic operation; train 1 will first acquire and use crossing A and then, later, crossing B. This might create a situation where each train has a hold on its first crossing, but it's waiting for the train ahead to free the second crossing. Since the train tracks are set up in a way that creates a circular resource (a crossing) dependency, a deadlock situation might arise. A sample deadlock is shown in figure 11.4.

Just as goroutines can get stuck waiting forever for a resource to be freed, a train operator might not even know that the system is stuck in a deadlock. From that person's

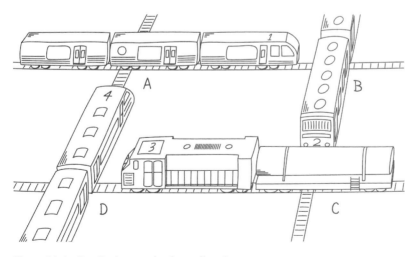

Figure 11.4   Deadlock occurring in a rail system

point of view, they are waiting for the train in front to move along so that they can free the crossing. Again, we can identify that the system is in a deadlock by using a resource allocation graph, as shown in figure 11.5.

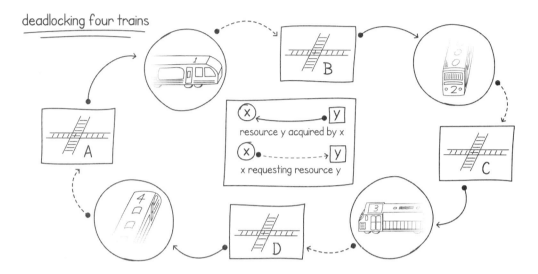

Figure 11.5   Resource allocation graph for a rail deadlock

The resource allocation graph clearly shows us that there is a cycle, signifying that we have a deadlock. Each train has acquired the use of a crossing but is waiting on the next train to release the next crossing. This is an example of a deadlock with four separate executions (the trains), though a deadlock can happen with any number greater than one. We can easily come up with a train layout that would involve any number of trains simply by adding more crossings and trains in a circular fashion.

In a 1971 paper titled "System Deadlocks," Coffman et al. illustrate four conditions that must *all* be present for deadlocks to occur:

- *Mutual exclusion*—Every resource in the system is either being used by one execution or is free.
- *Wait for condition*—Executions holding one or more resources can request more resources.
- *No preemption*—Resources being held by an execution cannot be taken away. Only the execution holding the resources can release them.
- *Circular wait*—There is a circular chain of two or more executions in which each is blocked while waiting for a resource to be released from the next execution in the chain.

In real life, we can see plenty of other examples of deadlocks. Examples include relationship conflicts, negotiations, and road traffic. In fact, road engineers spend a great deal of time and effort designing systems to minimize the risks of traffic deadlocks. Let's now look at a more complex example of deadlocking in software.

11.1.2 Deadlocking in a ledger

Imagine we work at a bank and are tasked with implementing software that reads ledger transactions to move funds from one account to another. A transaction subtracts the balance from a source account and adds it to a target account. For example, Sam paying Paul $10 means that we need to

1 Read Sam's account balance
2 Subtract $10 from Sam's account
3 Read Paul's account balance
4 Add $10 to Paul's balance

Since we want to be able to handle large volumes of transactions, we will be using multiple goroutines and shared memory to process transactions concurrently. To avoid race conditions, we can use mutexes on both the source and target accounts. This ensures that the goroutines are not interrupted while the money is being subtracted from one account and added to another. Figure 11.6 shows the logic of a goroutine handling a ledger transaction. The procedure is to acquire first the mutex on the source account and then the mutex on the target account, and only then to move the money.

concurrent ledger

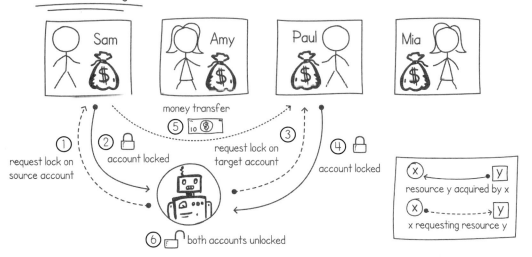

Figure 11.6   Using mutexes to lock source and target accounts when handling ledger transactions

Separate mutex locks, one for each account, are used so that when we are processing transactions, we only lock the accounts that are needed. Listing 11.3 shows a `BankAccount` type structure containing this mutex, an identifier, and a balance. The listing also contains a `NewBankAccount()` function, which instantiates a new bank account with a default balance of $100 and a new mutex.

```
package listing11_3_4

import (
    "fmt"
    "sync"
)

type BankAccount struct {
    id      string
    balance int
    mutex   sync.Mutex
}

func NewBankAccount(id string) *BankAccount {          ◁——┐  Creates a new instance of
    return &BankAccount{                                      a bank account with $100
        id:      id,                                          and a new mutex
        balance: 100,
        mutex:   sync.Mutex{},
    }
}
```

Listing 11.4 shows how we can implement a `Transfer()` function with the logic outlined in figure 11.6. The function transfers money, in the `amount` parameter, from the source (`src`) to a target (`to`) bank account. For logging purposes, the function also accepts an `exId` parameter. This parameter represents the execution that is calling this function. A goroutine calling this function passes a unique ID so we can log it on the console.

```
func (src *BankAccount) Transfer(to *BankAccount, amount int, exId int) {
    fmt.Printf("%d Locking %s's account\n", exId, src.id)
    src.mutex.Lock()                            ◁—— Locks mutex on the source account
    fmt.Printf("%d Locking %s's account\n", exId, to.id)
    to.mutex.Lock()          ◁——┐  Locks mutex on the target account
    src.balance -= amount
    to.balance += amount       Subtracts money from the source
    to.mutex.Unlock()          and adds it to the target account
    src.mutex.Unlock()
    fmt.Printf("%d Unlocked %s and %s\n", exId, src.id, to.id)
}
```
Unlocks both target and source accounts

We can now have a few goroutines executing randomly generated transfers, simulating a scenario where we are receiving a high volume of transactions. Listing 11.5

creates four bank accounts and then starts four goroutines, each executing 1,000 transfers. Each goroutine generates a transfer by randomly selecting a source and target bank account. If the source and target accounts happen to be the same, another target account is picked. Each transfer has a value of $10.

Listing 11.5 Goroutines executing randomly generated transfers

```go
package main

import (
    "fmt"
    "github.com/cutajarj/ConcurrentProgrammingWithGo/chapter11/listing11.3_4"
    "math/rand"
    "time"
)

func main() {
    accounts := []listing11_3_4.BankAccount{
        *listing11_3_4.NewBankAccount("Sam"),
        *listing11_3_4.NewBankAccount("Paul"),
        *listing11_3_4.NewBankAccount("Amy"),
        *listing11_3_4.NewBankAccount("Mia"),
    }
    total := len(accounts)
    for i := 0; i < 4; i++ {
        go func(eId int) {
            for j := 1; j < 1000; j++ {
                from, to := rand.Intn(total), rand.Intn(total)
                for from == to {
                    to = rand.Intn(total)
                }
                accounts[from].Transfer(&accounts[to], 10, eId)
            }
            fmt.Println(eId, "COMPLETE")
        }(i)
    }
    time.Sleep(60 * time.Second)
}
```

Annotations:
- Creates a goroutine with a unique execution ID
- Executes 1,000 randomly generated transfers
- Selects a source and a target account for the transfer
- Performs the transfer
- Once all the 1,000 transfers are complete, outputs the complete message
- Waits 60 seconds before terminating the program

Running listing 11.5, we expect to see 1,000 transfers for each of our four goroutines printed on the console and then the message COMPLETE outputted. Unfortunately, our program gets itself into a deadlock, and the final message is not printed:

```
$ go run ledgermutex.go
1 Locking Paul's account
1 Locking Mia's account
1 Unlocked Paul and Mia
. . .
2 Locking Amy's account
0 Locking Sam's account
3 Locking Mia's account
3 Locking Paul's account
```

```
3 Unlocked Mia and Paul
3 Locking Paul's account
3 Locking Sam's account
0 Locking Amy's account
2 Locking Paul's account
1 Unlocked Amy and Mia
1 Locking Mia's account
1 Locking Paul's account
```

NOTE Every time we run listing 11.5, we get slightly different output, not always resulting in a deadlock. This is due to the non-deterministic nature of concurrent executions.

From our output, we can observe that some goroutines are holding locks on some accounts and trying to acquire locks on others. The deadlock in our example happens between goroutines 0, 2, and 3. We can create a resource allocation graph to better understand the deadlock (see figure 11.7).

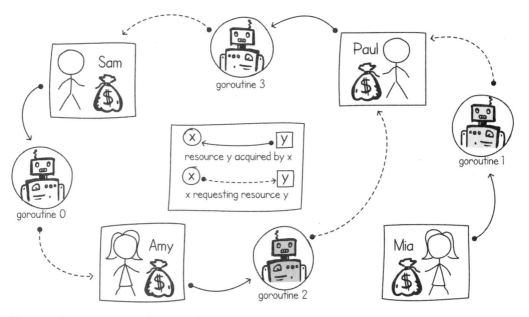

Figure 11.7   Deadlocking while processing ledger transactions

Our resource allocation graph in figure 11.7 shows that the deadlock is caused by goroutines 0, 2, and 3 since it contains a cycle with these goroutines as nodes. It also shows that a deadlock can affect other goroutines by blocking access to their resources. In this example, goroutine 1 is blocked while trying to acquire a lock on Paul's account.

11.2 Dealing with deadlocks

What should we do so that our programming does not suffer from deadlocks? We have three main approaches: detection, using mechanisms that avoid deadlocks, and writing our concurrent programming in a manner to prevent deadlock scenarios. In the following sections, we'll explore these three options.

It's also worth noting that there is one other approach when dealing with deadlocks: do nothing. Some textbooks refer to this as the *ostrich method*, with reference to ostriches sticking their heads in the sand when in danger (although this is a popular misconception). Doing nothing to prevent deadlocks only makes sense if we know for certain that in our system, deadlocks are rare, and when they do occur, the consequences are not costly.

11.2.1 Detecting deadlocks

The first approach we can adopt is detecting deadlocks so that we can do something about them. For example, after detecting that a deadlock has occurred, we can have an alert that calls someone who can restart the process. Even better, we can have logic in our code that is notified whenever there is a deadlock and performs a retry operation.

Go has some deadlock detection built in. Go's runtime checks to see which goroutine it should execute next, and if it finds that all of them are blocked while waiting for a resource (such as a mutex), it will throw a fatal error. Unfortunately, this means that it will only catch a deadlock if all the goroutines are blocked.

Consider listing 11.6, in which the main goroutine is waiting on a waitgroup for the two child goroutines to finish their work. Both goroutines are repeatedly locking mutexes A and B at the same time to increase the risk of a deadlock occurring.

Listing 11.6 Triggering Go's deadlock detection

```go
package main

import (
    "fmt"
    "sync"
)

func lockBoth(lock1, lock2 *sync.Mutex, wg *sync.WaitGroup) {
    for i := 0; i < 10000; i++ {
        lock1.Lock(); lock2.Lock()        | Locks and unlocks
        lock1.Unlock(); lock2.Unlock()    | both mutexes
    }
    wg.Done()    <——— Marks the waitgroup as done
}

func main() {
    lockA, lockB := sync.Mutex{}, sync.Mutex{}
    wg := sync.WaitGroup{}
    wg.Add(2)
```

```
    go lockBoth(&lockA, &lockB, &wg)      Starts two goroutines, locking
    go lockBoth(&lockB, &lockA, &wg)      both mutexes at the same time
    wg.Wait()
    fmt.Println("Done")                   Waits for the goroutine to terminate
}
```

When running the previous listing, if a deadlock occurs, all the goroutines will be blocked, including the main goroutine. The two goroutines will be blocked in a deadlock waiting for each other, and the `main()` goroutine will be stuck waiting on the waitgroup to be done. Here is a summary of the error message given by Go:

```
$ go run deadlockdetection.go
fatal error: all goroutines are asleep - deadlock!

goroutine 1 [semacquire]:
. . .
    /usr/local/go/src/sync/waitgroup.go:139 +0x80
main.main()
    /deadlockdetection.go:22 +0x13c

goroutine 18 [semacquire]:
. . .
sync.(*Mutex).Lock(...)
    /usr/local/go/src/sync/mutex.go:90
main.lockBoth(0x1400011c008, 0x1400011c010, 0x0?)
    /deadlockdetection.go:10 +0x104
. . .

goroutine 19 [semacquire]:
. . .
sync.(*Mutex).Lock(...)
    /usr/local/go/src/sync/mutex.go:90
main.lockBoth(0x1400011c010, 0x1400011c008, 0x0?)
    deadlockdetection.go:10 +0x104
. . .

exit status 2
```

In addition to telling us that we have a deadlock, Go outputs the details of what the goroutines were doing when our program got stuck. In this example, we can see that goroutines labeled 18 and 19 were both trying to lock a mutex while our `main()` goroutine (labeled goroutine 1) was waiting on the waitgroup.

We can easily write a program that works around this deadlock detection mechanism. Consider the next listing, in which we have modified the `main()` function to create another goroutine to wait for the waitgroup. The `main()` goroutine then sleeps for 30 seconds, simulating doing some other work.

Listing 11.7   Going around Go's deadlock detection

```
func main() {
    lockA, lockB := sync.Mutex{}, sync.Mutex{}
    wg := sync.WaitGroup{}
    wg.Add(2)
```

```
    go lockBoth(&lockA, &lockB, &wg)
    go lockBoth(&lockB, &lockA, &wg)
    go func() {
        wg.Wait()
        fmt.Println("Done waiting on waitgroup")
    }()
    time.Sleep(30 * time.Second)
    fmt.Println("Done")
}
```

Waits for 30 seconds

Creates a goroutine that waits on the waitgroup before outputting a message

Outputs a message, and then the program terminates

Since we now have the `main()` goroutine not really blocked but waiting on the `sleep()` function, Go's runtime will not detect the deadlock. When a deadlock occurs, the message `"Done waiting on waitgroup"` is not returned; instead, 30 seconds later, the `main()` goroutine outputs the `"Done"` message, and the program terminates without any deadlock errors:

```
$ go run deadlocknodetection.go
Done
```

A more complete way to detect a deadlock is to programmatically build a resource allocation graph representing all the goroutines and resources as nodes connected by edges, as you saw in figures 11.2, 11.5, and 11.7. We can then have an algorithm that detects cycles in the graph. If the graph contains a cycle, the system is in a deadlock state.

To detect a cycle in a graph, we can modify a depth-first search algorithm to look for cycles. If we keep track of the nodes visited while performing the traversal and we come across a node that was already visited, we know we have a cycle.

This is the approach adopted by some other frameworks, runtimes, and systems such as databases. The following is an error example returned by MySQL, a popular open source database. In this case, the deadlock happens when we have two concurrent sessions running transactions and trying to acquire the same locks at the same time. MySQL keeps track of all its sessions and allocated resources, and when it detects any deadlock, it returns the following error to the clients:

```
ERROR 1213 (40001): Deadlock found when trying to get lock;
try restarting transaction
```

If our runtime or system gives us deadlock detection, we can perform various actions whenever it detects a deadlock. One option is to terminate the executions stuck in the deadlock. This is similar to the approach Go's runtime takes, with the difference that Go terminates the entire process with all the goroutines.

Another option is to return an error to the executions that are requesting the resources whenever the request leads to a deadlock. The execution can then decide to perform some action in response to the error, such as releasing the resources and retrying after some time passes. This is the approach commonly adopted when using many databases. Typically, when a database returns a deadlock error, the database client can roll back the transaction and retry.

Why doesn't Go's runtime provide full deadlock detection?

Having a mechanism to detect a deadlock by checking for any cycles in a resource allocation graph is a relatively expensive operation in terms of performance. Go's runtime would have to maintain a resource allocation graph, and each time there was a resource request or release, Go would have to run the cycle-check algorithm on the graph. In an application where we have large numbers of goroutines requesting and releasing resources, this deadlock detection check would slow things down. It would also be unnecessary in many cases when the goroutines were not using multiple exclusive resources at the same time.

Implementing full deadlock detection in database transactions doesn't typically affect performance. This is because the detection algorithm is fast relative to the slow database operations.

11.2.2   Avoiding deadlocks

We can try to avoid deadlocks by scheduling executions in a manner that doesn't give rise to deadlocks. In figure 11.8, we again use the example of the train deadlock, but this time, we show the timelines of each train when they get stuck in the deadlock situation.

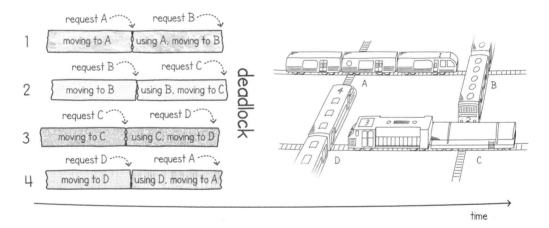

Figure 11.8   Train timelines leading to a deadlock

The system that is allocating resources (train crossings, in this example) can have smarter logic to assign resources so as to avoid deadlocks. In our train example, we know in advance the journey of each train and each train's length. So, when train 1 requests crossing A, we already know that crossing B might soon be requested. When train 2 comes along and requests crossing B, instead of assigning it and allowing the train to proceed, we can instruct the train to stop and wait.

The same can happen between trains 3 and 4. When train 4 comes along and asks for crossing D, we already know that it might later request crossing A, which is currently being used by train 1. So, again, we instruct train 4 to stop and wait. However, train 3 can proceed with no interruption, since both crossings C and D are free. No train is currently using a crossing that might request either of them in the future.

This train scheduling example is shown in figure 11.9. Trains 1 and 3 pass through the crossings uninterrupted while trains 2 and 4 stop and wait. Once the crossings are free again, trains 2 and 4 can continue on their journey.

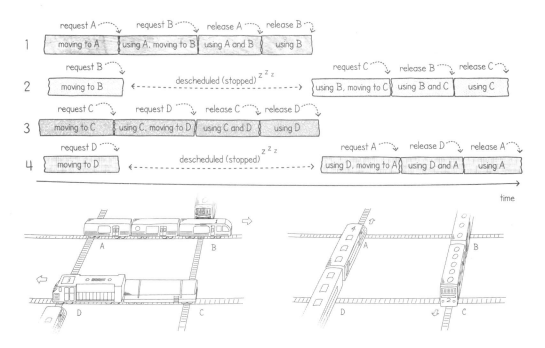

Figure 11.9   Avoiding deadlocks in the rail-crossing scenario

The *banker's algorithm*, developed by Edsger Dijkstra, is one such algorithm that can be used to check if a resource is safe to allocate and avoid deadlock. The algorithm can be used only if the following information is known:

- The maximum number of each resource that each execution can request
- What resources each execution is currently holding
- The available number of each resource

DEFINITION   Using this information, we can decide if the system is in a *safe* or *unsafe* state. Our system state is only safe if there is a way to schedule our executions in which they all reach completion (thus avoiding deadlocks), even if they request their maximum number of resources. Otherwise, the system state is said to be unsafe.

The algorithm works by deciding whether to grant a request for resources. It will grant a request for resources only if the system will still be in a safe state after the resource is assigned. If it leads to an unsafe state, the execution requesting the resources is suspended until it is safe to grant its request.

As an example, consider a resource that can be used by multiple executions in a limited fashion, such as a database connection pool with a fixed number of sessions. Figure 11.10 shows both a safe and an unsafe scenario. In scenario A, if execution a requests and is granted another database session resource, the system ends up in the unsafe state, shown in scenario B. This is because there is no way to grant any execution its maximum number of resources. In scenario B, we only have two resources left but executions a, b, and c can request a further five, three, and five resources. There is now an unavoidable risk of ending up in a deadlock.

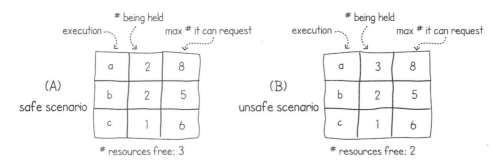

Figure 11.10   Examples of safe and unsafe state scenarios

Scenario A is said to still be in a safe state because there is scheduling that we can apply that will lead all of the executions to complete. In scenario A, we are still at a point where we can avoid a deadlock with careful resource allocation. Applying the banker's algorithm in scenario A of figure 11.10, we could suspend the executions a and c when they request more resources because granting the requests would lead to unsafe states. The algorithm would only allow requests from b because granting these would leave the system in a safe state. Once b frees enough resources, we can then grant them to c and later to a (see figure 11.11).

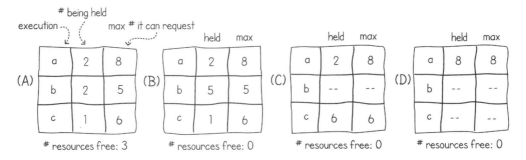

Figure 11.11   Sequence of safe resource allocations

The banker's algorithm can also work with multiple resources, such as locking the different bank accounts from our ledger application, described in section 11.1.2. However, for our application, we do not need to implement the full banker's algorithm because we know in advance the full set of resources each goroutine will need. Since we're only locking two specific bank accounts, the source and target accounts, our system can suspend the execution of a goroutine if either of its two accounts are currently being used by another goroutine.

To implement this, we can create an arbitrator whose job it is to suspend the execution of goroutines if they are requesting accounts that are currently in use. Once the accounts become available, the arbitrator can then resume the goroutines. The arbitrator can be implemented by using a condition variable to block the execution of a goroutine until all accounts become available. This logic is shown in figure 11.12.

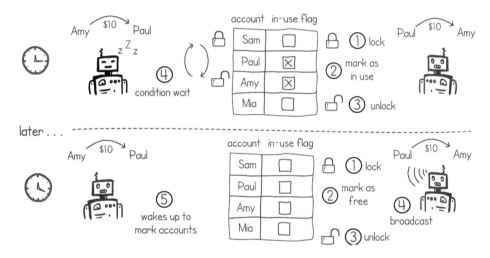

Figure 11.12 Using a condition variable to suspend goroutines when accounts are unavailable

When a goroutine requests resources that are in use from an arbitrator, the goroutine is made to wait on a condition variable. When another goroutine frees resources, it broadcasts so that any suspended goroutine can check to see if the required resource has become available. In this way, we avoid deadlocking, since the resources are locked only if they are all available.

In listing 11.8, we define the structure that will be used in the arbitrator. We also include a function to initialize the fields in the structure. The `accountsInUse` map is there to mark any accounts that are currently being used for money transfers, while the condition variable is used to suspend executions when accounts are in use.

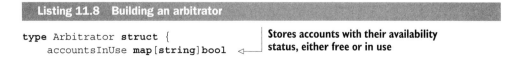

Listing 11.8 Building an arbitrator

```
type Arbitrator struct {
    accountsInUse map[string]bool
```

Stores accounts with their availability status, either free or in use

```
    cond *sync.Cond
}
```
⟵ **Condition variable to be used to suspend goroutines if accounts are not available**

```
func NewArbitrator() *Arbitrator{
    return &Arbitrator{
        accountsInUse: map[string]bool{},
        cond:          sync.NewCond(&sync.Mutex{}),
    }
}
```

Next, we need to implement a function that allows us to block the accounts if they are free or to suspend the execution of the goroutine if they're not. This is shown in listing 11.9, which contains the `LockAccounts()` function. The function acquires the mutex lock associated with the condition variable and checks to see if all the accounts are free by using the `accountsInUse` map. If any of the accounts are in use, the goroutine calls `Wait()` on the condition variable. This suspends the execution of the goroutine and unlocks the mutex. Once the execution is resumed, the goroutine reacquires the mutex, and this check is repeated until all the accounts are free. At this point, the map is updated to indicate that the resources are in use, and the mutex is unlocked. In this way, the goroutine never gets to execute the transfer logic until it has acquired all the accounts it needs.

Listing 11.9   Suspending executions to avoid deadlocks

```
func (a *Arbitrator) LockAccounts(ids... string) {
    a.cond.L.Lock()
    for allAvailable := false; !allAvailable; {
        allAvailable = true
        for _, id := range ids {
            if a.accountsInUse[id] {
                allAvailable = false
                a.cond.Wait()
            }
        }
    }
    for _, id := range ids {
        a.accountsInUse[id] = true
    }
    a.cond.L.Unlock()
}
```

Locks mutex on condition variable

Loops until all accounts are free

If an account is in use, suspends the execution of the goroutine

Once all accounts are available, marks requested accounts as in use

Unlocks the mutex on the condition variable

Once the goroutine is done with its transfer logic, it needs to mark the accounts as no longer in use. Listing 11.10 shows the `UnlockAccounts()` function. A goroutine calling this function holds the condition variable's mutex, marks all required accounts as free, and then broadcasts on the condition variable. This has the effect of waking up any suspended goroutines, which will then go ahead and check to see if their accounts have become available.

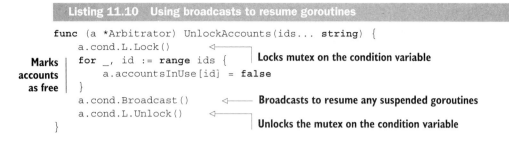

Listing 11.10   Using broadcasts to resume goroutines

```
func (a *Arbitrator) UnlockAccounts(ids... string) {
    a.cond.L.Lock()                    ◁──────┐
    for _, id := range ids {                  │   Locks mutex on the condition variable
        a.accountsInUse[id] = false
    }
    a.cond.Broadcast()            ◁────── Broadcasts to resume any suspended goroutines
    a.cond.L.Unlock()             ◁──────┐
}                                         │   Unlocks the mutex on the condition variable
```

Marks accounts as free

We can now use these two functions in our money-transfer logic. The next listing shows the modified `Transfer()` function that calls `LockAccounts()` before making the money transfer and calls `UnlockAccounts()` afterward.

Listing 11.11   Using the arbitrator to lock accounts during transfers

```
func (src *BankAccount) Transfer(to *BankAccount, amount int, tellerId int,
    arb *Arbitrator) {
    fmt.Printf("%d Locking %s and %s\n", tellerId, src.id, to.id)
    arb.LockAccounts(src.id, to.id)
    src.balance -= amount                   Performs the transfer once
    to.balance += amount                    both locks are obtained
    arb.UnlockAccounts(src.id, to.id)
    fmt.Printf("%d Unlocked %s and %s\n", tellerId, src.id, to.id)
}
```

Locks both the source and target accounts

Unlocks both accounts after transfer

Finally, we can update our `main()` function to create an instance of the arbitrator and pass it to the goroutines so that it can be used during the transfers. This is shown in the following listing.

Listing 11.12   `main()` function using arbitrator (imports omitted for brevity)

```
package main

import (...)

func main() {
    accounts := []BankAccount{
        *NewBankAccount("Sam"),
        *NewBankAccount("Paul"),
        *NewBankAccount("Amy"),
        *NewBankAccount("Mia"),
    }
    total := len(accounts)              Creates a new arbitrator to
    arb := NewArbitrator()    ◁─────┘   be used in the transfers
    for i := 0; i < 4; i++ {
        go func(tellerId int) {
            for i := 1; i < 1000; i++ {
                from, to := rand.Intn(total), rand.Intn(total)
```

```
            for from == to {
                to = rand.Intn(total)
            }
            accounts[from].Transfer(&accounts[to], 10, tellerId, arb)
        }
        fmt.Println(tellerId,"COMPLETE")
    }(i)
}
time.Sleep(60 * time.Second)
}
```

Deadlock avoidance in operating systems and language runtimes

Can deadlock avoidance algorithms be implemented in operating systems or in Go's runtime to schedule executions in a manner that avoids deadlocks? In practice, deadlock avoidance algorithms, such as the banker's algorithm, are not very useful when it comes to using them in operating systems and language runtimes because they require advance knowledge of the maximum number of resources that an execution will require. This requirement is unrealistic because operating systems and runtimes cannot be expected to know what resources each process, thread, or goroutine might ask for in advance.

In addition, the banker's algorithm assumes that the set of executions does not change. This is not the case for any realistic operating system in which processes are constantly being started up and terminated.

11.2.3 *Preventing deadlocks*

If we know in advance the full set of exclusive resources that our concurrent execution will use, we can use ordering to prevent deadlocks. Consider again the simple deadlock outlined in listing 11.1. That deadlock happens because the red() and blue() goroutines are each acquiring the mutexes in a different order. The red() goroutine is using lock 1 and then lock 2, while blue() is using lock 2 and then lock 1. If we change the listing so that they use the locks in the same order, as shown in the following listing, the deadlock won't occur.

Listing 11.13 Ordering mutexes prevents deadlocks

```
func red(lock1, lock2 *sync.Mutex) {
    for {
        fmt.Println("Red: Acquiring lock1")
        lock1.Lock()
        fmt.Println("Red: Acquiring lock2")
        lock2.Lock()
        fmt.Println("Red: Both locks Acquired")
        lock1.Unlock(); lock2.Unlock()
        fmt.Println("Red: Locks Released")
    }
}
```

```go
func blue(lock1, lock2 *sync.Mutex) {
    for {
        fmt.Println("Blue: Acquiring lock1")
        lock1.Lock()
        fmt.Println("Blue: Acquiring lock2")
        lock2.Lock()
        fmt.Println("Blue: Both locks Acquired")
        lock1.Unlock(); lock2.Unlock()
        fmt.Println("Blue: Locks Released")
    }
}
```

The deadlock doesn't occur because we never get in a situation where both goroutines are holding different locks and requesting the other one. In this scenario, when they both try to obtain lock 1 at the same time, only one goroutine will succeed. The other one will be blocked until both locks are available again. This creates a situation where a goroutine can obtain either all the locks or none.

We can apply this rule to our ledger application. Whenever we get a transaction to execute, we can define a simple rule that specifies the order in which to acquire the mutex locks. The rule could be that we should acquire the locks in alphabetical order based on the account ID. For example, if we have a transaction to transfer $10 from Mia to Amy, we should lock Amy's account first and then Mia's because Amy's account ID is alphabetically first. If, at the same time, we have another transaction that is transferring $10 from Amy to Mia, this transaction will be blocked on its first lock request, that of Amy. This example is shown in figure 11.13.

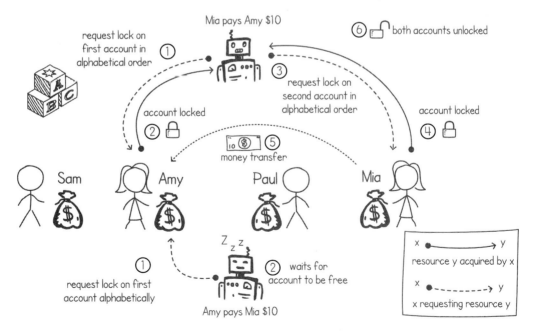

Figure 11.13 Using ordering to avoid deadlocks in the ledger application

In our ledger application example, we have made the account IDs equivalent to the account holder's name for simplicity. In a real-life application, the account ID might be numeric or a version 4 UUID, both of which can be ordered. The following listing shows the modified transfer function for our application where we are sorting the accounts by their IDs and then locking them in order.

Listing 11.14 Ordering accounts transfer function

```go
func (src *BankAccount) Transfer(to *BankAccount, amount int, tellerId int) {
    accounts := []*BankAccount{src, to}
    sort.Slice(accounts, func(a, b int) bool {
        return accounts[a].id < accounts[b].id
    })
    fmt.Printf("%d Locking %s's account\n", tellerId, accounts[0].id)
    accounts[0].mutex.Lock()
    fmt.Printf("%d Locking %s's account\n", tellerId, accounts[1].id)
    accounts[1].mutex.Lock()
    src.balance -= amount
    to.balance += amount
    to.mutex.Unlock()
    src.mutex.Unlock()
    fmt.Printf("%d Unlocked %s and %s\n", tellerId, src.id, to.id)
}
```

Places the source and target accounts into a slice

Sorts the slice containing both accounts by their ID

Locks the account with the lower order by ID

Locks the account with the higher order by ID

Unlocks both accounts

We can now run the preceding function and see that the accounts are always being locked in alphabetical order. In addition, all the goroutines complete without getting into any deadlocks. Here's a sample of the output:

```
$ go run ledgermutexorder.go
3 Locking Amy's account
2 Locking Amy's account
3 Locking Paul's account
3 Unlocked Amy and Paul
. . .
1 Locking Mia's account
1 Locking Paul's account
. . .
2 COMPLETE
. . .
0 COMPLETE
. . .
3 COMPLETE
. . .
1 COMPLETE
```

We can also use this ordering strategy to prevent deadlocks if we don't know in advance which exclusive resources we need to use. The idea here is not to acquire resources that have a lower order than the ones we're currently holding. When a situation happens that requires us to acquire a higher-order resource, we can always release the resources being held and request them again in the correct order.

In our ledger application, consider a goroutine that is executing a special transaction, such as "Pay Paul $10 from Amy's account; if Amy's account lacks sufficient funds, use Mia's account instead." In this scenario, we can write logic into our goroutine to perform the following steps:

1 Lock Amy's account.
2 Lock Paul's account.
3 If Amy's balance is sufficient to cover the transfer:
   a Subtract money from Amy's account and add it to Paul's.
   b Unlock both Amy's and Paul's accounts.
4 Otherwise:
   a Unlock both Amy's and Paul's accounts.
   b Lock Mia's account.
   c Lock Paul's account.
   d Subtract money from Mia's account and add it to Paul's.
   e Unlock both Mia's and Paul's accounts.

The important rule here is to never lock a lower-order resource if the execution holds a higher one. In this example, we had to release Paul's and Amy's accounts before locking Mia's. This ensures that we never get into a deadlock situation.

11.3 *Deadlocking with channels*

It's important to understand that deadlocks aren't limited to the use of mutexes. Deadlocks can occur whenever executions hold mutually exclusive resources and request other ones—this also applies to channels. A channel's capacity can be thought of as a mutually exclusive resource. Goroutines can hold a channel while also trying to use another one (by sending or receiving messages).

We can think of a channel as being a collection of read and write resources. Initially, a non-buffered channel has no read and write resources. A read resource becomes available when another goroutine is trying to write a message. A write operation makes one read resource available while trying to acquire a write resource. Similarly, a read operation makes one write resource available while trying to acquire one read resource.

Let's look at an example of a deadlock involving two channels. Consider a simple program that needs to recursively output file details, such as the filename, file size, and last modified date of all files under a directory. One solution is to have one goroutine that handles files and another that deals with directories. The directory goroutine's job is to read the directory contents and feed each file to the file handler using a channel. This is shown in the following `handleDirectories()` function.

Listing 11.15 Directory handler (error handling omitted for brevity)

```
package main

import (
```

```
    "fmt"
    "os"
    "path/filepath"
    "time"
)

func handleDirectories(dirs <-chan string, files chan<- string) {
    for fullpath := range dirs {
        fmt.Println("Reading all files from", fullpath)
        filesInDir, _ := os.ReadDir(fullpath)
        fmt.Printf("Pushing %d files from %s\n", len(filesInDir), fullpath)
        for _, file := range filesInDir {
            files <- filepath.Join(fullpath, file.Name())
        }
    }
}
```

Reads the full directory path from the input topic

Reads the contents of a directory

Feeds each item of the directory contents onto the output topic

The reverse happens in the file handler goroutine. When the file handler meets a new directory, it sends it to the directory handler's channel. The file handler consumes items from an input channel if the item is a file, and it outputs information about it, such as the file size and last modified date. If the item is a directory, it forwards the directory to the directory handler. This is shown in the following listing.

Listing 11.16 Files handler (error handling omitted for brevity)

```
func handleFiles(files chan string, dirs chan string) {
    for path := range files {
        file, _ := os.Open(path)
        fileInfo, _ := file.Stat()
        if fileInfo.IsDir() {
            fmt.Printf("Pushing %s directory\n", fileInfo.Name())
            dirs <- path
        } else {
            fmt.Printf("File %s, size: %dMB, last modified: %s\n",
                fileInfo.Name(), fileInfo.Size() / (1024 * 1024),
                fileInfo.ModTime().Format("15:04:05"))
        }
    }
}
```

Reads the full path of a file

If the file is a directory, writes it to the output channel

Reads information about the file

If the file is not a directory, displays file information on the console

We can now wire the two goroutines together with a `main()` function. In listing 11.17, we create the two channels and pass them to the newly created file and directory handler goroutines. We then feed the initial directory read from the arguments to the directory channel. To simplify the listing (for demonstration purposes), we have the `main()` goroutine sleep 60 seconds instead of using waitgroups to wait for the goroutines to complete.

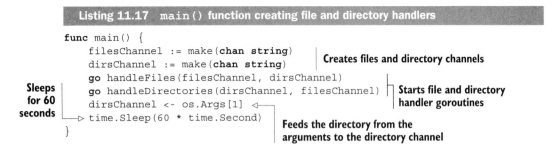

Listing 11.17 `main()` **function creating file and directory handlers**

```
func main() {
    filesChannel := make(chan string)          Creates files and directory channels
    dirsChannel := make(chan string)
    go handleFiles(filesChannel, dirsChannel)
    go handleDirectories(dirsChannel, filesChannel)   Starts file and directory
    dirsChannel <- os.Args[1]                          handler goroutines
    time.Sleep(60 * time.Second)
}
```

Sleeps for 60 seconds

Feeds the directory from the arguments to the directory channel

When we run all the listings together on a directory that has some subdirectories, we immediately get into a deadlock. The following example output shows the goroutines deadlocking soon after the directory handler tries to push 26 files onto the channel, and the file handler's goroutine tries to send the directory named `CodingInterview-Workshop`:

```
$ go run allfilesinfo.go ~/projects/
Reading all files from ~/projects/
Pushing 26 files from ~/projects/
File .DS_Store, size: 8.00KB, last modified: Mon Mar 13 13:50:45 2023
Pushing CodingInterviewWorkshop directory
```

The deadlocking problem here is shown in figure 11.14. We have created a circular wait condition between our two goroutines. The directory handler is waiting for a file handler's goroutine to read from the `files` channel while it's blocking any writes to the `dirs` channels. The file handler is waiting for a directory handler's goroutine to read from the `dirs` channel while it's blocking any writes to the `files` channel.

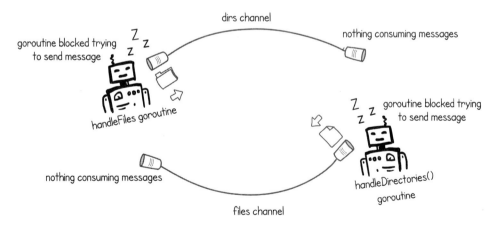

Figure 11.14 Deadlock with two channels

We might be tempted to think that we can solve the deadlock problem by having a buffer on the file or directory channel. This, however, will only postpone the deadlock. The problem will still occur once we encounter a directory that has more files or subdirectories than our buffer can handle.

We can also attempt to increase the number of goroutines that are running our file handlers. After all, a typical filesystem has substantially more files than directories. Again, however, this would only delay the problem. Once our program navigates to a directory that contains more files than the number of goroutines executing `handle-Files()`, we will again get into a deadlock situation.

We can prevent the deadlock in this scenario by removing the circular wait. An easy way to do this is to change one of our functions so that we send on the channel by using a newly spawned goroutine. Listing 11.18 adapts the `handleDirectories()` function so that it starts up a new goroutine every time it needs to push new files onto the `files` channel. In this way, we have freed the goroutine from having to wait for the channel to become available, and we have delegated the wait to another goroutine, breaking the circular wait.

Listing 11.18   Using a separate goroutine to write on a channel

```go
func handleDirectories(dirs <-chan string, files chan<- string) {
    for fullpath := range dirs {
        fmt.Println("Reading all files from", fullpath)
        filesInDir, _ := os.ReadDir(fullpath)
        fmt.Printf("Pushing %d files from %s\n", len(filesInDir), fullpath)
        for _, file := range filesInDir {
            go func(fp string) {          // Starts new goroutine that sends
                files <- fp               // each file to the files channel
            }(filepath.Join(fullpath, file.Name()))
        }
    }
}
```

An alternative solution that doesn't involve creating loads of separate goroutines is to read and write from our channels at the same time by using the `select` statement. Again, this will break the circular wait that causes deadlocks while using channels. We can adopt this approach in either the directories or the files goroutines. The following listing shows this for the `handleDirectories()` goroutine.

Listing 11.19   Using `select` to break the circular wait

```go
func handleDirectories(dirs <-chan string, files chan<- string) {
    toPush := make([]string, 0)          // Creates a slice to store files
    appendAllFiles := func(path string) {//  that need to be pushed to
        fmt.Println("Reading all files from", path)   // the file handler's channel
        filesInDir, _ := os.ReadDir(path)
        fmt.Printf("Pushing %d files from %s\n", len(filesInDir), path)
        for _, f := range filesInDir {
            toPush = append(toPush, filepath.Join(path, f.Name()))
        }
    }
}
```

Appends all files in a directory to the slice

```
        for {
            if len(toPush) == 0 {                   If there are no files to push, reads directory from
                appendAllFiles(<-dirs)              the input channel and adds all files in the directory
            } else {
                select {
                case fullpath := <-dirs:            Reads the next directory from the input
                    appendAllFiles(fullpath)        channel and adds all files in the directory
                case files <- toPush[0]:
                    toPush = toPush[1:]
                }
            }
        }
    }
```

Pushes the first file on the slice to the channel

Removes the first file on the slice

Having our goroutine complete the receive or send operation depending on which channel is available gets rid of the circular wait that was causing the deadlock. If the file handler's goroutine is busy sending a directory path on its output channel, our directory goroutine is not blocked and can still receive the directory path. The `select` statement lets us wait for two operations at the same time. The contents of a directory are appended to a slice so that when the output channel is available, they are pushed onto the channel.

NOTE Having deadlocks in message-passing programs is often a sign of bad program design. Having a deadlock while using channels means that we have programmed a circular flow of messages going through the same goroutines. Most of the time, we can avoid possible deadlocks by designing our programs so that the flow of messages is not circular.

11.4   Exercises

NOTE Visit http://github.com/cutajarj/ConcurrentProgrammingWithGo to see all the code solutions.

1   In the following listing, `incrementScores()` might produce a deadlock if it's run concurrently with multiple goroutines. Can you change the function so that it avoids or prevents deadlocks?

Listing 11.20   Deadlocking on player scores

```
type Player struct {
    name  string
    score int
    mutex sync.Mutex
}

func incrementScores(players []*Player, increment int) {
    for _, player := range players {
        player.mutex.Lock()
    }
    for _, player := range players {
```

```
        player.score += increment
    }
    for _, player := range players {
        player.mutex.Unlock()
    }
}
```

2 In listing 11.19, we changed the `handleDirectories()` function so that it uses the `select` statement to avoid a circular wait between the two goroutines. Can you also change the `handleFiles()` function from listing 11.16 in the same way? The goroutine should use the `select` statement to both receive and send on the two channels.

Summary

- A deadlock is when a program has multiple executions that block indefinitely, waiting for each other to release their respective resources.
- A resource allocation graph (RAG) shows how executions are using resources by connecting them with edges.
- In an RAG, an execution requesting a resource is represented by a directed edge from the execution to the resource.
- In an RAG, an execution holding a resource is represented by a directed edge from the resource to the execution.
- When an RAG contains a cycle, it signifies that the system is in a deadlock.
- A graph cycle detection algorithm can be used on the RAG to detect a deadlock.
- Go's runtime provides deadlock detection, but it only detects a deadlock if all the goroutines are blocked.
- When Go's runtime detects a deadlock, the entire program exits with an error.
- Avoiding deadlocks by using scheduling executions in a specific manner can only be done in special cases where we know beforehand which resources will be used.
- Deadlocks can be prevented programmatically by requesting resources in a pre-defined order.
- Deadlocks can also occur in programs that are using Go channels. A channel's capacity can be thought of as a mutually exclusive resource.
- When using channels, take care to avoid circular waits to prevent deadlocks.
- With channels, circular waits can be avoided by sending or receiving using separate goroutines, by combining channel operations with a `select` statement, or by better designing programs to avoid circular message flows.

12
Atomics, spin locks, and futexes

This chapter covers

- Synchronizing with atomic variables
- Developing mutexes with spin locks
- Improving spin locks with futexes

In previous chapters, we have used mutexes to synchronize access to shared variables amongst threads. We have also seen how to use mutexes as primitives to build more complex concurrent tools, such as semaphores and channels. We haven't yet explored how these mutexes are built.

In this chapter, we'll cover the most primitive of the synchronization tools: the atomic variable. We'll then explore how we can use it to build a mutex using a technique called *spin locking*. Later, we'll see how we can optimize the mutex implementation by making use of a futex—an operating system call allowing us to reduce the CPU cycles while waiting for a lock to become free. Finally, we'll focus on how Go implements the bundled mutex.

12.1 *Lock-free synchronization with atomic variables*

Mutexes ensure that critical sections of our concurrent code are executed by only one goroutine at a time. They are used to prevent race conditions. However, mutexes have the effect of turning parts of our concurrent programming into sequential bottle-necks. If we are just updating the value of a simple variable, such as an integer, we can make use of an atomic variable to keep it consistent amongst goroutines without need-ing to rely on mutexes that turn our code into a sequential block.

12.1.1 *Sharing variables with atomic numbers*

In previous chapters, we looked at an example with two goroutines, named Stingy and Spendy, that were sharing an integer variable representing their bank account. Access to the shared variable was protected with a mutex. Every time we wanted to update the variable, we would acquire the mutex lock. Once we were finished with the update, we would release it.

Atomic variables allow us to perform certain operations that execute without inter-ruption. For example, we can add to the value of an existing shared variable in a sin-gle atomic operation, which guarantees that concurrent add operations do not interfere with each other. Once the operation is executed, it is fully applied to the value of the variable without interruption. We can use atomic variables to replace mutexes in certain scenarios.

As an example, we can easily change our Stingy and Spendy program to use these atomic variable operations. Instead of using mutexes, we will simply call the atomic `add()` operation on our shared money variable. This guarantees that the goroutines do not produce race conditions that produce inconsistent results (see figure 12.1).

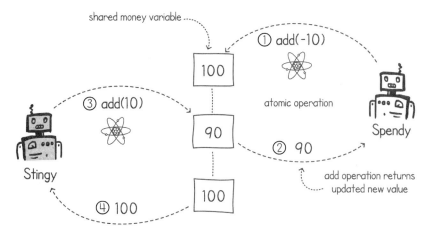

Figure 12.1   **Using atomic variables on Stingy and Spendy**

In Go, the atomic operations are in the `sync/atomic` package. All calls in this package accept a pointer to a variable on which the atomic operation is to be performed.

Here's a list of functions (from the `sync/atomic` package) that can be applied to 32-bit integers:

```
func AddInt32(addr *int32, delta int32) (new int32)
func CompareAndSwapInt32(addr *int32, old, new int32) (swapped bool)
func LoadInt32(addr *int32) (val int32)
func StoreInt32(addr *int32, val int32)
func SwapInt32(addr *int32, new int32) (old int32)
```

NOTE   The same `atomic` package contains similar operations for other datatypes, such as Booleans and unsigned integers.

For our Stingy and Spendy application, we can replace the mutex locks and instead use the `AddInt32()` operation every time we want to add to or subtract from the shared variable, as shown in the following listing. In addition to changing the addition and subtraction to use atomic operations, we also remove the need to use any mutexes.

Listing 12.1   Stingy and Spendy using atomic operations

```
package main

import (
    "fmt"
    "sync"
    "sync/atomic"     <─────  Imports the atomic package
)

func stingy(money *int32) {
    for i := 0; i < 1000000; i++ {
        atomic.AddInt32(money, 10)    <───┐  Adds $10 atomically to the
    }                                      │  shared money variable
    fmt.Println("Stingy Done")
}

func spendy(money *int32) {
    for i := 0; i < 1000000; i++ {
        atomic.AddInt32(money, -10)   <───┐  Subtracts $10 atomically from
    }                                      │  the shared money variable
    fmt.Println("Spendy Done")
}
```

NOTE   The `AddInt32()` function returns the new value after we add the delta. However, in our Stingy and Spendy goroutines, we're not making use of the return value.

We can modify our `main()` function to read the atomic variable's value by using the `LoadInt32()` function call. The following listing uses a waitgroup to wait for the goroutines to complete, and then it reads the shared `money` variable.

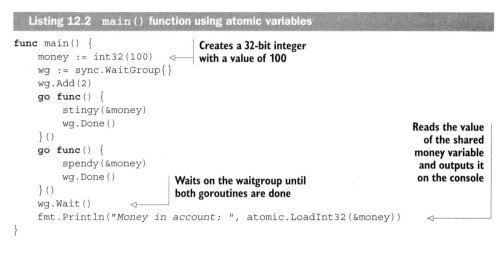

Listing 12.2   `main()` function using atomic variables

```go
func main() {
    money := int32(100)        ⟵  Creates a 32-bit integer
    wg := sync.WaitGroup{}          with a value of 100
    wg.Add(2)
    go func() {
        stingy(&money)
        wg.Done()
    }()
    go func() {
        spendy(&money)
        wg.Done()              Waits on the waitgroup until
    }()                        both goroutines are done
    wg.Wait()  ⟵
    fmt.Println("Money in account: ", atomic.LoadInt32(&money))  ⟵
}
```

Reads the value of the shared money variable and outputs it on the console

As expected, when we run listings 12.1 and 12.2 together, we don't get any race conditions, and the final value of the shared money variable is \$100:

```
$ go run atomicstingyspendy.go
Spendy Done
Stingy Done
Money in account:  100
```

12.1.2   *Performance penalty when using atomics*

Why don't we just use atomic operations for everything to eliminate the risk of sharing a variable and accidentally forgetting to use synchronization techniques? Unfortunately, there is a performance penalty to pay whenever we use these atomic variables. Updating a variable in a normal way is quite a bit faster than updating variables with atomic operations.

Let's look at this performance difference. Listing 12.3 uses Go's built-in benchmarking tools to test how fast it is to update a variable atomically compared with a normal update. In Go, we can write a benchmark unit test by prefixing the function signature with Benchmark and making the function accept a testing.B type. Listing 12.3 shows an example of this. In the first benchmark function, we update the total 64-bit integer using a normal read and update operation, and in the second, we update it using an atomic AddInt64() operation. When using Go's benchmark functions, bench.N is the number of iterations that our benchmark will execute. This value changes dynamically to ensure that the test runs for the specific duration (1 second by default).

Listing 12.3   Micro-benching the atomic addition operator

```go
package main

import (
    "sync/atomic"
```

```
    "testing"
)

var total = int64(0)    ◁─── Creates a 64-bit integer

func BenchmarkNormal(bench *testing.B) {
    for i := 0; i < bench.N; i++ {
        total += 1                  ◁─── Adds to the total variable using
    }                                    the normal add operator
}

func BenchmarkAtomic(bench *testing.B) {
    for i := 0; i < bench.N; i++ {          Adds to the total variable using
        atomic.AddInt64(&total, 1)   ◁───┘  the atomic operation function
    }
}
```

We can now run this benchmark by adding the -bench flag to the go test command. This test will tell us the performance difference between an atomic and a normal variable operation. Here's the output:

```
$ go test -bench=. -count 3
goos: darwin
goarch: arm64
pkg: github.com/cutajarj/ConcurrentProgrammingWithGo/chapter12/listing12.3
BenchmarkNormal-10        555129141              2.158 ns/op
BenchmarkNormal-10        550122879              2.163 ns/op
BenchmarkNormal-10        555068692              2.167 ns/op
BenchmarkAtomic-10        174523189              6.865 ns/op
BenchmarkAtomic-10        175444462              6.902 ns/op
BenchmarkAtomic-10        175469658              6.869 ns/op
PASS
ok      github.com/cutajarj/ConcurrentProgrammingWithGo/chapter12/listing12.3
➥ 9.971s
```

The results of our micro-benchmark indicate that the atomic addition on 64-bit integers is more than three times slower than using the normal operator. These results will vary on different systems and architectures, but on all systems, there is a substantial difference in performance. This is because when using atomics, we are forfeiting many compiler and system optimizations. For example, when we access the same variable repeatedly, like we do in listing 12.3, the system keeps the variable in the processor's cache, making access to the variable faster, but it might periodically flush the variable back to main memory, especially if it's running out of cache space. When using atomics, the system needs to ensure that any other execution running in parallel sees the update to the variable. Thus, whenever atomic operations are used, the system needs to maintain the cached variables consistently. This can be done by flushing to main memory and invalidating any other caches. Having to keep various caches consistent ends up reducing our program performance.

12.1.3 *Counting using atomic numbers*

A typical application of using atomic variables is when you need to count occurrences of the same thing from multiple executions. In chapter 3, we developed a program that used multiple goroutines to download web pages and count the frequencies of English alphabet letters. The total count of each letter was maintained in a shared slice data structure. Later, in chapter 4, we added a mutex to ensure that the updates to the shared slice were consistent.

We can change the implementation to use atomic updates every time we need to increment the count of a letter in the slice. Figure 12.2 shows that we're still using memory sharing, but this time, we're simply sending atomic updates to the variables. The previous approach used the two steps of reading the value and then writing the update, forcing us to use a mutex. By using an atomic update, we do not have to wait for another goroutine to release the mutex if we need to update a count. Our goroutines will run without any blocking interruptions from other goroutines. Even if two goroutines try to apply an atomic update at exactly the same time, the two updates are applied sequentially without conflicting.

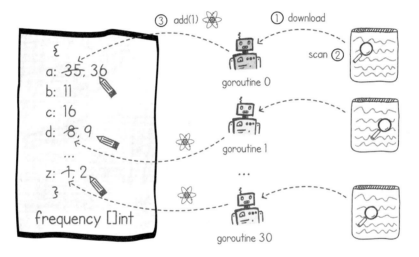

Figure 12.2   Using atomic operations for our letter-frequency program

Listing 12.4 modifies the previous implementation of the `countLetters()` function by removing the mutex lock and unlock and instead uses the atomic variable operation. In the listing, we use the reference of the integer contained in the slice directly and increment the count by 1 every time we encounter a letter.

Listing 12.4   Atomic variables in `countLetters()` (imports omitted)

```
package main

import (...)
```

```
const allLetters = "abcdefghijklmnopqrstuvwxyz"

func countLetters(url string, frequency []int32) {
    resp, _ := http.Get(url)
    defer resp.Body.Close()
    if resp.StatusCode != 200 {
        panic("Server returning error code: " + resp.Status)
    }
    body, _ := io.ReadAll(resp.Body)
    for _, b := range body {
        c := strings.ToLower(string(b))
        cIndex := strings.Index(allLetters, c)
        if cIndex >= 0 {
            atomic.AddInt32(&frequency[cIndex], 1)
        }
    }
    fmt.Println("Completed:", url)
}
```

Reads the body of the web page → `body, _ := io.ReadAll(resp.Body)`

Iterates over every letter contained in the body of the document → `for _, b := range body {`

Checks to see if the letter is part of the English alphabet

Uses an atomic add operation to increment the count of the letter

Next, we need to slightly modify the `main()` function so that the slice data structure uses 32-bit integers. This is required since atomic operations only work on specific data types such as `int32` or `int64`. In addition, we need to read the results by using the atomic function `LoadInt32()`. The following listing shows a `main()` function with these changes and uses a waitgroup to wait for all goroutines to complete.

Listing 12.5 `main()` function for atomic letter counter

```
func main() {
    wg := sync.WaitGroup{}
    wg.Add(31)
    var frequency = make([]int32, 26)
    for i := 1000; i <= 1030; i++ {
        url := fmt.Sprintf("https://rfc-editor.org/rfc/rfc%d.txt", i)
        go func() {
            countLetters(url, frequency)
            wg.Done()
        }()
    }
    wg.Wait()
    for i, c := range allLetters {
        fmt.Printf("%c-%d ", c, atomic.LoadInt32(&frequency[i]))
    }
}
```

Creates a slice with size 26 of type 32-bit integers

Waits until all goroutines are complete → `wg.Wait()`

Loads the value of each count from the frequency slice and outputs them on the console

NOTE Using the `LoadInt32()` function is not strictly necessary in the preceding listing because all the goroutines are finished by the time we read the results. However, it's good practice to use atomic load operations when working with atomics to ensure that we read the latest value from main memory and not an outdated cached value.

In chapter 3, when we ran our letter-frequency application without any mutex locks (listings 3.2 and 3.4), it produced inconsistent results. Using the atomic variables has the same effect as eliminating the race condition by using a mutex. However, this time, our goroutines are not blocking each other. Here is the output when we run listings 12.4 and 12.5 together:

```
$ go run atomiccharcounter.go
Completed: https://rfc-editor.org/rfc/rfc1018.txt
. . .
Completed: https://rfc-editor.org/rfc/rfc1002.txt
a-103445 b-23074 c-61005 d-51733 e-181360 f-33381 g-24966 h-47722 i-103262 j-
    3279 k-8839 l-49958 m-40026 n-108275 o-106320 p-41404 q-3410 r-101118 s-
    101040 t-136812 u-35765 v-13666 w-18259 x-4743 y-18416 z-1404
```

12.2   *Implementing a mutex with spin locks*

In the previous scenario, we modified the letter-frequency program to use atomic variables. The changes were simple because we only needed to update one variable at a time. What about when we have an application that requires us to update multiple variables together? In the previous chapter, we had one such scenario—the ledger application needed to subtract money from one account and add it to another. In that example, we used mutexes to protect multiple accounts. We have used mutexes throughout this book, but we've never looked at the details of how they're implemented. Let's pick a different scenario where we must use mutexes and then use atomic operations so we can build our own implementation of a mutex using a technique called *spin locking*.

Imagine that we're developing flight-booking software for an airline. When booking flights, customers want to purchase tickets for either their entire route or none at all if parts of the route are not available. Figure 12.3 shows the problem we're trying to solve. When we show a user that the full route has seats available and someone else books the last seats for part of the route in the meantime, the full purchase needs to be canceled. Otherwise, we risk irking customers by having them buy useless tickets that don't take them to their intended destinations. Even worse, we might end up stranding passengers at their destination if the outward booking was successful but the return flight booking failed when seats filled up. The flight-booking software needs to have controls to avoid these types of race conditions.

To implement such a booking system, we can model each flight as a separate entity containing details such as point of origin and destination, remaining seats on the flight, departure time, flight time, and so on. Using atomic operations to update the remaining seats on a flight will not solve the race condition outlined in figure 12.3 because when a customer books multiple flights together, we need to ensure that we update all the remaining seat variables on the flights booked together in an atomic unit. Atomic variables only guarantee atomic updates to one variable at a time.

To solve this problem, we can adopt the same approach we adopted for the ledger application, that of having a lock on each account. In this case, before adjusting each flight, we will obtain locks on each flight that is in the customer's booking. Listing 12.6

Figure 12.3 **A poorly written concurrent program for a flight-booking system results in race conditions.**

shows how we can model the details of each flight using a `struct` type. In this implementation, we're keeping things simple and only storing the flight's origin and destination and the seats left on the flight. We also use the `Locker` interface, which contains just two functions: `Lock()` and `Unlock()`. This is the same interface that a mutex implements.

Listing 12.6 Struct type representing a flight

```
package listing12_6

import (
    "sync"
)

type Flight struct {
    Origin, Dest string
    SeatsLeft int
    Locker    sync.Locker    ◁─┐  Provides an interface containing
}                                 lock and unlock functions
```

We can now develop a function that adjusts the `SeatsLeft` variable when given a booking containing a list of flights. Listing 12.7 implements this function, returning `true` only if all flights on the input slice contain enough seats for the booking request. The implementation starts by sorting the input list of flights in alphabetical order using the origin and destination. This ordering is done to avoid deadlocks (see chapter 11). The function proceeds by locking all the requested flights so that the number of seats remaining on each flight does not change while we're updating them. Then we check to see if each flight contains enough seats to fulfill the requested booking. If they all do, we reduce the seats on each flight by the number of seats the customer wants to buy.

Listing 12.7   Flight-booking function

```
package listing12_7

import (
    "github.com/cutajarj/ConcurrentProgrammingWithGo/chapter12/listing12.6"
    "sort"
)

func Book(flights []*listing12_6.Flight, seatsToBook int) bool {
    bookable := true
    sort.Slice(flights, func(a, b int) bool {
        flightA := flights[a].Origin + flights[a].Dest
        flightB := flights[b].Origin + flights[b].Dest
        return flightA < (flightB)
    })
    for _, f := range flights {
        f.Locker.Lock()
    }
    for i := 0; i < len(flights) && bookable; i++ {
        if flights[i].SeatsLeft < seatsToBook {
            bookable = false
        }
    }
    for i := 0; i < len(flights) && bookable; i++ {
        flights[i].SeatsLeft-=seatsToBook
    }
    for _, f := range flights {
        f.Locker.Unlock()
    }
    return bookable
}
```

— **Sorts flights in alphabetical order based on their origin and destination**

— **Locks all the requested flights**

— **Checks to see that all the requested flights have enough seats**

— **Subtracts the seats from each flight only if there are enough seats for the entire booking**

— **Unlocks all the locked flights**

— **Returns the result of the booking**

We could use Go's `sync.mutex`, as this gives us both the `Lock()` and `Unlock()` functions, but instead, let's take this opportunity to implement our own `sync.Locker` implementation. In doing so, we'll learn how mutexes can be implemented.

12.2.1   Comparing and swapping

Can any of the operations on the atomic variable help us to implement our mutex? The `CompareAndSwap()` function can be used to check and set a flag indicating that a resource is locked. This function works by accepting a value pointer and `old` and `new` parameters. If the `old` parameter is equal to the value stored at the pointer, the value is updated to match that of the `new` parameter. This operation (like all operations in the `atomic` package) is atomic and thus cannot be interrupted by another execution.

Figure 12.4 shows the `CompareAndSwap()` function when used in two scenarios. On the left side of the figure, the value of the variable is what we expect, equal to the `old` parameter. When this happens, the value is updated to that of the `new` parameter, and the function returns `true`. The right side of the figure shows what happens when we call the function on a value not equal to the `old` parameter. In this case, the update is not applied, and the function returns `false`.

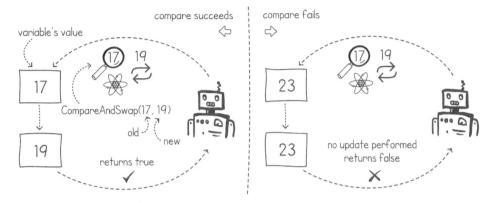

Figure 12.4 The `CompareAndSwap()` function operating in two scenarios

The two scenarios can be seen in action in listing 12.8. We call the same function twice with the same parameters. For the first call, we set the variable to have the same value as the old parameter, and for the second call, we change the value of the variable to be different.

Listing 12.8   Applying the `CompareAndSwap()` function

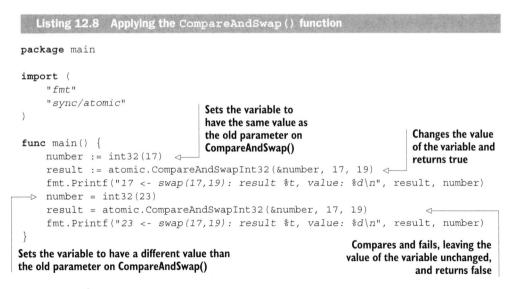

When we run the preceding listing, the first call succeeds, updating the variable and returning `true`. After we change the value of the variable, the second call fails, and the

CompareAndSwap() function returns `false`, leaving the variable unchanged. Here is the output:

```
$ go run atomiccompareandswap.go
17 <- swap(17,19): result true, value: 19
23 <- swap(17,19): result false, value: 23
```

Now that we know how the CompareAndSwap() function works, let's see how it can help us to implement our Locker interface.

12.2.2 *Building a mutex*

We can use the CompareAndSwap() function to implement a mutex completely in user space without having to rely on the operating system. We'll start by using an atomic variable as an indicator showing whether the mutex is locked. We can then use the CompareAndSwap() function to check and update the value of the indicator whenever we need to lock the mutex. To unlock the mutex, we can call the Store() function on the atomic variable. Figure 12.5 shows this concept.

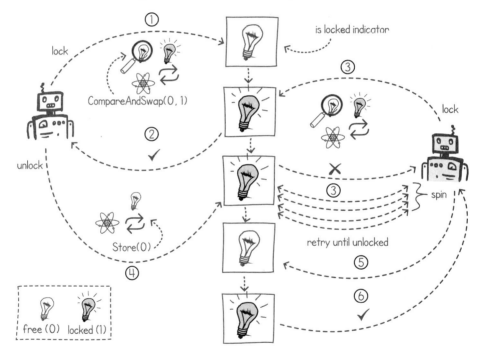

Figure 12.5   Implementing spin locks

If the indicator is showing as free, CompareAndSwap(unlocked, locked) will succeed, and the indicator will be updated to locked. If the indicator is showing as locked, the CompareAndSwap(unlocked, locked) operation will fail, returning `false`. At this point, we can keep retrying until the indicator changes value and becomes unlocked. This type of mutex is called a spin lock.

DEFINITION   A *spin lock* is a type of lock in which an execution will go into a loop to try to get hold of a lock repeatedly until the lock becomes available.

To implement our spin lock's indicator, we can make use of an integer variable. The integer can have a value of `0` it the lock is free and a value of `1` if it's locked. In listing 12.9, we use a 32-bit integer as our indicator.

The listing also shows how we can implement both the `lock()` and `Unlock()` functions, fully implementing the `Locker` interface. In the `lock()` function, the `CompareAndSwap()` operation is called in a loop until the call returns successfully and the atomic variable is updated to `1`. This is the spinning part of our lock. The goroutine locking the spin lock will continue looping until the lock is free. In the `Unlock()` function, we simply call the atomic `Store()` function to set the value of the indicator to `0`, signifying that the lock is free.

Listing 12.9   Spin lock implementation

```
package listing12_9

import (
    "runtime"
    "sync"
    "sync/atomic"
)

type SpinLock int32
```
A value of 0 indicates that the lock is free, while 1 indicates that the lock is locked.

```
func (s *SpinLock) Lock() {
    for !atomic.CompareAndSwapInt32((*int32)(s), 0, 1) {
        runtime.Gosched()
    }
}
```
Loops until CompareAndSwap() succeeds and sets the value to 1

Calls the Go scheduler to give execution time to other goroutines

```
func (s *SpinLock) Unlock() {
    atomic.StoreInt32((*int32)(s), 0)
}
```
Updates the integer value to 0, marking the lock as free

```
func NewSpinLock() sync.Locker {
    var lock SpinLock
    return &lock
}
```

In our spin lock implementation, we are calling the Go scheduler every time the goroutine finds that the lock is already being used by another goroutine. This call is not strictly necessary, but it should give other goroutines a chance to execute and possibly unlock the spin lock. In technical speak, we can say that the goroutine is *yielding* its execution.

Listing 12.9 includes a function to create our spin lock, returning a pointer to the `Locker` interface. We can use this implementation in our flight-booking program. The following listing shows the implementation for creating a new, empty flight using the spin locks.

> **Listing 12.10 Creating a new flight using spin locks**

```
package listing12_10

import (
    "github.com/cutajarj/ConcurrentProgrammingWithGo/chapter12/listing12.6"
    "github.com/cutajarj/ConcurrentProgrammingWithGo/chapter12/listing12.9"
)

func NewFlight(origin, dest string) *listing12_6.Flight {
    return &listing12_6.Flight{
        Origin:    origin,
        Dest:      dest,
        SeatsLeft: 200,
        Locker:    listing12_9.NewSpinLock(),   ⟵——— Creates a new spin lock
    }
}
```

> **DEFINITION** *Resource contention* is when an execution (such as a thread, process, or goroutine) uses a resource in a way that blocks and slows down another execution.

The problem with implementing mutexes using spin locks is that when we have high resource contention, such as a goroutine hogging a lock for a long time, other executions will be wasting valuable CPU cycles while spinning and waiting for the lock to be released. In our implementation, the goroutines will be stuck in the loop, executing CompareAndSwap() repeatedly until another goroutine calls unlock(). This waiting in a loop wastes valuable CPU time that could be used to execute other tasks.

12.3 *Improving on spin locking*

How can we improve our Locker implementation so that we don't have to loop continuously when the lock is not available? In our implementation, we called runtime.Gosched() to provide the opportunity for other goroutines to execute instead. This is known as *yielding* the execution, and in certain other languages (such as Java), the operation is called yield().

The problem with yielding is that the runtime (or operating system) doesn't know that the current execution is waiting for a lock to become available. It is likely that the execution waiting for the lock will be resumed multiple times before the lock is released, wasting valuable CPU time. To help with this, operating systems provide a concept known as a futex.

12.3.1 *Locking with futexes*

Futex is short for *fast userspace mutex*. However, this definition is misleading, as futexes are not mutexes at all. A *futex* is a wait queue primitive that we can access from user space. It gives us the ability to suspend and awaken an execution on a specific address. Futexes come in handy when we need to implement efficient concurrency primitives such as mutexes, semaphores, and condition variables.

When using futexes, we might use several system calls. The names and parameters vary on each operating system, but most operating systems provide similar functionality. For simplicity's sake, let's assume we have two system calls named `futex_wait(address, value)` and `futex_wake(address, count)`.

> ### Implementations of futexes on different operating systems
>
> On Linux, `futex_wait()` and `futex_wake()` can both be implemented with the system call `syscall(SYS_futex, ...)`. For the wait and wake functionality, we can use the `FUTEX_WAIT` and `FUTEX_WAKE` parameters respectively.
>
> On Windows, for `futex_wait()`, we can use the `WaitOnAddress()` system call. The `futex_wake()` call can be implemented by using either `WakeByAddressSingle()` or `WakeByAddressAll()`.

When we call `futex_wait(addr, value)`, we specify a memory address and a value. If the value at the memory address is equal to the specified parameter `value`, the execution of the caller is suspended and placed at the back of a queue. The queue parks all the executions that have called `futex_wait()` on the same address value. The operating system models a different queue for each memory address value.

When we call `futex_wait(addr, value)` and the value of the memory address is different from the parameter value, the function returns immediately, and the execution continues. These two outcomes are shown in figure 12.6.

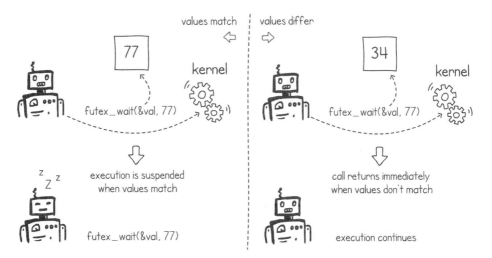

Figure 12.6   Calling `futex_wait()` with two different outcomes

The `futex_wake(addr, count)` wakes up suspended executions (threads and processes) that are waiting on the address specified. The operating system resumes a total of `count` executions, and it picks up the executions from the front of the queue. If the count parameter is `0`, all the suspended executions are resumed.

These two functions can be used to implement a user space mutex that only switches to the kernel when it needs to suspend the execution. This is when our atomic variable, representing the lock, is not free. The idea is that when an execution finds the lock marked as locked, the current execution can go to sleep by calling `futex_wait()`. The kernel takes over and places the execution at the back of the futex wait queue. When the lock becomes available again, we can call `futex_wake()`, and the kernel resumes one execution from the wait queue so that it can obtain the lock. This simple algorithm is shown in listing 12.11.

NOTE   In Go, we have no access to the futex system calls. The next code listings are pseudocode in Go to illustrate how runtimes can use the futexes to implement efficient locking libraries.

Listing 12.11   Locking and unlocking using futexes, attempt #1 (pseudo Go)

```go
package listing12_11

import "sync/atomic"

type FutexLock int32

func (f *FutexLock) Lock() {
    for !atomic.CompareAndSwapInt32((*int32)(f), 0, 1) {    // Tries to mark the atomic variable as locked by setting it to 1 if it is 0
        futex_wait((*int32)(f), 1)    // If the lock is not available, waits, but only if the lock variable has a value of 1
    }
}

func (f *FutexLock) Unlock() {
    atomic.StoreInt32((*int32)(f), 0)    // Updates the atomic variable to have a value of 0, freeing the lock
    futex_wakeup((*int32)(f), 1)    // Wakes up 1 execution
}
```

Passing a value of `1` to `futex_wait()` ensures we avoid a race condition where the lock is released just after we call `CompareAndSwap()` but before `futex_wait()`. If this happens, since `futex_wait()` is expecting a value of `1` but finds `0`, it will return immediately, and we'll go back to check again if the lock is free.

Our mutex implementation in the previous listing is an improvement on the spin lock implementation. When there is resource contention, the executions will not loop needlessly, wasting CPU cycles. Instead, they will wait on a futex. They will be queued until the lock becomes available again.

Although we have made the implementation more efficient in scenarios when we have contention, we have slowed it down in the reverse case. When there is no contention, such as when we are using a single execution, our `Unlock()` function is slower than the spin lock version. This is because we are always making an expensive system call in `futex_wakeup()`, even when no other executions are waiting on the futex.

System calls are expensive because they interrupt the current execution, switch context to the operating system, and then, once the call completes, switch back to the user space. Ideally, we want to find a way to avoid calling `futex_wakeup()` when nothing else is waiting on the futex.

12.3.2 Reducing system calls

We can further improve the performance of our mutex implementation if we change the meaning of our atomic variable that stands for the lock and instead have it tell us if there is an execution waiting for the lock. We can take the value of 0 as meaning unlocked, 1 as locked, and 2 as telling us that it is locked with executions waiting for the lock. In this way, we will only call `futex_wakeup()` when we have a value of 2, and we'll save time whenever there is no contention.

Listing 12.12 shows the unlocking function using this new system. In this listing, we unlock the mutex by first updating the atomic variable to 0, and then, if its previous value was 2, we wake up any waiting execution by calling `futex_wakeup()`. In this way, we will make this system call only when it's needed.

Listing 12.12 Waking up a futex only when it's needed

```
package listing12_12

import "sync/atomic"

type FutexLock int32

func (f *FutexLock) Unlock() {                          Marks the lock as unlocked,
    oldValue := atomic.SwapInt32((*int32)(f), 0)    ◁── storing the old value
    if oldValue == 2 {                      ◁─
        futex_wakeup((*int32)(f), 1)           If the old value was 2, it means
    }                                          executions are waiting.
}
```

Wakes up one execution

To implement the `lock ()` function, we can use both the `CompareAndSwap()` and `Swap()` functions working together. Figure 12.7 shows the idea. In this example, the execution on the left first does a normal `CompareAndSwap()` and marks the atomic variable as locked. Once it's done with the lock, it calls `Swap()` with a value of 0 to unlock. Since the `Swap()` function returns 2, it calls `futex_wakeup()`. On the right, after another execution finds that the atomic variable is already locked, it swaps the value of 2, and since the `Swap()` function returned a non-zero value, we call `futex_wait()`. In this way, while we're marking the variable as locked with waiters (a value of 2), we also check again that the lock didn't become free in the meantime. This `Swap()` step is repeated until it returns 0, signifying that we have acquired the lock.

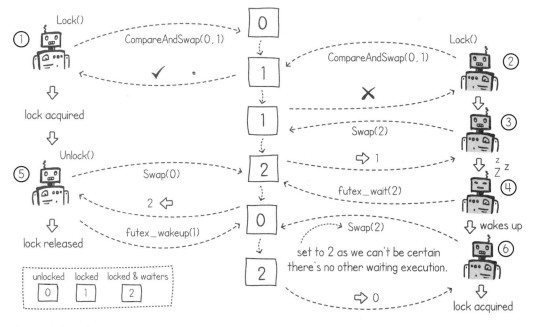

Figure 12.7   Using futexes only when there is contention

Listing 12.13 shows the `Lock()` function. The function first tries to acquire the lock by doing a normal `CompareAndSwap()`. If the lock is not available, it goes into a loop where it tries to acquire the lock and at the same time marks it as locked with waiters. It does this by using the `Swap()` function. If the `Swap()` function returns a non-zero result, it calls `futex_wait()` to suspend the execution.

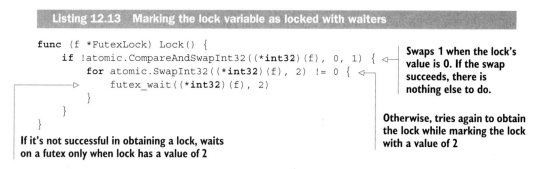

Listing 12.13 Marking the lock variable as locked with waiters

```
func (f *FutexLock) Lock() {
    if !atomic.CompareAndSwapInt32((*int32)(f), 0, 1) {
        for atomic.SwapInt32((*int32)(f), 2) != 0 {
            futex_wait((*int32)(f), 2)
        }
    }
}
```

Swaps 1 when the lock's value is 0. If the swap succeeds, there is nothing else to do.

Otherwise, tries again to obtain the lock while marking the lock with a value of 2

If it's not successful in obtaining a lock, waits on a futex only when lock has a value of 2

NOTE   After the execution wakes up from `futex_wait()`, it will always set the variable to a value of 2. This is because there is no way of knowing if there is another execution waiting. For this reason, we play it safe and set it to 2 at the cost of occasionally doing an unnecessary `futex_wakeup()` system call.

12.3.3 Go's mutex implementation

Since we now know how to implement an efficient mutex, it's worth investigating Go's mutex implementation to understand how it works. Calling a wait on a futex results in the operating system suspending the kernel-level thread. Since Go uses a user-level threading model, Go's mutex does not use futexes directly, as this would result in the underlying kernel-level thread being suspended.

The use of user-level threads in Go means that a queuing system, similar to our implementation using futexes, can be implemented completely in the user space. Go's runtime queues goroutines just as the operating system would do for kernel-level threads. This means we save time by not switching to kernel mode every time we need to wait for a locked mutex. Whenever a goroutine requests a mutex that is already locked, Go's runtime can put that goroutine into a waiting queue to wait for the mutex to become available. The runtime can then pick up another goroutine to execute. Once the mutex is unlocked, the runtime can pick up the first goroutine from the waiting queue, resume it, and make it attempt to acquire the mutex again.

To do all of this, the implementation of `sync.mutex` in Go makes use of a semaphore. This semaphore implementation takes care of queuing goroutines in cases when the lock is not available. This semaphore is part of the internals of Go and cannot be accessed directly, but we can explore it to understand how it works. The source code can be found here: https://github.com/golang/go/blob/master/src/runtime/sema.go.

Just like our mutex, the implementation of this semaphore uses an atomic variable to store the permits available. It first does a `CompareAndSwap()` on the atomic variable representing the permit available to reduce the permits by one. When it finds that there aren't enough permits (acting like a locked mutex), it puts the goroutine on an internal queue and parks the goroutine, suspending its execution. At this point, Go's runtime is free to pick up another goroutine from its run queues and execute it without the need to switch to kernel mode.

The code in Go's semaphore implementation is hard to follow because there is extra functionality to make it work with Go's runtime and deal with numerous edge cases. To help us understand how the semaphore works, the following listing shows pseudocode that implements a semaphore acquire function using atomic variables. The listing shows the core functionality of the `semacquire1()` function in Go's source code.

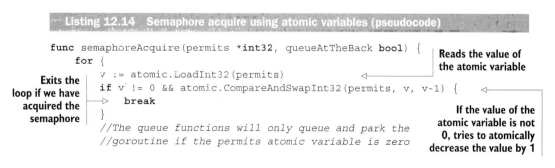

Listing 12.14   Semaphore acquire using atomic variables (pseudocode)

```
func semaphoreAcquire(permits *int32, queueAtTheBack bool) {          Reads the value of
    for {                                                             the atomic variable
        v := atomic.LoadInt32(permits)
        if v != 0 && atomic.CompareAndSwapInt32(permits, v, v-1) {
            break
        }
    }
    //The queue functions will only queue and park the
    //goroutine if the permits atomic variable is zero
```

Exits the loop if we have acquired the semaphore

If the value of the atomic variable is not 0, tries to atomically decrease the value by 1

```
        if queueAtTheBack {
            queueAndSuspendGoroutineAtTheEnd(permits)
        } else {
            queueAndSuspendGoroutineInFront(permits)
        }
    }
}
```

> **Queues and suspends the goroutine at the back or front only when permits is 0**

In addition, this semaphore implementation has functionality to prioritize a goroutine by placing it at the front of the queue instead of at the back. This can be used when we want to give a higher priority to a goroutine so that it's picked up first when a permit becomes available. We will see that this comes in handy in the full `sync.mutex` implementation.

The `sync.mutex` acts as a wrapper to the semaphore and, in addition, adds another level of sophistication on top with the aim of improving performance. Just like a normal spin lock, Go's mutex attempts first to grab hold of the lock by doing a simple `CompareAndSwap()` on an atomic variable. If it fails, it falls back on the semaphore to put the goroutine to sleep until the unlock is called. In this way, it's using the internal semaphore to implement the functionality of the futex we saw in previous sections. This concept is shown in figure 12.8.

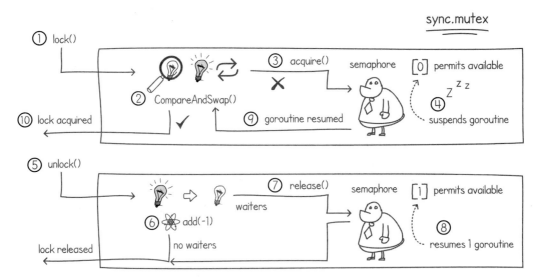

Figure 12.8   The internals of Go's mutex

This is still not the full story. The `sync.mutex` has an additional layer of complexity—it has two modes of operation: normal and starvation mode. In normal mode, when the mutex is locked, goroutines are queued up normally to the back of the semaphore queue. Go's runtime resumes the first waiting goroutine in this queue whenever a lock is released.

A mutex running in normal mode has a problem: a waiting goroutine, whenever resumed, has to compete with new arriving goroutines. These are goroutines that have just called the lock () function and haven't yet been placed into the waiting queue. The newly arriving goroutines have an advantage over the resumed goroutine: since they are already running, they are more likely to acquire the lock than a goroutine that is being taken out of the queue and resumed. This can create a situation where the first goroutine in the waiting queue is resumed in vain because by the time it tries to perform the CompareAndSwap(), it will find the mutex already taken by the newly arrived goroutine. This can happen multiple times, making the mutex prone to starvation; the goroutines will remain stuck in the queue for as long as we have newly arriving goroutines acquiring the lock (see figure 12.9).

Figure 12.9 Newly arriving goroutines have an advantage over waiting ones.

In the implementation of sync.mutex, when a resumed goroutine fails to acquire the mutex, the same goroutine is suspended again, but this time it is placed at the front of the queue. This ensures that the next time the mutex is unlocked, the goroutine is picked up first. If this repeats for a while and the goroutine fails to acquire the lock after a certain period (set to 1 ms), the mutex switches to starvation mode.

When the mutex is in starvation mode, the mutex acts in a fairer manner. As soon as the mutex is unlocked, it is passed to the goroutine at the front of the waiting queue. Newly arriving goroutines do not try to acquire the mutex, but instead go directly to the tail of the queue and get suspended until it's their turn. The mutex switches back to normal mode once the queue is empty or a waiting goroutine spends less than 1 ms acquiring the lock.

NOTE The source for Go's `mutex` can be found at https://go.dev/src/ sync/mutex.go.

The purpose of this extra complexity is to improve performance while avoiding goroutine starvation. In normal mode, when we have low contention, the mutex is very efficient, as goroutines can acquire the mutex quickly, without having to wait on the queue. When we have high contention and we switch to starvation mode, the mutex ensures that goroutines do not get stuck on the wait queue.

12.4   Exercises

NOTE Visit http://github.com/cutajarj/ConcurrentProgrammingWithGo to see all the code solutions.

1 In listing 12.9, we implemented a spin lock by using integers. Can you change this implementation so that it uses the atomic Boolean type found in the `sync/atomic` Go package? Just like in listing 12.9, the implementation needs to provide the `Lock()` and `Unlock()` functions found in `sync.Locker`.

2 Go's mutex implementation also includes a `TryLock()` function. Use the previous implementation of the spin lock with an atomic Boolean to include this extra `TryLock()` function. This function should attempt to acquire the mutex and immediately return `true` if the mutex was acquired and `false` otherwise. Here is the full function signature:

```
func (s *SpinLock) TryLock() bool
```

3 Atomic variables can also be used to implement spinning semaphores. Write an implementation of a semaphore that can be initialized with a specified number of permits. The semaphore can use atomic variables to implement the following function signatures:

```
func (s *SpinSemaphore) Acquire()
```

The `Acquire()` function reduces the number of permits available by 1. If no more permits are available, it will spin on the atomic variable until one is available:

```
func (s *SpinSemaphore) Release()
```

The `Release()` function increments the number of permits available by 1:

```
func NewSpinSemaphore(permits int32) *SpinSemaphore
```

The `NewSpinSemaphore()` function creates a new semaphore with the specified number of permits.

Summary

- Atomic variables provide the ability to perform atomic updates on various data types, such as atomically incrementing an integer.
- Atomic operations cannot be interrupted by other executions.
- Applications in which multiple goroutines are updating and reading a variable at the same time can use atomic variables instead of mutexes to avoid race conditions.
- Updating an atomic variable is slower than updating a normal variable.
- Atomic variables work on only one variable at a time. If we need to protect updates to multiple variables together, we need to use mutexes or other synchronization tools.
- The `CompareAndSwap()` function atomically checks to see whether the value of the atomic variable has a specified value and, if it does, updates the variable with another value.
- The `CompareAndSwap()` function returns `true` only when the swap succeeds.
- A spin lock is an implementation of a mutex completely in the user space.
- Spin locks use a flag to indicate whether a resource is locked.
- If the flag is already locked by another execution, the spin lock will repeatedly try to use the `CompareAndSwap()` function to determine whether the flag is unlocked. Once the flag indicates that the lock is free, it can then be marked as locked again.
- When there is high contention, spin locks waste CPU cycles by looping until the lock becomes available.
- Instead of endlessly looping on the atomic variable to implement a spin lock, a futex can be used to suspend and queue the execution until the lock becomes available.
- To implement a mutex with an atomic variable and a futex, we can have the atomic variable store three states: unlocked, locked, and locked with waiting executions.
- Go's mutexes implement a queuing system in the user space to suspend goroutines that are waiting to acquire a lock.
- The mutexes in the `sync` package wrap around a semaphore implementation that queues and suspends goroutines when no more permits are available.
- The mutex implementation in Go switches from normal to starvation mode in situations where newly arriving goroutines are blocking queuing goroutines from acquiring the lock.

index

A

abstractions 14, 17, 20, 40, 43, 89
Actor model 190
Add() 123, 137
Akka 189–190
algorithm 11, 130–132, 150, 183, 210, 217, 222,
    230, 257–260, 288
  banker's algorithm 259–261, 264
  compiler algorithm 48
  deadlock avoidance algorithms 264
  detection algorithm 258
  galactic algorithms 131
  graph cycle detection algorithm 272
  matrix multiplication algorithm 115, 131
  pipeline algorithm 210, 240
  scheduling algorithm 18
Amdahl's law 11–13, 15, 70, 74
API 27, 78
artificial intelligence 130
asynchronous 31
atomic 59, 70, 93, 127, 273–279, 282–285,
    288–291, 294–295
  atomic operation 59, 249, 274–280
  atomic package 274–275, 282
  atomic update 278, 280
  definition 59

B

barriers 114–115, 126–130, 133–137
  barrier group 127
  barrier size 127–129, 135
  barriers or no barriers? 136
  barriers type 115
  barriers vs. waitgroups 126
  cyclic barrier 127
  explanation 126
  implementation 127
  introduction 114
  sharing 130
batch-processing systems 19
blocking 75, 77, 80, 85–86, 88, 102, 104, 112, 136,
    158, 160–167, 170–172, 174–176, 186, 254,
    269, 278, 280, 295
  blocking calls 36, 136
  blocking function 74
  blocking I/O operation 39
  blocking operations 36, 166
  I/O calls 34
  non-blocking calls 34, 75
  read calls 34
broadcast 98, 125, 207
  condition variable 128–129
  instead of signal 124
  pattern 207, 214
  resume 262
  to a waiting goroutine 95
  to multiple channels 204, 206–207
  unblocking goroutines 101
  unlock 107
Broadcast() 93, 96, 99–101, 107–108, 110, 113,
    125, 129, 207, 263
buffer 24, 146–148, 154–162, 232, 242, 269
  buffer capacity 146, 148
  buffer data structure 157
  buffered channel 146
  capacity buffer 243
  channel buffer 148
  empty buffer 147
  full buffer 146

buffer *(continued)*
  memory buffer 227
  message buffer 146
  queue buffer 159
bus 43–45, 70
  architecture 43
  interface 19
  system 43

C

cache 19, 34, 43–45
  coherence 45
  consistency 277
  CPU 45
  layer 44
  processor 44, 59, 277
  write-through 45
cache-coherency protocols 45
case statement 165, 177
channel struct 156
channels 142, 144–145, 147–178, 180–182, 184,
    186–187, 189–204, 206–208, 210, 212–214,
    226, 228–232, 234, 238, 242, 245, 267–273
  as concurrency tools 10
  buffered channel 146, 148, 154, 162
  closed channel 152
  description 9
  directory channel 268
  dirs. channel 269
  files channel 269–270
  Go channels 4, 141–142, 146
  input and output channels 179
  input channel 193, 195–200, 204, 206–207,
    212–213, 232, 238–239, 268, 271
  message passing 142
  messages channel 172
  multiple channels 163–164
  nil channel 174–175, 177, 186
  non-blocking 166
  non-buffered channel 267
  output channel 175, 177, 181, 184–185,
    193–194, 196–198, 200–201, 203, 205,
    207, 213, 228–229, 238–239, 268, 271
  patterns 187
  quit channel 191–195, 197, 208–209, 212–213,
    238–239
  read 145
  result channel 170
  synchronized channels 9
  Timer channel 186
  unbuffered 189
  use 142–144
    creating 143
    reading 143

work queue channel 232–234
  zero-buffer channel 159
  zero-capacity channel 160
circular resource 249
client handler 28–29, 78, 82
clone() 27
close() 162, 168, 191, 208
cloud computing 6
coherency wall 45
command line 23, 40
communication sequential processes (CSP) 9–10,
    14–15, 141, 166, 187–190, 210, 212, 214
CompareAndSwap() 282–286, 288–293, 295
compiler 48–49, 59, 61–62, 69, 277
computer graphics 130
concurrency
  concurrency patterns 5, 190, 217, 219
  concurrency tools 10, 108, 113, 136, 162
  concurrent application 4, 10, 89, 178, 220
  concurrent interference 159
  concurrent program 47, 56, 60, 72, 214, 220,
    225, 245, 281
  concurrent programming 3–5, 9, 14, 23, 39, 52,
    179, 182, 217, 243
    and Amdahl's law 13
    avoiding race conditions 61–63
    bottlenecks 274
    concurrent code 4, 7, 13, 19, 26, 55, 88,
      188, 274
    concurrent programs 5, 7, 17, 27, 38–39, 54
      deadlocks 245
    CSP 189
    CSP-style 10
    deadlocks 247, 255
    goroutines 9
    locks 66
    memory sharing 43
    message passing 179
    resource allocation 16
    responsiveness 8
    shared memory 188
    using channels 153
    worker pool 230
  concurrent programming vs. sequential
    programming 5
  concurrent reads 66, 80, 108
condition variable 10, 53, 87, 89–90, 92–96,
    98–102, 104–107, 109–114, 123–125,
    127–129, 137, 162, 188, 190, 261–263, 287
connection 28, 52–54, 132, 199, 231–233, 235
  client connection 232–233
  database connection 260
context switch 19, 33–34, 59–60
Copy on write 23

core 26, 34–35, 55, 83, 214, 291
  CPU core 5
  dual-core processor 19
  multicore processors 6
  multicore system 20
  multicore technology 6
  multiple cores 19, 82, 136, 154
  parallel processing cores 13
  single core 82
  single-core 19
core.async 189
CPU 5–7, 17–20, 23, 26–27, 29–30, 34, 37–39,
    43–44, 59, 69, 92, 134, 273, 286, 288, 295
CreateProcess() 22–23
CreateThread() 27
critical section 59, 61, 63, 65–69, 73, 75, 77, 80, 82,
    85–88, 95, 102, 104, 179, 274
  mutex protection 67
curl 23–24, 233, 235

D

database 51, 108, 257–258
database session resource 260
deadlocks 144–145, 175, 245, 247–250, 253–258,
    260, 264–265, 269, 271–272, 281
  avoiding 258–260, 262, 264
  blocking access 254
  channels 267, 269–271
  circular dependency 249
  dealing with 255
  detection 175, 255–258, 272
  error 257
  examples 250
  identifying 245, 250
  introduction 245
  preventing 264–267, 270–271
  resource allocation graphs 247–248, 250, 254
decomposition 217, 219–222, 243
  data decomposition 220, 243
  input data decomposition 220
  output data decomposition 220
  task decomposition 219
device driver 18
Dijkstra, Edsger 110, 259

E

environment variable
  GOMAXPROCS 35
Erlang 9, 189–190
escape analysis 47–48
exec() 23

execution 67, 69–71, 74, 108, 150, 208, 221, 250,
    252, 287–288
  blocking 53, 72, 84, 93, 102, 155, 175, 186
  boundaries 179–180
  concurrent 3, 5, 9, 14, 31, 55, 62, 65, 88, 108,
    113, 155, 159, 162, 179, 182–183, 189, 203,
    220–221, 245, 247, 254, 264
  copy 22
  CSP 190
  error 257
  holding a mutex 109
  interruption 59–61, 282, 289
  locking 295
  loop 285
  main thread 20, 30
  memory 24
  message passing 180
  multiplexing 166
  order 33
  parallel 39, 220, 222, 227, 277
  pausing 8, 18
  pipeline 193, 198
  resources 259–260, 264, 267, 272, 286
  resuming 61, 101, 113, 127–128
  sequential 70, 88, 198
  sleep 30
  slow down 58
  starvation 103, 113
  state 17, 186
  stopping 168, 214, 245
  suspend and awaken 287
  suspended executions 128, 137, 288
  suspending 68, 83, 92–93, 95, 99, 104, 113, 118,
    127, 130, 137, 201, 260–262, 287–288, 290–291
    queuing 295
  switching 34
  terminating 191–192
  threads 24, 27, 33–34, 42, 67, 188–189, 233
  unblocking 89
  units 19–20
    actors 190
  waiting 96, 289
  waking 289–290
  yielding 60, 285–286

F

fan-in pattern 178, 200–202, 214
fan-out pattern 199–200, 204, 214
first in first out 155
first-class objects 164–165, 187–188, 190, 210,
    212, 214
flag
  -bench 277
  -race 62, 69

flag *(continued)*
  closed channels 177
  data 195, 197
  locked 70, 295
  locked resource 282
  moreData 197
  open channel 152, 162, 177–178
  status 152
  writeActive 106
  writer active indicator 104
fork() 22–23
ForkExec() 23
futex 273, 286–292, 295
futex_wait() 287–290
futex_wake() 287–288
futex_wakeup() 289–290

G

garbage collection 48
global interpreter lock 27
global run queue (GRQ) 35
globalLock 84–87
Go 4, 10, 14, 34, 60, 233
  abstractions 9
  atomic operations 274
  barriers 115, 127
    implementation 127
  benchmarking tools 276
  blocking 36
  bundled mutex implementation 273
  channel 231
  channels 149, 160, 162, 164, 187, 214, 245
    closing 150, 152
    implementation 161
    nil values 174
    synchronous 162
  close channel 191
  common patterns 190
  communication 187
  compiler 47
  condition variable 93–94
    implementation 93
  context switching 37
  CSP 9–10, 189–190, 214
  deadlock 272
  deadlock detection 175, 255–258, 272
  deadlock prevention 264
  documentation 61, 104
  execution termination 27, 31
  exiting process 103
  exiting processes 38
  futex 288
  generics 156, 238

GitHub 161
Go mutex 75
Go slice 51, 53, 78, 155, 180
Go vs. CSP 210, 212
goroutine
  lock 37
goroutine resumption 292
goroutines 9, 27, 29, 33–34
  hybrid threading 35
goroutines vs. barriers 136
heap vs. stack 48
hybrid system 34
locks 81
message passing 142
monitor pattern 96
mutexes 67, 70, 75, 77, 291–292, 294
  implementation 291, 294–295
nonblocking operations 166
os.ReadDir() 226
processes 23
race detector 62–65
runtime 35, 41, 48, 60, 98, 134, 144, 257
runtime error 145
RWMutex 104
scheduler 37–38, 60–61
select statement 163, 166
semaphore 109
  implementation 291
slice 53
struct 128
sync.mutex 282, 291
terminating processes 52
threads 43
threads vs. barriers 136
tools 10
WaitGroup 115
waitgroups 114–115, 118, 120, 122, 137
worker pool 233, 244
go keyword 47, 49, 52
Go scheduler 65, 285
goroutines 40, 66, 78, 80, 82, 84, 91, 102,
    144, 146–147, 164, 168, 175–177, 180–182,
    191–195, 197, 200–201, 203–204, 207–208,
    211–214, 223–224, 226, 228–232, 235,
    238–239, 242–244, 247–248, 268–270,
    275, 278, 286, 291–295
  anonymous 154, 164, 173
  atomic 278–280, 285
  barriers 126–130, 133–137
    matrix multiplication 131–132
  basics of 9
  bidirectional 149
  blocked goroutine 157
  blocking 74–75, 80, 155, 157

goroutines *(continued)*
  channels 187
    quitting 191, 208
    reusing patterns 190
  child 32, 40, 98, 162
  client handler 79–83
  concurrency 9, 14, 23, 31, 43
  concurrent 82, 154, 162
  condition variables 90
  creating 29, 31, 75
  critical section 67, 80
  CSP 190
  deadlocks 245–249, 251–258, 261–264, 267, 269–271
    circular wait 269, 272
    preventing 261, 264–267
    resuming 262–263
  download goroutine 200
  downloadPage() 198
  downloadPages() 199–200
  doWork() 111, 115
  explanation 29
  extractWords() 200
  fan-in pattern 200
  file handler 268–269
  file hash 226
  forked goroutine 228–230
  frequentWords() 205
  generateUrls() 198–199
  infinite loop 103
  input-to-output channel 200
  join goroutine 228, 230
  kernel space 34, 37, 41
  lock 82
  lock-free synchronization 274
  locks 75, 86–87, 285–286
  longestWords() 202–204, 207
  loosely coupled 180
  LRQ 35
  main() 71, 75–76, 98, 103, 112, 117, 119, 130, 133–136, 143–144, 148, 153, 162, 165, 174–175, 177, 192, 212, 226, 228, 231–232, 234, 242, 247, 256–257, 268
  match-recorder 78–79
  memory sharing 46–47
  memory space 48–49
  message passing 141–142, 180, 182–185
  monitor 75
  mostFrequentWords() 207
  multiple 49, 52–53, 56–57, 59, 65, 198, 200–201, 204
    broadcast 204, 207
    broadcasting 204
    issues 59–60

  mutexes 70
    waiting 99
  multiple channels 163
    reading 164
  mutex
    critical section 77
  mutex lock
    acquisition 124
  mutexes 67–69, 291
    locking 67–68
  password discovery 169–170
  pipeline 193–194, 196–198, 202, 211, 213
  player handler 100
  prime-filtering 212
  primeMultipleFilter() 212
  queue 36
  race conditions 61–62, 67
    preventing 274
  reader 84–88, 102, 104, 107–108, 238
  reader and writer 106
  receiver 144–148, 151, 154, 157–161, 177
  receiver() 143
  release 106
  resource sharing 62–63, 65, 69
  sales and expenses goroutines 176
  scheduling 37–38
  semaphores 108–112
  sender 144–147, 157–158, 161
  shared resources 84
  signal 95–98
    missing 96
  single processor 60
  sleep 91–93, 292
  starting 79
  starvation 294
  stopping 168–169
  suspended 113, 119, 124–125, 128–129, 161, 292, 295
  suspending
    with semaphores 161
  Take(n) 208–209
  timing out 171
  user space 33
  using channels 9
  vs. sequential programming 54
  waitgroups 137, 275–276
  waiting 98–101, 115, 117–121
  work stealing 36, 41
  worker goroutine 231
  worker pool 231–235
  writer 85–88, 102–104, 106, 108
  yielding 60
goroutines extractWords() 200
Gosched() 37–38, 60–61, 98, 285–286
Gustafson's law 13–15

H

hash code 223–226
    computation 224
hash function 223
heap 26, 47–49, 53, 58
Heisenbug 58
horizontal scaling 6
HTTP 142, 231–232, 235
    HTTP header 232
    HTTP requests 231–232
    HTTP server 230–231, 233
hybrid threading 35, 41

I

I/O 5, 7, 14, 18, 20, 27, 36, 39, 60, 166
IEEE 27
immutability 189–190
independent computations 217
inlining 49
instruction pointer 26–27
inter-process communication (IPC) 42
inter-thread communication (ITC) 42–43, 141
interrupt 18–19, 37, 69
    clock interrupts 37
    interrupt controller 18

J

Java 27, 34, 96, 190, 286
JSON 79

K

kernel 288
kernel mode 291

L

latency 240–241, 244
    system latency 241–242
lifecycle 17
linked list 155–157, 159
load-balancing 198–199, 231
local run queue (LRQ) 35–36
Lock() 67–69, 71, 73–75, 78–79, 81–82, 85–86,
        88, 91–95, 97, 99, 101, 104, 106–107, 110,
        117, 124–125, 129, 158–159, 246, 252, 255,
        262–266, 271, 281–282, 285, 288, 290, 294
locks 66–69, 73–76, 81, 85–86, 88, 93, 102–106,
        136, 166, 246, 248, 254, 256–257, 261, 263,
        265–267, 273, 280–281, 285–286, 288–292, 295
    acquiring 293, 295

exclusive 81, 89, 247
futexes 288
global 84–87
globalLock 85
incorrect way 72
mutex 66–67, 70, 74, 76, 80, 84, 98–100, 112,
        124–125, 128, 136, 246, 251, 255–256, 262,
        265, 274–275, 278, 280, 284
    non-blocking 74
    read 80, 82, 104, 106
    reader 82, 88, 102–103, 106
    readers-writer 66, 80–81, 84, 87–89, 102–103,
        113, 183
    readersLock 85
    recursive read 104
    spin locking 273
    spin locks 273, 280, 284–286, 288–289, 292,
        294–295
    write locks 80, 82
    write-preferred 104
    writer 84, 88, 102–106
loop 30, 47, 61, 69, 73, 79, 95, 101, 131, 134–135,
        150, 167–168, 176, 178, 223–224, 226, 239,
        285–286, 288, 290–291
    for loop 51, 95, 143, 152
    for range loop 162
    infinite loop 103, 233, 238–239, 246
    select loop 178
loop-carried dependence 224–225
loop-level parallelism 223
loop-level parallelism pattern 223–224
loosely coupled 179–180, 186
loosely coupled vs. tightly coupled 179

M

main() 30–33, 35, 37–38, 46–48, 51–53, 57,
        63–64, 68–69, 71, 74, 76, 79, 81, 87, 91, 94,
        96–100, 103, 108, 111–112, 115–120, 122, 130,
        134–135, 143–145, 148–149, 151–154, 162,
        165, 167, 170, 172, 174–175, 177, 180–182,
        184–185, 192–199, 201–204, 207, 209, 212,
        214, 223–226, 228–229, 231, 233–234, 237,
        239, 243, 246–247, 253, 255–256, 263,
        268–269, 275–276, 279, 283
master/worker. *See* worker pool pattern
matrix multiplication 39, 130–133, 135–136, 220
McIlroy, Douglas 210
memory 4, 6–7, 16, 19–27, 29, 33, 40, 42–48, 53,
        58–59, 62–63, 65, 70, 88, 131, 141–142, 178,
        180–183, 186, 189–190, 192, 203, 214, 279, 287
    main memory 277
    shared memory 46, 182, 187–188, 251
memory sharing 5, 10, 42–44, 54, 61, 163,
        178–180, 182–183, 186–190, 193, 196, 278

message passing 5, 42, 141–142, 163, 178–183, 186–187, 189–190, 193, 196, 214
monitor 19, 76, 96, 166
multicore system 34, 39, 43, 61
multiple processors 4, 7, 26, 41, 60, 69, 132
multiprocessing 17, 19, 40
multiprocessor 34, 45
multiprogramming 17
multithreaded 27–28, 43
mutex.Lock() 247
mutexes 10, 66–69, 71–73, 75–76, 78–80, 82, 84–85, 87–88, 90, 92–96, 98–108, 110, 113, 123–125, 129, 155, 157, 159, 162, 179, 188, 190, 251–252, 255, 262, 267, 273–274, 278, 280–281, 284, 288, 291–295
  acquiring 75–76
  avoiding 182
  building 284
  bundled mutex 273
  calls 74
  combining 90
  condition variable 104, 123, 262
  creating 71
  deadlocks 246, 248, 251, 264
  definition 67
  documentation 75
  implementation 69–70
  implementing 282
    atomic variable 295
    Go 291
    spin locks 280, 286, 295
  improve performance 289
  initial state 69
  introduction 67
  locking 68, 71, 88, 92, 99, 101, 252, 262–263
  locking and unlocking 70–71, 255
  locks
    non-blocking 74
  non-blocking 75
  normal mode 293
  performance cost 73
  race conditions 158–159, 295
  read 82
  read and write locks 81
  read-write 82
  reader 81
  readers-writer 66, 77, 81–86, 88, 103, 105, 108, 113
  release 98
  releasing 76
  replacing 274
  shared 68
  spin locking 273
  spin locks 284
  starvation 293

sync.mutex 293
synchronization 69
unlocking 72, 78–79, 91, 93, 99, 101, 113, 262–263, 284, 289
user space 288
using 67
vs. semaphores 108–109
write 82
MySQL 257

N

network connections 23, 27
Newsqueak 166
non-blocking 75, 136, 166, 172, 234
non-deterministic environment 188

O

Occam 9, 189
operating system 5, 8, 16–25, 27, 29, 33–39, 43, 60–61, 69–70, 98, 166, 188–189, 264, 273, 284, 286–289, 291
ostrich method 255
output channel 228

P

parallel 7, 11–13, 15–16, 21, 27, 29, 31–32, 34–35, 39, 41, 44, 46, 49, 54, 58, 60–61, 69–70, 74, 82, 132, 154, 210, 218–219, 223, 225, 227, 235, 241, 243–244
  parallel computing 13, 131
  vs. sequential execution 237
parallelism 9, 13, 19–20, 38–39, 134, 222–223, 243
  concurrency vs. parallelism 38–39
  loop-level parallelism 244
performance scalability 11
permit 108–113, 119, 122, 137, 156–160, 291–292
pipe 24
pipeline pattern 13, 193, 195–198, 201–205, 207–214, 235–236, 238–241, 244
pointers 26, 190
poison pill message 150
POSIX 27
prime number 173–174, 210–212
primitives 9–10, 14–15, 154, 179, 188, 273, 287
process context block (PCB) 19
processes 5, 10, 16, 20–26, 29, 31, 33–34, 38, 41–43, 48–49, 52, 54, 69, 80, 150, 189–190, 210–211, 235, 255, 257, 264, 286, 288
  child 22
  concurrency 16, 20
  concurrent processes 23

processes *(continued)*
  creating 22
  creating and forking 23
  CSP 189
  curl 24
  definition 20
  memory 43, 47
  multiple 29
  multithreaded 25
  parent 22–23
  sequential processes 14, 189–190
  terminating 23, 27, 31, 52, 108, 144
  vs. threads 24–26, 29, 40
  word count 24
processor 4, 6–9, 14, 18–19, 26, 34, 36, 39, 41, 43, 45, 54, 58, 61, 69–70, 224
  multicore 83
  single 60
production environment 63
program counter 19, 22, 25–27
pseudo-parallel execution 39
pthreads 27
Python 27

Q

queue 18, 34–37, 154–158, 162, 199, 230–232, 235, 242, 286–288, 291–295
  ready queue 18
  shared queue 155
  wait queue 288, 294
  waiting queue 18, 291, 293

R

race conditions 4–5, 9, 42, 53–65, 69–70, 187–188, 190, 245, 281
  detecting 63–65
  preventing 65–67, 69, 72, 77, 80, 101, 142, 158–159, 187, 189–190, 203, 251, 274, 276, 280, 288, 295
race detector 64
read operations 77, 164
read-preferring 87, 102
readersLock 84–87
ReadLock() 83, 85, 103, 106
ReadUnlock() 83, 86, 103, 107
real-time processing 19
receiver 143–152, 155–156, 158–162, 177
regex 196–197, 231
register 19, 58
Release() 110–112, 118, 120, 157–160, 294
replicated workers. *See* worker pool pattern

requests 18, 26–28, 51, 78–79, 83, 108, 199, 230, 235, 243, 258, 260–261
  read requests 80
  user requests 28, 78
resource allocation graph 247–248, 250, 254, 257–258, 272
resource contention 286
return statement 169
RFC 51
runtime
  of Go 9
runtime package 161
runtime.LockOSThread() 37
runtime.UnlockOSThread() 37
RWMutex 81, 104

S

Scala 189–190
scalability 11–13, 15, 70, 77, 222, 243
scalability limit 11–12
scheduling 33, 38, 40, 60, 72, 258–260, 272
  preemptive 37
  user-level 60
select statement 152, 164–167, 169, 171–172, 174–178, 184, 186, 191–192, 195, 197, 234, 270–272
semaphores 10, 53, 89, 108–114, 118–120, 155, 157, 160, 162, 179, 188, 190, 273, 287, 294
  binary semaphore 108
  buffer semaphore 155–160
  capacity semaphore 156–160
  weighted semaphore 112–113
Semi-Automatic Ground Environment (SAGE) 19
sender 145–149, 152, 154–162, 190
sentinel value 150
sequential execution 189
sequential program 29, 31, 49, 64, 168, 224, 228, 237
sequential programming 5, 153, 223
  sequential program vs. goroutine 54
serial 13, 15, 223
sha256 223–226
shared data structure 43, 78, 81, 136, 155, 220
shared memory 26, 43, 58, 180
shared state 80, 93
shared variables 26, 45–47, 49, 58–59, 61, 69, 71, 87, 100, 154, 273–275
sieve of Eratosthenes 210
signal 24, 89, 92, 95–99, 110–113, 124, 167–168, 191, 226
Signal() 93, 95–97, 99, 110–111, 113
sleep() 115, 117, 257
software performance 13
spin locking 280

spinning locks 5
SRC model 188
stack 22, 25–27, 33, 47–49, 192
StartProcess() 23
starvation mode 292–295
states 17–18, 27, 126, 260, 295
Strassen, Volker 131
stream reader 28
sync package 67, 83, 109, 115, 120, 295
sync.Cond 93–95, 97, 99, 101, 105, 110, 124,
    128, 262
sync.mutex 291–292
sync.RWMutex 81–82
synchronization 10, 39, 69–70, 87, 89, 96, 99, 114,
    141, 187, 222, 225, 243, 276
  barriers 133
  executions 9, 55
  lock-free 274
  logic 190
  primitives 188
  race conditions 61–62, 65, 80
  threads 26, 38
  tools 183, 273, 295
synchronous 31, 144, 146, 158, 161, 190
syscall package 23
system call 22–23, 27, 37, 166, 273, 287, 289–290
System/360 19

T

task dependency graph 218–219
task granularity 221–222
tasks
  coarse-grained 221
  fine-grained 221
TCP 233
test and set operation 70
thread communication 26, 42–43, 141, 179
thread pool pattern. *See* worker pool pattern
threads 16, 20–22, 24–29, 33–39, 42–44, 48, 53–54,
    62, 65, 69, 96, 100, 103, 136, 188, 273, 288
  definition 20
  green threads 34
  kernel-level 9, 33–37, 41, 43, 49, 61, 67, 75, 136,
    166, 291
  user-level 9, 33–35, 41, 60, 291
throughput 6, 14, 62, 82, 240–242, 244
  throughput rate 240
tightly coupled 179, 186
time sharing 19–20
time.Sleep() 40, 96, 129, 147

timeouts 163
TryLock() 75–76, 81, 88, 136, 294

U

UNIX 17, 22–23, 27, 166
UnLock() 81–82, 88
Unlock() 67–69, 71–74, 76, 78–79, 81–82,
    85–87, 91–95, 97, 99, 101, 106–108, 110,
    118, 124–125, 129, 158–159, 246, 252, 255,
    262–266, 272, 281–282, 285, 288–289, 294
user space 33, 37, 284, 287, 289, 291, 295

V

variables
  atomic variables 273–276, 278, 280, 282,
    284–285, 288–289, 291–292, 294–295
virtual threads 34

W

Wait() 93, 95–101, 106, 110–111, 113, 115–120,
    122–125, 127–129, 134–135, 137, 148, 201,
    224, 230, 256–257, 262, 276, 279
waitgroups 10, 53, 57, 114–127, 136–137, 147–148,
    154, 201, 223, 228–229, 242, 255–257, 268,
    275–276, 279
WaitGrp 120, 123–125
WaitOnAddress() 287
WakeByAddressAll() 287
WakeByAddressSingle() 287
web server 26, 28, 77, 231
Windows 22–23, 27, 287
work stealing 36
worker pool pattern 230–235, 242, 244
worker-crew model. *See* worker pool pattern
write-preferring 89, 104–105, 113
write-starvation 102
writeEvery() 165
WriteLock() 83, 85, 103–104, 106
writer active indicator 104
writer-preferred 108
WriteUnlock() 83, 86–87, 107

Y

yield 37, 60–61, 286
yielding 285–286

RELATED MANNING TITLES

100 Go Mistakes and How to Avoid Them
by Teiva Harsanyi

ISBN 9781617299599
384 pages, $69.99
August 2022

Go in Action, Second Edition
by Andrew Walker with William Kennedy

ISBN 9781633439702
400 pages *(estimated)*, $59.99
Spring 2024 *(estimated)*

Grokking Concurrency
by Kirill Bobrov

ISBN 9781633439771
304 pages *(estimated)*, $49.99
December 2023 *(estimated)*

Parallel and High Performance Computing
by Robert Robey and Yuliana Zamora

ISBN 9781617296468
704 pages, $69.99
May 2021

For ordering information go to www.manning.com